MILITARY
AIRCRAFT
OF THE WORLD

Gordon Swanborough

Charles Scribner's Sons
NEW YORK

Contents

Addenda

Aérospatiale TB30 Epsilon (p128): The Armée de l'Air placed an initial order for 30.

Beech T-34C Turbine Mentor (p135): The Uruguayan Navy ordered three. The US Navy has ordered an additional 41.

Boeing 727 (p142): The Royal New Zealand Air Force purchased three 727-100s from United Airlines in 1981, using one to provide spares for the other two to be operated by No 40 Squadron.

Boeing 737 (p141): A maritime surveillance version, with side-looking radar in the rear fuselage, extra fuel tankage and other special features, was ordered in 1981 by the Indonesian Air Force. The first of three was to be delivered in May 1982.

British Aerospace Bulldog (p145): Recent orders brought the total for the Nigerian Air Force to 36 and the Royal Jordanian Air Force (and Air Academy) to 23.

British Aerospace Hawk (p19): The Indonesian Air Force ordered four more, plus another four on option. The United Arab Emirates Air Force is negotiating a contract for 18.

CASA C101 Aviojet (p148): The Chilean Air Force has ordered eight with eight more on option.

Dassault Breguet Alpha Jet (p37): The Cameroon Air Force has ordered six.

Dassault-Breguet Atlantic NG (p31): The first of two prototypes of the Atlantic New Generation (converted from Atlantic No 42) flew at Toulouse/Blagnac on 8 May 1981.

Photo Credits

Copyright © Ian Allan Ltd 1971, 1973, 1975, 1979, 1981

U.S. edition published by Charles Scribners Sons

Copyright under the Berne Convention.

Printed in Great Britain
Library of Congress Catalog Number: 81-84021
ISBN: 0-684-17284-4

Dassault-Breguet Guardian (p154): The first of five Mystère-Falcon 20H Guardians for Aéronavale flew on 15 April 1981.

General Dynamics F-16 (p46): Additional customers for the Fighting Falcon are South Korean Air Force, for 36, and the Pakistan Air Force, for about 42.

HAL HJT-16 Kiran II (p170): The Indian Air Force has authorised production of 24 Kiran IIs to follow on the Kiran Is.

IAI Lavi: Israel Aircraft Industries is building four prototypes of a new fighter destined for service with the Heyl Ha'Avir starting in January 1988. The Lavi will be powered by the General Electric F404 and first flight is expected in 1984.

Kaman SH-2F Seasprite (p176): The SH-2F interim LAMPS helicopter re-entered production in 1981 against a US Navy contract for 18, with follow-on orders expected.

McDonnell Douglas F-4 Phantom II (p77): Production of the Phantom II ended on 20 May 1981 with delivery of the final aircraft built in Japan by Mitsubishi.

McDonnell Douglas/BAe AV-8B: The RAF is to obtain 60 of these Advanced Harriers under plans for joint Anglo-US production announced in June 1981. Final assembly will take place in the UK, while McDonnell Douglas will be responsible for more than 300 AV-8Bs expected to be ordered by the US Marine Corps.

Northrop F-5 (p93): The Swiss government ordered during 1981 32 more F-5Es plus six two-seat F-5Fs.

Pilatus PC-7 Turbo Trainers (p194): An order for 40 has been placed by the Swiss Air Force. The United Arab Emirates Air Force ordered 14 for delivery in 1982.

Piper Chellan: To meet the requirements of the Chilean Air Force, Piper has developed a two-seat primary trainer known as the Chellan, based on the Piper Saratoga and powered by a 300hp Lycoming IO-540 engine. A prototype was flown in the USA in 1981 and up to 100 will be assembled by the Chilean Air Force workshops at El Bosque AFB from components supplied by Piper. The same workshop also is assembling a batch of 30 PA-28 Cherokee Dakotas for use as trainers.

Piper Cheyenne: Two examples of the Cheyenne II equipped for the maritime surveillance role were delivered to the Mauritanian Air Force in April 1981.

Siai-Marchetti S211 (p203): First flight of the prototype S211 was made at Milan-Malpensa airport on 10 April 1981.

Westland/Aérospatiale Lynx (p215): Newly-designated variants are the HAS Mk 3 (Royal Navy) and HAS Mk 4 (French Navy), similar to the HAS Mk 2 but with uprated engines. The HT Mk 3 designation for the RAF training variant has been cancelled.

Westland Wasp (p214): The Indonesian naval air arm purchased 10 Wasp anti-submarine helicopters from the Dutch Navy during 1981.

Introduction

A comparison of the contents of this new edition of *Military Aircraft of the World* with the previous edition published two years ago might, at first glance, suggest that there has been a slowing down of the international arms race. Not one major new type has emerged in that two-year interval and although a number of types have made their first flights in the period, and others have taken on new significance, every one of the major aircraft described in Part One of this volume received at least a mention in the 1979 edition. That is not to say, however, that this edition simply duplicates the earlier volume; not only has all the data and descriptive text been thoroughly revised and updated, and new photographs introduced throughout, but the opportunity has also been taken to include illustrations and details of many second-line aircraft (in Part Two) which have not previously been recorded, especially some basically civil types that are operated in military guise.

To make this possible, and at the same time to give extra space and added prominence in Part One to several types of major importance, it has been necessary to exclude entries for a few of the older and less significant second-line types. One of the difficulties confronting the editor of any volume such as this is that old military aeroplanes tend to linger on, performing odd jobs in odd corners of the world for many years after they have passed the prime of their importance. Details of these types can be found, if required, in one of the earlier editions of *Military Aircraft of the World*. It would be nice to record them all but, alas, to do so could well double the size and thus the price of this volume and thereby put it out of reach of a large portion of the readership for which it is intended. We must satisfy ourselves, therefore, with the claim that this is the most complete single-volume compact guide to the combat and support aircraft in service throughout the world in 1981. It describes and illustrates more than 300 different aircraft types: every effort has been made to ensure that the photographs show current service versions in the markings of a user-service in 1980.

Both in its completeness and its style, this edition follows the standards that have been set over a number of years. It differs from earlier editions, however, in that the name of John W. R. Taylor no longer appears as joint author. In order to devote his energies increasingly to the editorship of *Jane's All the World's Aircraft*, John Taylor has reluctantly relinquished his association with this title, the continuing high standard of which owes much to the groundwork he laid over many years. The present editor gladly acknowledges his indebtedness, in the preparation and presentation of this volume, to his friend and former associate.

GS

3

Aeritalia G91

Italy

Single-seat light tactical strike-reconnaissance fighter, in service

Data, photo and silhouette: G91Y
Powered by: Two 2,720lb (1,235kg) st General Electric J85-GE-13A turbojets
Span: 29ft 6.5in (9.01m)
Length: 38ft 3.5in (11.67m)
Empty weight: 8.598lb (3,900kg)
Gross weight: 19,180lb (8,700kg)
Max speed: 690mph (1,110km/h) at sea level
Typical combat radius: 466miles (750km) at sea level
Armament: Two 30mm cannon in sides of front fuselage; four underwing attachments for up to 4,000lb (1,816kg) of bombs, AS.20 missiles, air-to-ground rockets or 0.50in machine gun pods

The original G91 was the winner of a design competition for a standardised strike fighter for NATO forces. Three prototypes and 27 pre-production G91s were ordered initially by NATO. The first prototype, with a 4,050lb (1,837kg) st Orpheus BOr1, flew on 9 August 1956. After winning the NATO evaluation contest in October 1957, the G91 was ordered into production. The first pre-production model flew on 20 February 1958, and the Italian Air Force formed the first G91 development squadron in August 1958, equipped with the pre-production machines. These were the only pure fighter G91s, subsequent operational aircraft being G91Rs with three Vinten 70mm cameras in a less-pointed nose. Variants, all with 5,000lb (2,268kg) st Orpheus 803, are the G91R/1, R/1A and R/1B, of which 98 were built for the Italian Air Force, and the G91R/3 and R/4 of which 100 were built by Fiat for the German Air Force, with 282 more licence-built in Germany. The R/4s were subsequently acquired by the Portuguese Air Force, which has also now received from Germany 23 R/3s. Italian G91Rs have four 0.50in guns instead of the cannon fitted to the German versions. Tandem two-seat training versions with a larger wing and longer fuselage are the G91T/1 (more than 80 for Italy) and G91T/3 (66 for Germany; six later to Portugal). The G91Y was evolved from the G91T for the Italian Air Force, with the same enlarged wing and two J85s replacing the single Orpheus engine. The first of two prototypes flew on 27 December 1966. A pre-production batch of 20 was delivered and these were followed by series production of 45, work on which was completed during 1976; these aircraft currently equip two *Stormi* (Wings) of the Italian Air Force.

Aeritalia G222   Italy

**Medium-range tactical transport, in production
and service**

Photo: G222, Somalia
Data and silhouette: G222
Powered by: Two 3,400shp General Electric
T64-P-4D turboprops
Span: 94ft 6in (28.80m)
Length: 74ft 5.5in (22.70m)
Empty weight: 32,165lb (14,590kg)
Gross weight: 58,422lb (26,500kg)
Max speed: 336mph at 15,000ft (540km/h at
4,575m)
Range: 1,833 miles (2,950km) with 11,025lb
(5,000kg) load
Accommodation: Crew of three and 44 troops, 32
paratroops, or up to 36 stretchers and eight
attendants or seated casualties

Design studies began in 1963, under Italian Air Force
contracts, with a view to developing a V/STOL
tactical transport. Using a conventional high-wing
layout, with two turboprop engines, Fiat proposed to
obtain STOL performance by installing four direct-lift
engines in each nacelle. This project had the
capability of taking off in 230ft (70m) and carrying
its design payload a distance of 310 miles (500km),
but an alternative was also schemed in which the
lift-engines were deleted and the weight saved was
taken up by extra fuel, giving a greatly increased
range at the expense of take-off performance. Two
flying prototypes (and a static test specimen) of this
conventional version were eventually ordered by the
Italian government, with the stipulation that the
work be shared throughout the Italian industry under
Fiat direction. First flights of the two prototypes were
made on 18 July 1970 and 22 July 1971
respectively, and following evaluation in the early
months of 1972 the Italian Air Force has ordered a
total of 44 G222s. Production is spread throughout
the Italian aerospace industry, with final assembly by
Aeritalia (incorporating the former Fiat Aviation
Division) now undertaken near Naples. The first
G222s were assembled in the Fiat works in Turin,
where the first production G222 made its maiden
flight on 23 December 1975. The fourth aircraft was
the first example exported, to the United Arab
Emirates Air Force at the end of 1976, and the first
of three ordered by the Argentine Army was
delivered in March 1977. Two examples designated
G222 VS acquired by the Italian Air Force are
equipped for the ECM mission, with radomes under
the nose and atop the fin. Six G222 RM for service
with the 14° *Stormo Radio misure* have equipment
for radio and radar calibration. 20 G222Ls ordered
by Libya in 1978 have Tyne 101 engines and the
first of these flew on 13 May 1980. One G222 was
delivered to the Somalia Air Force in 1980.

5

Aermacchi MB326, EMBRAER AT-26 Xavante and Atlas Impala

Italy

Basic trainer and light attack aircraft, in production and service

Silhouette and photo: Xavante
Data: MB326K
Powered by: One 4,000lb (1,814kg) st Rolls-Royce Viper 632-43 turbojet
Span: 35ft 7in (10.85m)
Length: 35ft 0.25in (10.67m)
Gross weight: 13,000lb (5,897kg)
Max speed: 553mph (890km/h) at 5,000ft (1,525m)
Typical combat radius: 81 miles (130km) with max weapon load
Armament: Two 30mm DEFA cannon in lower front fuselage; six underwing pylons for up to 4,000lb (1,814kg) of external stores

The first of two prototypes of this widely-used tandem two-seat basic trainer flew on 10 December 1957 powered by a 1,750lb (794kg) st Rolls-Royce Viper 8 turbojet. Production models had the 2,500lb (1,134kg) st Viper 11 and the first of 100 for the Italian Air Force flew on 5 October 1960. Delivery of this batch was completed in 1966 but 28 more were ordered subsequently, including, in 1974, 12 MB326Es (six of them conversions) with new equipment and strengthened wing with six weapon attachments. Five MB326RMs are equipped for radio calibration duties. Eight MB326Bs and nine MB326Fs, delivered to the Tunisian and Ghana Air Forces respectively, are similar. In the spring of 1967, Aermacchi flew the prototype MB326G, an armed version with a 3,410lb (1,547kg) st Viper 540 engine. Production versions are known as the MB326GB and orders include 17 for Zaïre, eight for the Argentine Navy, 23 for the Zambian Air Force and 167 similar MB326GCs for the Brazilian Air Force (the majority made by Embraer in Brazil as the AT-26 Xavante). Brazil has supplied six Xavantes to Togo and nine to Paraguay. MB326H is the version for the Royal Australian Air Force and Navy, with Viper 11 engine; 12 were supplied by Aermacchi, with the balance of orders totalling 87 for the RAAF and 10 for the RAN built by CAC in Australia. In South Africa, Atlas Aircraft built 151 MB326M Impala Is, similar to the MB326G with armed capability, and subsequently put into production a batch of 100 of the Impala 2, similar to the MB326K. The latter is a single-seat attack/trainer version with Viper 632 engine, first flown on 22 August 1970; its two-seat counterpart is the MB326L. Orders for these later variants included six Ks and two Ls for the United Arab Emirates Air Force (Dubai), six Ks for Ghana, eight Ks and four Ls for Tunisia, six Ks for Zaïre and seven Ks for South Africa pending delivery of the locally-produced Impala 2s.

Aermacchi MB339 (and Veltro II) Italy

Two-seat basic/advanced trainer in production and single-seat strike aircraft under development

Data, photo and silhouette: MB339A
Powered by: One 4,000lb (1,814kg) st Piaggio-built Rolls-Royce Viper 632-43 turbojet
Span: 35ft 7.5in (10.86m) over tip tanks
Length: 35ft 0in (10.97m)
Empty weight: 6,780lb (3,075kg)
Gross weight: 13,000lb (5,897kg)
Max speed: 558mph (898km/h) at sea level
Max range: 1,093 miles (1,760km) with internal fuel only, and 1,310 miles (2,110km) with two underwing drop tanks

Closely related to the MB326, the MB339 was evolved during 1973/4 after a close study of the future requirements of the Italian *Aeronautica Militare,* and of military users in general, for an advanced trainer with secondary close-support capabilities. The outward similarity between the MB339 and the earlier Aermacchi product, with the exception of the forward fuselage, belies the extent of internal redesign to improve the structure and to introduce new equipment and systems. The front fuselage was redesigned to raise the rear (instructor's) seat, giving the MB339 a profile similar to that of the BAe Hawk, Dassault-Breguet/Dornier Alpha Jet and other contemporary trainer designs. The MB339 has provision to carry an extensive range of ordnance under the wings in addition to a 7.62mm multi-barrel gun pod under the fuselage. The first of two prototypes flew on 12 August 1976, followed by the second on 20 May 1977. Initial production orders were placed by the Italian Air Force in 1977 and the first production aircraft flew on 20 July 1978 against a total requirement for 100. Export orders have been placed by the Peruvian Air Force (for 14) and the Argentine Navy (for 10). On 30 May 1980, Aermacchi flew the prototype of a light strike version of the MB339; known as the MB339K Veltro II, this has a similar single-seat front fuselage to the MB326K and can carry a wide variety of armament on the six wing hardpoints.

Antonov An-12 (NATO code-name 'Cub')   USSR

Medium/long-range transport, in service

Photo: An-12, India
Data and silhouette: 'Cub A'
Powered by: Four 4,000ehp Ivchenko AI-20K turboprops
Span: 124ft 8in (38.0m)
Length: 108ft 3in (33.0m)
Gross weight: 134,480lb (61,000kg)
Max cruising speed: 373mph (600km/h)
Range: 2,110miles (3,400km) at 342mph (550km/h) with 22,050lb (10,000kg) payload
Accommodation: Crew of five and troops, vehicles or freight
Armament: Two 23mm cannon in tail turret

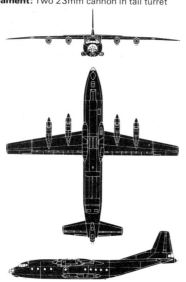

Developed from the An-10 commercial airliner, this turboprop transport has been standard equipment in the Soviet Air Force for paratroop-dropping, air supply and heavy transport duties for many years. Its undercarriage has four-wheel bogie main units, retracting into fairings on each side of the cabin, and is fitted with low-pressure tyres, enabling the An-12 to operate from unprepared airfields. Take-off and landing runs are uner 2,500ft (750m.) A loading ramp for vehicles and freight forms the undersurface of the up-swept rear fuselage and can be opened in flight for air-dropping of troops and supplies. Size of the main cabin is 44ft 3.5in (13.50m) long, by 9ft 10in (3.0m) wide and 7ft 10.5in (2.40m) high.

Foreign air forces which have been supplied with troop and cargo transport An-12s ('Cub-A') include those of Algeria, Bangladesh, Egypt, India, Iraq, Poland, Syria and Yugoslavia. A civil version, known as the An-12V, without the tail gun turret, is operated on pure freight services by Aeroflot and has been supplied to several other nations in the Soviet bloc. At least one Aeroflot An-12 has been operated on skis during service in the Arctic and is one of the largest aeroplanes ever equipped in this way.

Current Soviet Air Force An-12s have an enlarged under-nose radome. A version apparently equipped for electronic intelligence (ELINT) and data collecting is in service with Soviet Naval Aviation ('Cub-B'). A special ECM 'jamming' version is known to NATO as 'Cub-C'; examples have been operated by the Egyptian Air Force as well as the Soviet Air Force.

Antonov An-22 (NATO code-name 'Cock')   USSR

Long-range heavy strategic transport, in service

Powered by: Four 15,000shp Kuznetsov NK-12MA turboprops
Span: 211ft 4in (64.40m)
Length: 189ft 7in (57.80m)
Max payload: 176,350lb (80,000kg)
Gross weight: 551,160lb (250,000kg)
Max speed: 460mph (740km/h)
Range: 6,800 miles (10,950km) with max fuel and 99,200lb (45,000kg) payload; 3,100 miles (5,000km) with max payload
Accommodation: Crew of five or six: 28-29 passengers plus freight

First flown on 27 February 1965, the Antonov An-22 was the world's largest transport aircraft until the appearance of the Lockheed C-5A and Boeing 747. A natural progression from the An-10/12 series, the An-22 was in service with Aeroflot and the Soviet Air Force by mid-1967, at which time two prototypes in civil markings were operating an experimental freight service and three others in military markings took part in the display at Domodedovo. The latter disgorged, after landing, batteries of 'Frog-3' and 'Ganef' missiles on tracked launchers. The An-22 has a normal payload of 176,350lb (80,000kg) but in a series of record flights in October 1967, a max load of 221,443lb (100,445kg) was lifted. In two other series of record flights in 1972 and 1974, An-22s carried payloads of up to 110,230lb (50,000kg) over distances of up to 3,108 miles (5,000km) at speeds up to 378mph (608km/h). A feature of the An-22 design is that four gantries are installed on overhead rails running the entire length of the cabin to facilitate freight handling through the rear door ramp. Early examples carried the scanner for a navigational radar in a radome under the starboard wheel housing, but later service versions have it relocated under the nose. By 1969, An-22s were in service with several Soviet Air Force units, and in 1970 one was lost in the Atlantic during relief flights after the Peruvian earthquake. Production was terminated in 1974, after about 50 had been built.

Antonov An-26 (and An-24 and An-32)   USSR
(NATO code-names 'Curl', 'Coke' and 'Cline')

Tactical personnel and supply transport, in production and service

Photo: An-26, Yugoslavia
Data and silhouette: An-26
Powered by: Two 2,820ehp Ivchenko AI-24T turboprops plus, in the starboard nacelle, one 1,985lb (900kg) st RU19-300 turbojet for standby use
Span: 95ft 9.5in (29.20m)
Length: 78ft 1in (23.80m)
Empty weight: 33,113lb (15,020kg)
Gross weight: 52,911lb (24,000kg)
Cruising speed: 264-270mph (425-435km/h)
Range: 560 miles (900km) with 9,920lb (4,500kg) payload
Accommodation: Flight crew of five (two pilots, radio operator, flight engineer and navigator) and up to 40 paratroops or 24 stretchers

The An-26 (NATO code-name 'Curl') is a variant of the An-24 (NATO code-name 'Coke') short-range general purpose transport, more specifically adapted to military needs, although civil versions have been seen in service. The An-24 itself was first flown in 1960 and was produced in large quantities, initially for use by Aeroflot and then for export to other airlines and for military use. The An-26, which made its appearance in 1969, differs primarily in having a redesigned rear fuselage with a 'beaver-tail' incorporating ramps and loading doors so that vehicles can be accommodated. The rear door forming the ramp for loading can also be swung down and forward beneath the fuselage to allow direct loading from trucks into the cabin, which has an electrically or manually operated conveyor fitted flush in the floor. Among the air forces known to have put An-24s or An-26s into service — mostly in small numbers — as troop and personnel carriers, in addition to the Soviet Air Force itself, are those of Bangladesh, the Congo Republic (Brazzaville), Czechoslovakia, Egypt, East Germany, Hungary, Iraq, North Korea, Mongolia, Peru, Poland, Romania, the Somali Republic, North Vietnam, South Yemen and Yugoslavia. During 1977, a development of the An-26 was offered to the Indian Air Force to meet its requirements for a tactical transport, this being designated An-32 (NATO 'Cline') and having uprated AI-20 engines to improve its performance in hot and high airfield conditions. The An-32 is not known to be in service with the Soviet Air Force and a projected Indian Air Force order for 95 had not been confirmed up to the end of 1980.

Avro Shackleton

Long-range maritime reconnaissance and AEW aircraft, in service

Photo: Shackleton MR Mk 3, SAAF
Data and silhouette: Shackleton AEW Mk 2
Powered by: Four 2,455hp Rolls-Royce Griffon 57A piston-engines
Crew: 10
Span: 119ft 10in (36.52m)
Length: 92ft 6in (28.19m)
Gross weight: 98,000lb (44,452kg)
Max speed: 260mph (418km/h). Patrol endurance, up to 10hrs
Armament: None

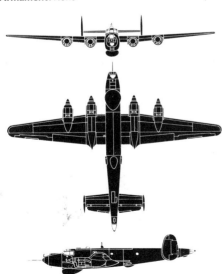

Only survivors of the 188 Shackletons built for the RAF are AEW Mk 2s, converted from MR Mk 2Cs and assigned to No 8 Squadron for long-range airborne early warning duties from RAF Lossiemouth. For this purpose, they have had all armament removed and a range of new equipment added, including AN/APS-20 (F) I search radar (transferred from retired Gannet AEW Mk 3s) in a radome under the forward fuselage, Orange Harvest wideband passive ECM, APX7 IFF and Doppler navigator. Since these Shackletons entered service, they have been further updated by the addition of AMTI (Airborne Moving Target Indicator) units. The first of 12 AEW Mk 2 conversions flew on 30 September 1971, and they will remain in service until the AEW Mk 3 version of the Nimrod is introduced in the 1980s. The Shackleton MR Mk 1 (77 built) first entered service with No 120 Squadron of RAF Coastal Command late in 1951. The Mk 1 aircraft could be distinguished from later versions by their shorter, more rounded nose with fixed undernose radome and blunt rear fuselage. The MR Mk 2 (prototype WB833) was developed in 1952 with a longer, more streamlined nose, pointed tail-cone and retractable ventral radar. With equipment brought up to Mk 3 standard, the Mk 2C continued in RAF service until 1972. The Shackleton MR Mk 3 had wingtip tanks, nose-wheel undercarriage in place of the former tail-wheel type and other refinements. 69 Mk 2 and 42 Mk 3 aircraft were built. To increase the capabilities of the RAF's Mk 3 Shackletons, they underwent extensive modification to Phase 3 standard, including structural strengthening, increase in fuel capacity and the addition of two Rolls-Royce Bristol Viper auxiliary turbojets, mounted in the rear of the outboard engine nacelles, to improve take-off performance. A squadron of Mk 3 Shackletons, without the Viper boost engines, serves with the South African Air Force.

11

BAC Lightning

UK

Single-seat supersonic fighter, in service

Silhouette: Lightning F Mk 53
Data and photo: Lightning F Mk 6
Powered by: Two 16,360lb (7,420kg) st
Rolls-Royce Avon 301 turbojets with afterburning
Span: 34ft 10in (10.61m)
Length: 55ft 3in (16.84m)
Gross weight: approx 50,000lb (22,680kg)
Max speed: Mach 21 (1,320mph; 2,124km/h)
Armament: Two Red Top or Firestreak air-to-air
missiles, or two packs of 24 air-to-air rockets plus,
optionally, two 30mm guns in ventral pack

The Lightning F Mk 1, evolved from the P1A research
aircraft, first flew on 4 April 1957. This version (20
built) and the F Mk 1A (28 built), with provision for
flight refuelling, equipped three RAF squadrons. The
F Mk 2, first flown on 11 July 1961, introduced
many improvements and could carry Red Top as well
as Firestreak. 30 were modified to F Mk 2A, with
some features of the F Mk 6, for service in RAF
Germany with Nos 19 and 92 Squadrons. First flown
on 16 June 1962, the F Mk 3 had Series 300 Avons,
a larger square-tip tail fin and much improved
equipment, although the two 30mm Aden guns
fitted in earlier marks were deleted. From it was
evolved the fully-developed F Mk 6 (prototype flown
on 17 April 1964), in which the outer portion of the
wing leading-edge had slightly less sweep and
incorporated conical camber, and the capacity of the
ventral fuel tank was more than doubled. This
version can carry two overwing fuel tanks for long-
range ferrying. By 1978, only two squadrons of Mk 6
aircraft remained operational in the UK. These and
the Lightning Training Squadron also use a few
T Mk 5s (prototype first flown 29 March 1962; 22
built) which are side-by-side dual-control fully-
operational counterparts of the F Mk 3. Saudi
Arabia purchased 35 Lightning F Mk 53 multi-role
interceptor/ground-attack fighters, six T Mk 55
trainers, and five ex-RAF Mk 2 and two Mk 4 as
F Mk 52 and T Mk 54 respectively. These remain
first-line equipment in 1980, but 12 F Mk 53 and
two T Mk 55 Lightnings bought by Kuwait were
withdrawn from service in 1977.

Beriev M-12 (Be-12) (NATO code-name 'Mail')

USSR

Maritime reconnaissance amphibian, in service

Data: Estimated
Powered by: Two 4,000shp Ivchenko AI-20D turboprops
Span: 97ft 6in (29.70m)
Length: 107ft 11.25in (32.9m)
Gross weight: 65,035lb (29,500kg)
Max speed: 379mph (610km/h)
Range: 2,485 miles (4,000km)
Armament: Attack weapons on four underwing pylons and in bomb-bay in rear of hull

Existence of this turboprop-engined amphibian became known in 1961, when a single example appeared during the Soviet Aviation Day fly-past over Moscow. This fleeting appearance revealed the type to be a close relative of the piston-engined Be-6 which was then standard equipment in flying-boat squadrons of the *Morskaya Aviatsiya* (Soviet Navy Aviation). The prototype is believed to have flown for the first time during 1960.

Little more was heard of the new type until October 1964 when a series of altitude records was established by the Be-12, named *Tchaika* (Seagull) and designated M-12 by the Soviet forces. These records showed that the Be-12 was capable of lifting a payload of 22,266lb (10,100kg) and of reaching nearly 40,000ft (12,185m) with no payload.

Several examples of the M-12 participated in the display at Domodedovo in July 1967, showing that it had entered service, presumably as a replacement for the Be-6. Although resembling the latter type in all general respects other than the engines and undercarriage, in detail it shows many design refinements. A speed record of 351mph (565km/h) around a 500km circuit was set up by an M-12 in April 1968, in the flying-boat, rather than amphibian, category; and M-12s now hold all 21 records for turboprop amphibians in the FAI Class C3 Group II, and all 17 records for turboprop flying-boats in Class C2 Group II.

About 100 M-12s are thought to have been built, and they are operational with units of the Soviet Northern and Black Sea fleets. For a period, some were based in Egypt for patrol duties over the Mediterranean.

13

Boeing B-52 Stratofortress

USA

Strategic heavy jet bomber, in service

Photo and silhouette: B-52G
Data: B-52H
Powered by: Eight 17,000lb (7,718kg) st Pratt & Whitney TF33-P-3 turbofans
Span: 185ft 0in (56.42m)
Length: 160ft 10in (49.05m)
Gross weight: over 488,000lb (221,350kg)
Max speed: About 600mph (957km/h) at 50,000ft (15,240m)
Range: 10,000 miles (16,093km)
Armament: One 20mm multi-barrel cannon in remote-control rear turret. Primary armament comprises eight SRAM internally and six under each wing, as alternative to conventional HE bombs internally
Accommodation: Crew of six

Development of the B-52 began in mid-1945, and production totalled 744 between 1954 and 1962. First operational version was the B-52B, in service from June 1955 onwards. By 1980, the number in service with SAC had been reduced to about 340, in the B-52D, B-52G and B-52H versions (plus about 190 in inactive storage) and these are expected to remain operational until the end of the century. In a major modification programme started in 1972, 281 B-52s of the G and H models were adapted to carry 20 Short Range Attack Missiles (SRAM) each, for continued service with SAC. Another programme, begun in 1973, introduced AN/ASQ-151 Electro-optical Viewing System (EVS) which provides forward-looking LLTV and IR capability and is indicated by two small steerable chin turrets under the nose. A further, and continuing, updating programme was started in 1974 under the code-name 'Rivet Ace' and includes the introduction of 'Phase VI' ECM, the many new features of which include a radome on the port tailplane tip. Following the selection, in 1980, of the Boeing AGM-86B air-launched cruise missiles, the USAF started a programme to allow B-52Gs to carry 12 of these missiles each, on wing pylons. Later in the 1980s, they will be adapted to carry eight more AGM-86Bs internally and the B-52Hs may receive the same modification. The 80 B-52Ds are assigned to give direct support to NATO.

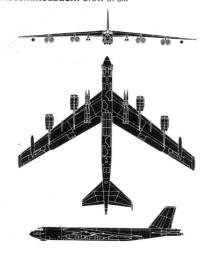

Boeing E-3A Sentry

USA

Seventeen-seat airborne warning and control system aircraft, in production and service

Powered by: Four 21,000lb (9,525kg) st Pratt & Whitney TF33-P-100/100A turbofans
Span: 145ft 9in (44.42m)
Length: 152ft 11in (46.61m)
Gross weight: About 330,000lb (149,685kg)
Search range: 7hr endurance at 29,000ft (8,840m) at a distance of 1,150 miles (1,850km) from base
Armament: None

Following evaluation of proposals by McDonnell Douglas and Boeing, the USAF selected the latter company as prime contractor for its new Airborne Warning and Control System (AWACS) aircraft on 8 July 1970. The Boeing proposal was based on the airframe of the commercial Model 707-320B, with the addition of an extensive range of equipment for the airborne early-warning command-and-control role, including a downward-looking radar in a large rotating dorsal radome. Two prototypes were ordered, and the first of these flew on 9 February 1972. Designated EC-137D, they were used for competitive evaluation of Hughes and Westinghouse radars, the latter being selected later in 1972. Two more 707 airframes were ordered subsequently for conversion to E-3A prototypes, this being the production designation, and these aircraft flew (without AWACS electronics) in February and July 1975. One of the EC-137Ds also became an E-3A prototype while the other was modified up to full production standard. The USAF intends to acquire 34 E-3As (including the three prototypes) eventually, although the programme suffered successive stretch-outs and by mid-1980 only 25 had been firmly ordered. The first production E-3A was delivered on 24 March 1977 and entered service with the 552nd Airborne Warning and Control Wing. On 6 December 1978, a Memorandum of Understanding was signed, providing for 18 E-3As to be acquired in 1982-85 for joint operation by the European NATO nations (except the UK). The first European AWACS was rolled out on 27 January 1981.

Boeing KC-135 Stratotanker and C-135 Stratolifter

USA

Refuelling tanker and strategic transport, in service

Photo: KC-135D
Data and silhouette: KC-135A
Powered by: Four 13,750lb (6,237kg) st Pratt & Whitney J57-P-59W turbojets
Span: 130ft 10in (39.88m)
Length: 136ft 3in (41.53m)
Empty weight: 98,466lb (44,663kg)
Gross weight: 316,000lb (143,464kg)
Max speed: 585mph (941km/h) at 30,000ft (9,144m)
Range: 1,150 miles (1,850km) with full load of transfer fuel
Accommodation: Crew of six and up to 80 passengers

The KC-135A jet tanker-transport first flew on 31 August 1956 and deliveries of 732 began in June 1957. Approximately 600 operational in 1980 with eight Air National Guard Wings and Groups, and two Reserve Squadrons, are standard flight refuelling tankers for Strategic Air Command bombers, each with a total fuel capacity of 31,200 US gallons (118,100 litres), and can also be used as cargo or personnel transports. The USAF plans to convert at least half, and perhaps all of this tanker fleet to have CFM56 turbofan engines, as KC-135REs, if a trial installation, to fly in October 1981, is successful.

For use by MATS as interim jet transports, the C-135A and TF33-P-5 turbofan engined C-135B were ordered in 1961, with tanker gear deleted and space for 87,100lb (39,510kg) of cargo or 126 troops; eleven C-135Bs became VC-135Bs when fitted with VIP interiors. France purchased 12 C-135F tankers similar to the KC-135A, to refuel Mirage IVs. Other aircraft in the KC-135A series were modified during production for special duties, bringing the total quantity built to 820. These special variants were 14 KC-135B (later EC-135C) SAC Airborne Command Posts; four RC-135A for photo-reconnaissance and mapping (later converted to KC-135D) and 10 RC-135B for electronic reconnaissance. Other designations were applied to various aircraft which changed their role after initial delivery; these included 10 WC-135Bs for weather reconnaissance, RC-135C, D, E, M, S, U and V electronic reconnaissance versions and EC-135G, H, J, K, L and P command posts. Eight EC-135Ns serve as advanced range instrumentation aircraft for space mission support. The KC-135Q variant is the KC-135A specially adapted to refuel Lockheed SR-71s; the KC-135R and KC-135T were for special reconnaissance. Military versions of the Boeing 707 are described separately on the next page.

Boeing Model 707 and VC-137

USA

VIP transport and flight refuelling tanker, in service

Photo: CC-137 tanker
Data and silhouette: 707-320C
Powered by: Four 19,000lb (8,626kg) st Pratt & Whitney JT3D-7 turbofans
Span: 145ft 9in (44.42m)
Length: approx 158ft 0in (48.16m)
Gross weight: 333,600lb (151,315kg)
Max speed: 620mph (998km/h)
Range: Over 7,000 miles (11,263km)

Although a close relative of the KC-135 (see previous page), the commercial Boeing 707 differs in several important respects, notably in the size of the fuselage, which is of greater diameter. Several Boeing 707 variants are in military service. The Canadian Armed Forces acquired five 707-320Cs in 1970, which are operated as CC-137s, and three have Beech underwing pods for in-flight refuelling of fighters, using the probe and drogue method. The Luftwaffe operates four standard 707-320Cs as personnel and freight carriers; the RAAF has acquired two 707s from Qantas and plans to acquire three more as FR tankers were made in 1980. One 707-320B is operated as a presidential and VIP transport by the Argentine Air Force, and another serves in the same rôle in Egypt. The most famous military 707, however, is Air Force One, the personal transport of the president of the USA. Basically a 707-320B, this has a VIP interior and is designated VC-137C. Air Force One is operated from Andrews AFB by the 89th Military Airlift Wing, which also has on strength a second similar VC-137C as a reserve and three smaller 707-120s bought by USAF for VIP duties as VC-137As and modified to VC-137Bs when turbofans replaced the original turbojet engines. In 1974, the Iranian Imperial Air Force began the acquisition of 12 Boeing 707-320Cs specially adapted to serve as flight-refuelling tankers as well as cargo or personnel transports. These Boeing 707-3J9Cs were basically commercial 707-320Cs with side-loading cargo doors and could be readily adapted to have full passenger or executive interior layouts. In addition, each carried a Beech Model 1080 refuelling pod under each wingtip, and had a Boeing 'flying boom' under the rear fuselage, with an operator's station below the cabin floor. The status of these aircraft in 1980, following the Iranian revolution, was uncertain.

Breguet Br1050 Alizé

France

Three-seat carrier-borne anti-submarine aircraft, in service

Powered by: One 2,100eshp Rolls-Royce Dart RDa21 turboprop
Span: 51ft 2in (15.6m)
Length: 45ft 6in (13.86m)
Empty weight: 12,565lb (5,700kg)
Gross weight: 18,100lb (8,200kg)
Max speed: 292mph (470km/h) at 10,000ft (3,050m)
Endurance: 5hr 10min at 144mph (230km/h) at 1,500ft (460m)
Armament: Internal weapon bay for three 353lb (160kg) depth charges or one torpedo. Racks under inner wings for two 160kg or 175kg depth charges. Racks under outer wings for six 5in rockets or two AS12 air-to-surface missiles. Sonobuoys in front of wheel housings

Development of the Alizé began in 1948 when Breguet designed the two-seat Br960 Vultur mixed power plant (turboprop and jet) strike aircraft to meet a French Navy requirement. When the Navy abandoned this concept in 1954, Breguet was given a contract to adapt the Vultur design into a three-seat single-engined anti-submarine aircraft, and this became the Br1050 Alizé. The first stage was to modify the second prototype Vultur into an aerodynamic prototype of the new design. A more powerful (1,650shp) Mamba turboprop was installed; the Nene turbojet was removed to make way for a large retractable 'dustbin' radome in the rear fuselage and dummy undercarriage/sonobuoy nacelles were fitted to the wings. This aircraft flew for the first time on 26 March 1955. Meanwhile, two genuine prototypes and three pre-production Alizés had been ordered, with Dart turboprop in place of the Mamba. The first of these flew on 6 October 1956, and the first of 75 production Alizés for the French Navy, with detail changes, was delivered on 26 March 1959. The remaining aircraft equip two French Navy squadrons, Flotilles 4F and 6F, for service on board the carriers *Foch* and *Clémenceau* and for training; of these, 28 Alizés are being updated to equip one Flotille on board the two carriers throughout the 1980s, with improved radio and navaids, ECM, and Thomson-CSF Iguane radar. 12 Alizés were supplied to the Indian Navy and more were acquired later, ex-Aéronavale; they continue to equip No 310 Squadron at INS *Garuda*, one detached flight of four aircraft from the squadron normally serving on board the carrier INS *Vikrant*, from which Alizés were in operational use during the 1971 Indo-Pakistan War.

British Aerospace Hawk   UK

Basic/advanced/weapons trainer and light strike aircraft, in production and service

Photo: Hawk Mk 53
Data and silhouette: Hawk T Mk 1
Powered by: One 5,340lb (2,425kg) st Rolls-Royce Turboméca RT172-06-11 Adour 151 turbofan
Span: 30ft 9.75in (9.39m)
Length: 36ft 7.75in (11.17m) (excluding nose probe)
Empty weight: 8,040lb (3,647kg)
Gross weight: trainer, clean, 11,100lb (5,035kg); trainer, armed, 12,284lb (5,572kg); max permissible, 17,097lb (7,755kg)
Max speed: approx 560mph (1,046km/h)
Combat radius: 345 miles (556km) with 5,600lb (2,540kg) weapon load
Max range: 1,922 miles (3,093km) with drop tanks

This Hawker Siddeley design (the HS1182) was selected by the RAF during 1972, after competitive evaluation with a BAC project, to provide a new basic/weapons trainer to replace the Gnat, Hunter and, in some rôles, the Jet Provost. An initial production order was placed immediately following this decision and was for 175 Hawk T Mk 1s; the RAF also plans to order 18 more. The first flight was made on 21 August 1974 and deliveries began on 4 November 1976, initially to replace Gnats at No 4 FTS, Valley. Subsequently, Hawks have also gone into service at the No 1 Tactical Weapons Unit (TWU) at Brawdy and No 2 TWU at Chivenor; in 1980, the Red Arrows aerobatic team also re-equipped on this type. RAF aircraft can carry the centre-line gunpod with a 30mm Aden and have two wing hardpoints, usually used (at the TWUs) to carry rocket pods; they can also carry a pair of Sidewinder AAMs to allow the RAF Hawks to serve in a defensive rôle in an emergency. The Hawk can carry up to 6,500lb (2,950kg) externally, using two additional wing pylons, as demonstrated by the Hawk T Mk 50 company demonstrator. During 1980, deliveries began of the Hawk Mk 52 (12 for Kenya), Hawk Mk 53 (eight for Indonesia) and Hawk Mk 51 (50 for Finland). Of the latter, 46 are to be assembled by Valmet OY at Halli in Finland. Zimbabwe was reported to have ordered eight Hawks early in 1981.

British Aerospace Harrier (and AV-8)   UK

Singe-seat V/STOL strike and reconnaissance aircraft, in production and service

Data and silhouette: Harrier GR Mk 3
Powered by: One 21,500lb (9,752kg) st Rolls-Royce Pegasus 103 vectored-thrust turbofan
Span: 25ft 3in (7.70m)
Length: 45ft 6in (13.87m)
Gross weight: VTOL, approx 17,000lb (7,710kg); STOL, approx 23,000lb (10,433kg); max, over 25,000lb (11,339kg)
Max speed: over 737mph (1,186km/h)
Typical radius of action: 500 miles (805km)
Armament: Three under-fuselage and four underwing attachments for 5,000lb (2,268kg) of stores. Typical load includes a 1,000lb bomb and two 30mm gun pods under fuselage; two pods of 19 68mm SNEB rockets and two 1,000lb bombs under wings

The Harrier is the operational development of the P1127 Kestrel, first aircraft to utilise the Pegasus vectored-thrust turbofan. The first of six pre-production Harriers made its first hovering flight on 3 August 1966, and the first of 114 single-seat Harriers for the RAF flew on 28 December 1967, with the designation GR Mk 1 and powered by the Pegasus 101 engine. Engines of this type were later modified to the more powerful Pegasus 102 standard, the aircraft being then designated GR Mk 1As; a further change of engine to 21,500lb (9,725kg) Pegasus 103 changed the designation to GR Mk 3, and aircraft with laser target-marking equipment in the nose are GR Mk 3A. The RAF also acquired 17 tandem two-seat Harrier T Mk 2s with revised front fuselage and tail unit; the first flew on 24 April 1969. The same engine changes as described above altered the designations to T Mk 2A and T Mk 4 respectively.

Deliveries of the Harrier GR Mk 1 to the RAF began in April 1969, and No 1 Squadron began working up on the type in the latter half of that year. Two Harrier squadrons are assigned to RAF Germany (Nos 3 and 4). The US Marine Corps received on 6 January 1971 the first of 102 Harriers ordered as AV-8As; eight two-seat TAV-8As have also been delivered. The first 10 had Pegasus 10 (F402-RR-400) engines; the remainder have the 21,500lb st Pegasus 11 (F402-RR-401). Under test in 1980, the AV-8C is a modified AV-8A with improved avionics, lift improvement devices and ECM; one example has also been tested with a 25mm GE cannon in one of the gun pods, with ammunition in the other. The Spanish Navy has ordered, through the US, eleven AV-8As and two TAV-8As, known in Spain as Matadors. Two trainers ordered by the Indian Navy are designated Harrier T Mk 60. A single Harrier Mk 52 has been built as a two-seat demonstrator.

After concluding an agreement with Hawker Siddeley, McDonnell Douglas at St Louis began development of the basic Harrier to meet US Marine

Above left: Harrier GR3

Above: AV-8B

Below: Harrier T2

Corps requirements for an improved V/STOL attack aircraft. This led to the AV-16 proposal, in which there was also RAF and RN interest, but because of funding restraints the less expensive AV-8B subsequently emerged. This retains the basic Harrier/AV-8A fuselage, with a raised cockpit similar to that of the Sea Harrier and with lift improvement devices (LIDS) under the fuselage. The engine is the 21,500lb (9,752kg) st F402-RR-404 version of the Pegasus, with redesigned air intakes, and the wing is all-new, with a supercritical section and increased span and area. This wing accommodates six pylons (compared with four on the basic Harrier) and the AV-8B therefore has a considerably increased weapon-carrying capability. The AV-8B has a span of 30ft 4in (9.24m) and length of 46ft 4in (14.12m); at a max STO weight of 28,750lb (13,041kg) it can lift an external load of 9,200lb (4,173kg). Two prototype YAV-8Bs were built by converting AV-8As, and the first of these flew on 9 November 1978. Funds were released for McDonnell Douglas to proceed with four full-scale development (FSD) AV-8Bs but approval for the full Marine Corps programme to acquire 336 AV-8Bs was still under consideration early in 1981, with an RAF order for this variant also a possibility.

British Aerospace HS748 and Andover UK

Short/medium-range tactical transport, in production and service

Photo and silhouette: HS748 srs 2A
Data: HS748 srs 2A
Powered by: Two 2,280ehp Rolls-Royce Dart 534-2 turboprops
Span: 98ft 6in (30.02m)
Length: 67ft 0in (20.42m)
Gross weight: 51,000lb (23,133kg) in overload condition
Cruising speed: 281mph (452km/h)
Range: 1,105 miles (1,778km) with max payload
Accommodation: Flight crew of two and up to 58 troops or 48 paratroops and despatchers

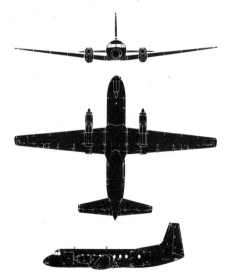

The Avro company (subsequently part of Hawker Siddeley, now British Aerospace) began design of this twin-Dart transport in January 1959, initially for commercial use, and the prototype flew on 24 June 1960. More than 300 examples have been built to date, some as military transports fitted with a large air-openable freight-loading door in the port side of the rear fuselage. Military operators include the RAAF (10), RAN (2), Belgian Air Force (3), Brazilian Air Force (12), Brunei (1), Cameroon (2), Colombian Air Force (2), Ecuadorean Air Force (4), Nepal (1), South Korea (2) Tanzania (3), Thailand (2), Upper Volta (1), Venezuela (3) and Zambian Air Force (1). The Indian Air Force has acquired a total of 72, of which the first four were lower-powered Srs 1s; these aircraft are assembled by HAL at Kanpur from British components. The RAF uses four HS748s as Andover C Mk 2s and two others assigned to the Queen's Flight are designated Andover CC Mk 2. The Andover C Mk 1 was a special version for the RAF with a redesigned rear fuselage incorporating a straight-in loading ramp. The first example flew on 21 December 1963, being a converted HS748, and the first of 31 Andover C Mk 1s for the RAF flew on 9 July 1965. The Andover C Mk 1 was retired as an RAF tactical transport in 1975, but six were subsequently modified to Andover E Mk 3s for radio and radar calibration duties and 10 others were sold to the RNZAF, of which one was modified to have a VVIP interior, one a VIP interior and the remainder are used as troop and supply transports. On 18 February 1977, Hawker Siddeley flew the prototype of an HS748 specially equipped for maritime surveillance, with MAREC radar in a radome under the centre fuselage, this version being known as the Coastguarder. None had been sold up to 1980, but the Royal Australian Navy has converted two of its standard HS748s for the electronic countermeasures role.

British Aerospace (HS801) Nimrod MR   UK

Four-engined long-range anti-submarine aircraft, in service

Photo: Nimrod MR Mk 2
Data and silhouette: Nimrod MR Mk 1
Powered by: Four 12,140lb (5,506kg) st Rolls-Royce Spey Mk 250 turbofans
Span: 114ft 10in (35.0m)
Length: 126ft 9in (38.63m)
Gross weight: 175,500lb (79,605kg)
Max speed: 575mph (926km/h)
Ferry range: 5,755 miles (9,265km)
Armament: Mines, bombs, depth charges and torpedoes in weapon-bay

The Nimrod has an airframe basically similar to that of the Comet 4C airliner, with an unpressurised pannier containing a weapon-bay added under the fuselage. The centre fuselage is fitted out as a navigational and tactical centre for the operators of the wide range of submarine detection devices. There is a searchlight in the front of the fuel pod on the starboard wing leading-edge and an electronic countermeasures pod on the fin-tip. The 12-man crew includes two pilots and an engineer on the flight deck, and two navigators and seven sensor operators in the forward cabin. Up to 45 passengers can be carried when the Nimrod is operated in its secondary trooping role. The first of two prototype Nimrods, converted from Comet transports, flew on 23 May 1967. A total of 46 MR Mk 1 production models was ordered to replace the RAF's Shackletons and the first of these (XV226) flew on 28 June 1968. Deliveries to No 201 Squadron of Strike Command, at Kinloss, began on 2 October 1969. Nimrods now equip four Strike Command squadrons (Nos 42, 120, 201 and 206) and the OCU (No 236). Three additional aircraft, designated Nimrod R Mk 1, serve in an electronic reconnaissance role with No 51 Squadron based at RAF Wyton and can be distinguished by the lack of MAD fairing behind the tail unit. During 1978, work began on the first of a planned total of 32 conversions of Nimrod MR Mk 1s to MR Mk 2 standard. This variant features the very advanced Searchwater radar, the AQS-901 acoustics system compatible with the Australian-developed Barra sonobuoy, a new central tactical system and a new communications system. Armament includes the Stingray torpedo, and ESM (Electronic Support Measures) pods are carried under the wings. The first MR Mk 2 was handed over to No 201 Squadron on 23 August 1979.

British Aerospace Nimrod AEW Mk 3   UK

Ten-seat airborne early-warning and control system aircraft, in production

Data, photo and silhouette: Nimrod AEW Mk 3
Powered by: Four 12,140lb (5,512kg) st Rolls-Royce RB 168-20 Spey Mk 250 turbofans
Span: 115ft 1in (35.08m)
Length: 137ft 5.5in (41.76m)
Gross weight: Not revealed
Mission speed: 350mph (563km/h)
Mission endurance: Over 10 hours
Armament: None

The Nimrod was selected in March 1977 to meet the British requirement for an airborne early warning aircraft to replace the squadron of Shackleton AEW Mk 2s that by 1980 were the last piston-engined aircraft in front-line service with the RAF. This decision was taken after protracted negotiations to adopt the Boeing E-3A Sentry for standardised NATO use and was necessary to ensure that the new aircraft became available in the required timescale. Much of the project design work had already then been completed, on the basis of the existing Nimrod maritime reconnaissance aircraft being used as the flight vehicle on which to mount the search radar and associated analytical and communications systems. The key equipment is the Marconi Avionics multi-mode pulse Doppler system, with large scanners mounted within massive radomes in the nose and tail of the aircraft. In the cabin are six consoles; one for the TACCO (tactical control officer), one for the communications control officer, one for the ESM operator and three for air direction officers. Prior to the completion of the first Nimrod AEW Mk 3, a converted (ex-commercial) Comet 4C was fitted with one half of the radar system, with nose radome only, and flew on 28 June 1977; a Nimrod MR Mk 1 began flight testing the new communications system in February 1980. The first of three development AEW Mk 3s flew on 16 July 1980; these, like eight full production standard aircraft to follow, are converted Nimrod AEW Mk 1 or 1A airframes and all will eventually serve in a single squadron to be based at RAF Waddington.

British Aerospace Sea Harrier   UK

Single-seat carrier-based fighter/strike/ reconnaissance aircraft, in production and service

Data, photo and silhouette: Sea Harrier FRS Mk 1
Powered by: One 21,500lb (9,760kg) st Rolls-Royce Pegasus 104 vectored-thrust turbofan
Span: 25ft 3.25in (7.70m)
Length: 47ft 7in (14.50m)
Gross weight: Over 25,000lb (11,340kg) for STO
Max speed: Over 737mph (1,186km/h) at low altitude
Radius of action: 100 miles (161km) plus loiter time on combat air patrol
Armament: Provision for two gun pods under fuselage, each carrying one 30mm Aden cannon, and four wing pylons plus one fuselage pylon to carry AAMs, ASMs, bombs, rockets, etc

Development of a version of the Harrier (separately described) more specifically intended for carrier-based operations in the naval strike fighter role began in the early 1970s, although the Harrier in unmodified form has proved fully capable of operating from carrier decks and is so used by the US Marines and Spanish Navy. As eventually ordered by the Royal Navy in May 1975 for operation from the new 'Invincible' class of through-deck carriers, the Sea Harrier FRS Mk 1 differs from the basic RAF Harrier in having a new front fuselage with a raised cockpit and changed avionics; a modified engine (Pegasus 104 instead of 103) in which two major magnesium components have been eliminated; a new cockpit conditioning system and single auto-pilot; increased roll power from roll control valves; increased tailplane incidence travel; revised liquid oxygen system; a hold-back system on the main undercarriage leg; an emergency brake system; updated Martin-Baker ejection seats; magnesium components eliminated from airframe structure; strengthened centre fuselage structure and provision for air-to-air and air-to-ground guided weapons to be carried under the wings, to RN requirements. The RN order for Sea Harriers is for 34 aircraft, of which the first made its maiden flight on 20 August 1978. Deliveries began in June 1979 for use by the Intensive Flying Trials Unit and No 700A Squadron. Operational squadrons, for service aboard the through-deck carriers are Nos 800 and 802, with a third (No 809) planned to form later. The Indian Navy has ordered six similar Sea Harrier FRS Mk 51s.

British Aerospace (BAC167) Strikemaster (and Jet Provost)

UK

Two-seat counter-insurgency strike aircraft and trainer, in service

Data, photo and silhouette: Strikemaster
Powered by: One 3,410lb (1,546kg) st Rolls-Royce Viper 535 turbojet
Span: 36ft 10in (11.23m)
Length: 33ft 8.5in (10.27m)
Gross weight: 11,500lb (5,215kg)
Max range: 1,382 miles (2,224km)
Max speed: 472mph (760km/h) at 20,000ft (6,100m)
Armament: Two 7.62mm FN machine guns in fuselage. Four wing strong points for maximum underwing load of 3,000lb (1,360kg)

The BAC 167 Strikemaster was developed from the basic armed Jet Provost to meet the needs of small air forces for a relatively cheap armed counter-insurgency aircraft and trainer. It differs from the RAF's Jet Provost T Mk 5 trainer primarily in having an uprated engine, permanently-attached tip-tanks and increased armament capability. Common to both the Strikemaster and the Jet Provost 5 is a pressurised cockpit. The first Strikemaster flew on 26 October 1967, and 141 have been built for the Saudi Arabian Air Force (25 Mk 80 and 22 Mk 80A), the South Yemen People's Republic (4 Mk 81, later sold to Singapore), the Sultan of Oman's Air Force (12 Mk 82 and 12 Mk 82A, of which five sold later to Singapore), the Kuwait Air Force (12 Mk 83), the Singapore Air Defence Command (16 Mk 84), the Kenya Air Force (6 Mk 87), the Royal New Zealand Air Force (16 Mk 88) and the Ecuadorean Air Force (16 Mk 89). In 1980, a final batch of 10 Strikemasters was in production at Hurn against expected future orders. A total of 110 Jet Provost T Mk 5s were built for the RAF, with 2,500lb (1,134kg) st Viper 202, pressure cabin and optional wingtip tanks. They replaced the Jet Provost T Mk 4, which was unpressurised. The T Mk 3 which had a 1,750lb (794kg) st Viper 102 engine remains in service alongside the T Mk 5; both of these variants have undergone a refit programme, completed in 1976, since when they have been redesignated T Mk 3A and T Mk 5A. Export models of the Jet Provost, with provision for two 0.303in machine guns in the air intake walls and limited underwing stores capability, were the T Mk 51 (Viper 102) for Ceylon, the Sudan and Kuwait and T Mk 52 (Viper 202) for Venezuela, Sudan, Iraq and the South Yemen. Five armed Jet Provost 55s (BAC 145) were sold to the Sudan to supplement its Mk 51s and 52s.

British Aerospace (BAC) VC10   UK

Long-range troop and freight transport, and flight refuelling tanker, in service

Data, photo and silhouette: VC10 C Mk 1
Powered by: Four 21,800lb (9,888kg) st Rolls-Royce Conway 301 (R Co 43 Mk 550) turbojets
Span: 146ft 2in (44.55m)
Length: 133ft 8in (40.47m) (without refuelling probe)
Gross weight: 323,000lb (146,510kg)
Max cruising speed: 581mph (935km/h)
Typical range: 3,900 miles (6,275km) with 57,400lb (26,030kg) payload at 425mph (683km/h) at 30,000ft (9,145m)
Accommodation: 150 passengers in rearward-facing seats, or freight

Although similar in overall dimensions to the original BOAC version, the RAF's VC10 C Mk 1 (Model 1106) has the more powerful Conway 550 engines and fin fuel tank of the Super VC10. Other changes include the installation of a large cargo door at the front of the cabin on the port side, an optional nose-probe for flight refuelling and an Artouste auxiliary power unit in the tail-cone for engine starting and electric power on the ground. The primary duty of the RAF's VC10s is to carry troops or personnel at high speed to any part of the world. The first C Mk 1 made its first flight on 26 November 1965. Deliveries began on 7 July 1966, and were completed in 1968; 14 originally went into service with No 10 Squadron, but this number was reduced to 11 as part of the 1976 defence cuts. The aircraft are named individually after holders of the Victoria Cross.

To fulfil the increased flight refuelling requirement anticipated with the phase-in of the Tornado, the RAF purchased in 1978 five VC10 and four Super VC10 airliners operated previously by Gulf Air and East African Airways respectively, for conversion into three-point flight-refuelling tankers by BAe at Bristol. The VC10 tankers were to enter service from 1982 onwards, equipping a new squadron; the converted Standard aircraft are designated K Mk 2 (Model 1112) and the Supers are K Mk 3 (Model 1164). One other VC10 operates in military colours, this being an ex-British Caledonian Airways standard VC10 used at the RAE Bedford for a variety of research tasks. Another standard VC10, sold by British Airways to the Sheik of Abu Dhabi, has operated as a VIP transport in the colours of the Federation of Arab Emirates.

Cessna A-37 Dragonfly (and T-37) USA

Light attack aircraft and basic jet trainer, in service

Data, photo and silhouette: A-37B
Powered by: Two 2,850lb (1,293kg) st General Electric J85-GE-17A turbojets
Span: 35ft 10.5in (10.93m)
Length: 29ft 3.5in (8.93m)
Gross weight: 14,000lb (6,350kg)
Max speed: 507mph (816km/h) at 16,000ft (4,875m)
Ferry range: 1,010 miles (1,628km)
Armament: One 7.62mm multi-barrel Minigun; eight underwing strong points for more than 5,000lb (2,270kg) of ordnance

Cessna's first design for a jet aeroplane won a competition in 1954 for a primary jet trainer for the USAF. The first of two XT-37 prototypes flew on

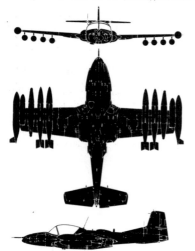

12 October 1954, and the first of an evaluation batch of 11 T-37s flew a year later. A total of 416 T-37As were built, with two Continental J69-T-9 turbojets, before being superseded in production by the T-37B with 1,025lb (465kg) st J69-T-25 engines and revised equipment. All T-37As were converted to 'B' standard, and production of the T-37B continued into 1976, side-by-side with the export T-37C. The latter has provision for underwing armament, including machine gun pods, rockets and bombs. T-37Bs were delivered to Thailand, Cambodia, Chile and Pakistan, while Germany purchased 47 for use in its training programmes based in the USA. Recipients of T-37Cs included Portugal, Peru, Brazil, Chile, Colombia, Greece, Pakistan, S. Korea, Thailand and Turkey. A total of 1,268 T-37s of all types was built.

The A-37 was evolved from the T-37 for service in Vietnam, following evaluation by the USAF of two YAT-37D prototypes (first flown on 22 October 1963). In August 1966 the USAF ordered Cessna to complete 39 T-37Bs then in production as A-37As and the first of these was delivered in May 1967. These aircraft had eight underwing hardpoints, J85-GE-17A engines each de-rated to 2,400lb (1,090kg) st, and other changes and were operational in Vietnam by 1969. Deliveries began in May 1968 of the A-37B, with fully-rated engines, in-flight refuelling provision, 6g airframe stressing, provision for increased fuel capacity and other operational improvements. A total of 538 A-37Bs was built, recipients in addition to the USAF being Peru, Chile, Guatemala and Honduras. Many A-37Bs were transferred by USAF to the Vietnamese Air Force and nearly 100 were left in Vietnam when the war ended; some of these later entered service with the VPAF. Others serve with the Air Force Reserve in four squadrons; in addition, two ANG squadrons were to re-equip in 1981/2 on the OA-37B, a version of the Dragonfly modified for Forward Air Control duty.

Convair F-106 Delta Dart

USA

Interceptor fighter, in service

Data, photo and silhouette: F-106A
Powered by: One 24,500lb (11,123kg) st Pratt &
Whitney J75-P-17 afterburning turbojet
Span: 38ft 3.5in (11.67m)
Length: 70ft 8.75in (21.56m)
Empty weight: 23,646lb (10,726kg)
Gross weight: About 35,000lb (15,875kg)
Max speed: Mach 2.3 (1,525mph; 2,450km/h) at
36,000ft (11,000m)
Range: 1,150 miles (1,850km)
Accommodation: Pilot only (pilot and observer in
F-106B)
Armament: One Douglas AIR-2A Genie or AIR-2B
Super Genie rocket and four Hughes AIM-4F or
AIM-4G Super Falcon air-to-air missiles in internal
weapons bay, supplemented by one 20mm M-61
cannon in modified aircraft

Development of the Convair F-102 to accommodate
the more powerful J75 engine began in 1955 under
the designation F-102B but this was later changed
to F-106. While the wing remained substantially
unchanged, the fuselage was extensively redesigned
with the air intakes moved farther aft and the cockpit
moved relatively farther forward. The shape of the fin
and rudder was changed, the undercarriage was
improved and provision was made for later weapons
in the bomb-bay. A Hughes MA-1 guidance and
control system was introduced to permit the F-106
to operate with SAGE defence system. The first
F-106A flew on 26 December 1956. Production of
277 was completed by the end of 1960, deliveries to
Air Defense Command having begun in mid-1959.
On 9 April 1958, the first of 63 F-106Bs flew; this
variant is a combat trainer with two seats in tandem
and full operational capability. Until 1977, the
F-106A and F-106B equipped the majority of
Aerospace Defense Command units, some 231 Delta
Darts being shared by six active and five ANG
squadrons. New drop tanks suitable for supersonic
operation and capable of being refuelled in flight
were added to the F-106s some years ago. Another
modification programme, started in 1973, made
most F-106As capable of carrying an M-61 multi-
barrel 20mm cannon, together with a Snap-Shoot
gunsight. This enhanced the dogfighting capability of
the F-106. During 1979, the USAF phased out
Aerospace Defense Command as a major command
and the active F-106 units were transferred to TAC,
then re-equipping on F-4s. By 1980, the F-106
therefore remained in service only with the five ANG
squadrons.

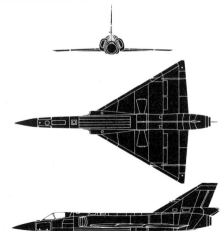

Dassault Mirage IV-A

France

Two-seat supersonic strategic bomber, in service

Powered by: Two 15,400lb (6,985kg) st SNECMA Atar 09K afterburning turbojets
Span: 38ft 10.5in (11.85m)
Length: 77ft 1in (23.50m)
Empty weight: 31,965lb (14,500kg)
Max gross weight: 73,800lb (33,475kg)
Max speed: Mach 2.2 (1,460mph; 2,350km/h) at 36,000ft (11,000m)
Tactical radius: 770 miles (1,240km)
Armament: One nuclear weapon recessed into bottom of fuselage, or 16 1,000lb bombs or four Martel air-to-surface missiles under fuselage and wings

To meet French Air Force requirements for a supersonic bomber to deliver France's atomic bomb, Dassault scaled up the Mirage III fighter design and the result was the prototype Mirage IV, which flew for the first time on 17 June 1959. Powered by two 13,225lb (6,000kg) st Atar 09 turbojets with afterburning, this aircraft exceeded Mach 2 during its 33rd test flight. It was followed by three pre-production Mirage IVs, of which the first flew on 12 October 1961. The first two had 14,110lb (6,400kg) st Atar 09Cs and introduced a circular under-fuselage radome and dummy missiles, some containing test equipment. The third pre-production machine, first flown on 23 January 1963, was to operational standard, with Atar 09Ks, flight-refuelling nose-probe and armament. A total of 62 production Mirage IV-As were ordered for the French Air Force. The first of these flew on 7 December 1963, and all had been delivered to the French Air Force by 1967. During the time that they made up the primary French nuclear strike force (*Force de Frappe*), the aircraft were kept in protective shelters, from which they could take off with their engines running at full power. As land-based and submarine-launched nuclear missiles have taken over the primary strike role, the Mirage IV-A force has been re-assigned to a low-level tactical strike role, carrying HE bombs or a tactical nuclear weapon with a 70KT yield. By the end of 1979, 47 Mirage IVs remained in service with nine squadrons in three wings, with no replacement expected before 1985. Four Mirage IV-As have been assigned to the strategic surveillance role, carrying reconnaissance equipment in a large pod, and 15 are to be modified to carry the French ASMP (*air-sol moyenne portée*) stand-off nuclear missile for service from 1985 onwards.

Dassault-Breguet Atlantic

France

Long-range maritime reconnaissance aircraft, in production and service

Photo and silhouette: Br1150 Atlantic
Data: Atlantic ANG
Powered by: Two 6,220ehp SNECMA/Rolls-Royce Tyne RTy20 Mk 21 turboprops
Span: 122ft 6.75in (37.36m)
Length: 104ft 2in (31.75m)
Max gross weight: 101,850lb (46,200kg)
Max speed: 409mph (658km/h)
Typical endurance: 8hrs at low altitude at 690 miles (1,110km) from base
Crew: 12
Armament: Internal weapon bay accommodates all standard NATO bombs, 385lb (175kg) depth charges, homing torpedoes and Exocet ASMs. Four underwing pylons for ASMs, unguided rockets etc.

Two prototypes of the Breguet Br 1150 Atlantic were ordered in December 1959, following a NATO design competition for a Neptune replacement which had attracted a total of 25 entries from manufacturers in several countries. The governments of France, Federal Germany, Belgium, the Netherlands and USA assumed joint responsibility for the programme, and design and manufacture of the aircraft was undertaken by a consortium of companies in several countries, under the overall leadership of Breguet. The first of the prototypes flew on 21 October 1961. Two pre-production aircraft (the first of which flew on 25 February 1963) introduced a 3ft (1m) longer front fuselage, giving more room in the operations control centre. Breguet then delivered 40 production machines for the French Navy, to equip three squadrons, and 20 for the German Navy; five of the latter are used for ECM duties with special equipment and 14 others are being upgraded by Dornier for service until the late 1980s. The first delivery of an operational Atlantic was made to Aéronavale on 10 December 1965. In 1968, further orders were placed by the Netherlands for nine aircraft, and by Italy for 18; and during 1974, Aéronavale sold three of its Atlantics to Pakistan. In the same year, work was started on converting an existing aircraft into a prototype Atlantic Mk II, planned to have AM39 Exocet air-to-surface missiles and a new standard of electronics primarily for an air-to-surface-vessel attack role. By 1977 this had evolved into the more refined Atlantic ANG (Atlantic Nouvelle Géneration), the full development phase of which was launched in October 1978 against a French Navy requirement for 42. Two prototype conversions of earlier Atlantics were to fly in 1981 and 1982 with delivery of the first production ANG in 1985.

Dassault-Breguet Etendard IV and Super Etendard

France

Single-seat carrier-based fighter-bomber and reconnaissance aircraft, in production and service

Data, photo and silhouette: Super Etendard
Powered by: One 11,025lb (5,000kg) st SNECMA Atar 8K-50 turbojet
Span: 31ft 6in (9.60m)
Length: 46ft 11.5in (14.31m)
Gross weight: 20,280-25,350lb (9,200-11,500kg)
Max speed: approx Mach 1 (660mph; 1,062km/h) at 36,000ft (11,000m)
Radius of action: 403 miles (650km) with AM39 missile
Armament: Two 30mm DEFA cannon. Four underwing attachments for 882lb (400kg) bombs, Magic air-to-air missiles or rocket pods. Alternatively, one Exocet AM39 air-to-surface missile under starboard wing and external fuel tank under port wing

The Etendard began life as a low-level land-based strike fighter to meet French Air Force and NATO requirements, prototypes of the Etendard II, IV and VI variants being built and flown. None of these models progressed beyond the prototype stage, but the French Navy decided to adapt the Etendard IV for service from its two attack carriers, the *Clémenceau* and *Foch*, and the prototype of the navalised Etendard IV-M flew on 21 May 1958. It was followed by five pre-production and 69 production IV-Ms, used to equip two seagoing squadrons (*Flot* 11F and 17F) and one shore-based training unit. Some of the IV-Ms were delivered with nose refuelling probes and 'buddy' refuelling packs. Also in service, with *Flot* 16F, is the Etendard IV-P, of which 21 were delivered (plus one prototype) as dual-purpose reconnaissance/tankers, with nose and ventral camera positions, no cannon, self-contained navigation system and flight refuelling nose-probe. During 1973, the French Navy ordered development of the Super Etendard, the principal new features being Agave X-band radar in a larger nose radome, uprated Atar 8K-50 non-afterburning turbojet instead of the 9,700lb (4,400kg) st Atar 8B of the Etendard IV, and improved wing leading-edge and trailing-edge flaps. The first of three prototype/trials aircraft converted from standard Etendard IVs flew on 28 October 1974 and the first of a planned production series of 71 Super Etendards flew on 24 November 1977. Deliveries to the Aéronavale began on 28 June 1978 and the Super Etendard is being used to equip *Flot* 11F and 17F, together with *Flot* 14F (previously flying F-8E(FN) Crusaders). An order for 14 Super Etendards has been placed by the Argentine's Comando de Aviacion Naval to replace A-4Q Skyhawks.

Dassault-Breguet Mirage III

France

Single-seat long-range fighter-bomber, in production and service

Data, photo and silhouette: Mirage III-E
Powered by: One 13,670lb (6,200kg) st SNECMA Atar 09C afterburning turbojet and, optionally, one 3,307lb (1,500kg) SEP 844 rocket-engine
Span: 27ft 0in (8.22m)
Length: 49ft 3.5in (15.03m)
Empty weight: 15,540lb (7,050kg)
Max gross weight: 29,760lb (13,500kg)
Max speed: Mach 2.2 (1,460mph; 2,350km/h) at 40,000ft (12,000m)
Tactical radius: 745 miles (1,200km) in ground attack configuration
Armament: Two 30mm cannon in fuselage and one AS.30 air-to-surface missile or Matra R530 air-to-air missile under fuselage, and two rocket pods or 1,000lb bombs under wings. Two Sidewinders can also be carried

The Mirage III was designed as an all-weather fighter capable of operating from short unprepared airstrips and has proved to be one of the most successful jet fighters of the 1960-1980 period, with about 1,400 sold to over 20 nations (including 480 Mirage 5 variants — see next page).

The prototype flew on 17 November 1956, with a 9,900lb (4,500kg) st Atar 101G turbojet. It was followed by the Mach 2 Mirage III-A with 13,225lb (6,000kg) st Atar 9B turbojet, of which 10 were built, and the generally-similar Mirage III-C (first flown 9 October 1960) of which 95 were built for all-weather interception and day ground attack duties with the French Air Force, with optional 3,307lb (1,500kg) thrust rocket-engine in the rear fuselage, and one for the Swiss Air Force. Others were delivered to Israel (III-CJ) and to South Africa (III-CZ). The Mirage III-C was followed by the III-E, first flown on 5 April 1961. This is a long-range fighter-bomber version with Atar 09C engine, fuselage lengthened by 1ft (30cm) and new nav/attack equipment. French orders for over 300 have been supplemented by export orders from the Argentine (III-EA), Brazil (III-EBR), Pakistan (III-EP), South Africa (III-EZ), Spain (III-EE; local designation C11), Lebanon (III-EL) and Venezuela (III-EV). Alongside the Mirage III-C, Dassault developed and produced the III-B, a tandem two-seat trainer which is 2ft (60cm) longer and retains the same strike capability as the III-C. This version first flew on 20 October 1959, and has been produced for the French Air Force, Israel (III-BJ), Lebanon (III-BL), Switzerland (III-BS), South Africa (III-BZ and III-DZ), Australia (III-D), Pakistan (III-DP), Brazil (III-DBR), Spain (III-DE; local designation CE11), and the Argentine (III-DA). The III-BE is a two-seat version of the III-E for the French Air Force. A reconnaissance version of the III-E is designated Mirage III-R and was first flown in prototype form in November 1961. It carries five cameras in the nose and has been built for the French Air Force (III-R and III-RD, the latter with improved equipment), Pakistan (III-RP), Switzerland (III-RS), South Africa (III-RZ and III-RDZ) and Abu Dhabi (III-RAD). A version of the III-C was built in Switzerland as the III-S, with Hughes radar and Falcon missiles; a version of the III-E built in Australia was designated III-O, a two-seat version being the III-D. Some late-production Mirage IIIs have the Atar 9K-50 engine, including the III-D2Z and III-R2Z for South Africa.

Dassault-Breguet Mirage 5 and 50 (and IAI Dagger)

France

Single-seat fighter-bomber, in production and service

Photo and silhouette: Mirage 5
Data: Mirage 50
Powered by: One 15,873lb (7,000kg) st SNECMA Atar 9K-50 afterburning turbojet
Span: 27ft 0in (8.22m)
Length: 51ft 0.5in (15.56m)
Empty weight: 15,765lb (7,150kg)
Gross weight: 30,200lb (13,700kg)
Max speed: Mach 2.2 (1,460mph; 2,350km/h) at 40,000ft (12,000m)
Combat radius: 430 miles (690km) with 1,760lb (800kg) bomb-load
Armament: Two 30mm cannon in fuselage. Typical external weapon load comprises two 1,000lb bombs, 10 500lb bombs and two 250lb bombs, plus two external fuel tanks. Other weapons can include one AS30 or R530 missile, rocket pods and Sidewinder missiles

By simplifying the electronics and other systems of the basic Mirage III-E airframe. Dassault produced a day fighter-bomber with increased internal fuel capacity, considerably greater weapon-carrying capability and reduced maintenance requirements, known as the Mirage 5. The prototype flew on 19 May 1967. Subsequently, 50 5-J Mirages were ordered by Israel, but delivery of these was blocked by the French government and in 1972 they were taken into service into the French Air Force as Mirage 5-Fs. Belgium ordered a total of 106 in three versions: the 5-BA for ground attack (27), the 5-BR reconnaissance model (63) and the 5-BD two-seater (16). The first of three Belgian Mirage 5s completed by Dassault flew on 6 March 1970; the remainder were then assembled in Belgium by SABCA. Other customers include Peru (5-P and 5-PD two-seaters); Libya (5-D, 5-DE, 5-DR and two-seat 5-DD); Colombia (5-COA, plus camera-equipped 5-COR and two-seat 5-COD); the United Arab Emirates Air Force-Abu Dhabi (5-AD and 5-RAD, plus two-seat 5-DAD); Venezuela (5-V and two-seat 5-DV); Gabon (5-G and two-seat 5DG); Zaïre (5-M and two-seat 5-DM); Pakistan (5-PA) and Saudi Arabia (5-SDE and two-seat 5-SDO). The Mirage 5s supplied to Saudi Arabia were transferred immediately to the Egyptian Air Force, on whose behalf they were bought. Dassault developed a derivative of the Mirage III/5 family known as the *Milan* (Kite), with retractable 'moustache' foreplanes which improve the low-speed handling. After trials on a Mirage III-R, a prototype Milan S-01 with Atar 09K-50 flew on 29 May 1970, but was not put into production. However, Sudan has ordered 24 Mirage 50s which are basically Mirage 5s with the Atar 09K-50 engine; and Chile has ordered 16 of this version, the prototype of which first flew on 15 April 1979. Israel Aircraft Industries has also offered for sale refurbished Mirage 5s with Atar 09C engines under the name of Dagger, and the Argentine Air Force placed an order for 26 of these aircraft during 1978.

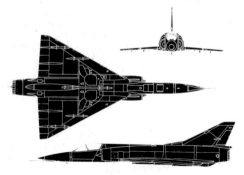

Dassault-Breguet Mirage F1

France

Single-seat all-weather multi-purpose fighter, in production

Data, photo and silhouette: Mirage F1-C
Powered by: One 15,798lb (7,166kg) st SNECMA Atar 09K-50 afterburning turbojet
Span: 27ft 6.75in (8.40m)
Length: 49ft 2.5in (15.00m)
Empty weight: 16,314lb (7,400kg)
Gross weight: 32,850lb (14,900kg)
Max speed: Mach 2.2 (1,460mph; 2,350km/h) at 40,000ft (12,000m). Mach 1.2 at low altitude
Endurance: 3hr 45min
Armament: Two 30mm DEFA cannon in forward fuselage. One under-fuselage strong point, and two under each wing, for max external load (in F1-E) of 8,820lb (4,000kg). Provision for Sidewinder missile attached to each wingtip

This multi-purpose fighter is a development of the Mirage III-E, with a basically similar fuselage and the same weapon systems. Its primary rôle is all-weather interception at all altitudes, but versions are also available with ground attack capability. The prototype flew for the first time on 23 December 1966, but was destroyed on 18 May 1967. Three replacements were ordered by the French Air Force, and the first of these, the F1-02, flew on 20 March 1969, followed by F1-03 on 18 September 1969 and F1-04 on 17 June 1970. The basic production model is the F1-C, the first production example of which flew on 15 February 1973. The F1-B is a two-seat variant, first flown on 26 May 1976. The F1-A has simplified electronics. The F1-E designation was first used for a single prototype, first flown on 22 December 1974, with 18,740lb (8,458kg) st M53 engine, but is now used for an Atar-engined advanced attack version, of which the F1-D is the two-seat equivalent. The F1-R reconnaissance version ordered by the French Air Force carries cameras internally and sensors in an underbelly pod. The French Air Force has ordered a total of 180 F1-Cs, 20 F1-Bs and 30 F1-Rs and funded 22 more in the 1981 defence budget; the first F1-Cs were delivered in March 1973 to the 30e *Escadre* at Reims. Export orders have brought total sales to 614 by end-1980, the customers comprising Spain (F1-CE; -EE and -BE; Spanish designations C14 and CE14), Greece (F1-CG), Kuwait (F1-CK and BK), Iraq (F1-EQ and -BQ), Ecuador (F1-JA and JB), Libya (F1-AD, -BD and -ED), Morocco (F1-CH and -BH), Jordan (F1-EJ and -BJ) and South Africa (F1-AZ and -CZ). Qatar has ordered 12 single-seat F1s and two two-seaters.

Dassault-Breguet Mirage 2000

France

Single-seater air superiority and long-range interdiction fighter, in production

Powered by: One 19,840lb (9,000kg) st SNECMA M53-5 turbofan with afterburning
Span: 29ft 6in (9.00m) (estimated)
Length: 50ft 3.5in (15.33m) (estimated)
Gross weight: 33,070lb (15,000kg)
Max speed: Approximately Mach 2.3 (1,520mph; 2,440km/h) above 40,000ft (12,000m)
Radius of action: 435 miles (700km) (air superiority role)
Armament: Built-in armament of two 30mm DEFA cannon. Two Matra Super 530 and two Matra 550 Magic air-to-air missiles in air superiority rôle (plus provision for two drop tanks). Four underwing pylons and five fuselage hardpoints for up to 11,000lb (5,000kg) of ordnance in interdiction rôle

The Mirage 2000 is being developed as the principal new tactical fighter for the Armée de l'Air, with which it is expected to enter service in 1983. The Mirage 2000 follows the delta-wing configuration of the highly successful Mirage III/5 series, but is designed for a high overall performance and increased combat capability. The initial version is intended for interceptor and air superiority rôles, in which it carries two 30mm DEFA cannon and two Matra 550 Magic missiles. A large Thomson-CSF/EMD pulse-doppler radar, the RDI, is being developed for service from 1985; earlier aircraft, and those for export from 1984, will have the RDM multi-rôle doppler radar. Carrying two drop tanks in addition to the four air-to-air missiles, it will have about twice the endurance of the Mirage F1 on combat air patrols, and in the secondary rôle of long-range low-altitude interdiction and reconnaissance it will be able to carry up to 11,000lb (5,000kg) of bombs on four wing and five fuselage hardpoints. The initial Armée de l'Air requirement is for 130 of the air superiority version, in single-seat and two-seat variants, in addition to about 200 long-range interdiction and tactical reconnaissance versions for which Aérospatiale is developing the nuclear ASMP (*air-sol moyenne portée*) stand-off missile. The first of four prototypes of the single-seat Mirage 2000 (including one company-funded) flew on 10 March 1978, followed by the others on 18 September 1978, 26 April 1979 and 12 May 1980. A prototype of the two-seat Mirage 2000B made its first flight on 11 October 1980.

Dassault-Breguet/Dornier Alpha Jet   France/Germany

Light strike aircraft and basic/weapons trainer, in production and service

Powered by: Two 2,975lb (1,350kg) st SNECMA-Turbomeca GRTS Larzac 04-C5 turbofans
Span: 29ft 11in (9.11m)
Length: 40ft 3in (12.29m)
Empty weight: 7,660lb (3,475kg)
Gross weight: trainer, 10,010lb (4,540kg); close support, 13,227lb (6,000kg); max permissible, 15,432lb (7,000kg)
Max speed: 616mph (991km/h) at sea level, Mach 0.84 at altitude
Radius of action: close support, 390 miles (630km)
Armament: Provision for gun pod under fuselage (one 30mm or two 0.50in), and four wing pylons carrying max combined load of 3,760lb (1,710kg)

The project to develop a new basic trainer to meet the joint requirements of France and Germany was initiated in July 1969, A basic Dornier design submitted jointly with Dassault was selected for development, having tandem seating and two SNECMA-Turboméca Larzac 02 engines. After development began in 1971 for the Armée de l'Air and the Luftwaffe, the latter changed its requirement to that of a close air-support, battlefield reconnaissance and anti-helicopter aircraft and the Alpha Jet A was developed around more powerful Larzac engines to have extra wing pylons and higher operating weights, as quoted above. This version is normally flown as a single-seater with ECM in the rear cockpit. The first of the two 'basic' prototypes flew in France on 26 October 1973, followed by the second in Germany on 9 January 1974. Prototype No 3, also flown in France, was first airborne on 6 May 1974 and represented the Luftwaffe configuration, while No 4, flown in Germany on 11 October 1974, was a French trainer. The first truly representative production French trainer flew on 19 May 1978; the first Alpha Jet A for the Luftwaffe had flown in Germany on 12 April 1978. The Armée de l'Air has ordered 144 Alpha Jet Es and first put the type into service with GE314 at Tours in May 1979 for advanced training. The Luftwaffe ordered 175 and the Technische Gruppe 31 began an intensive flying trial in March 1979 followed by inauguration of JaboG 49 as the first operational unit on 20 March 1980. The Belgian Air Force ordered 33 Alpha Jet Bs (first flight 20 June 1978; production aircraft assembled by SABCA) and service use began at the 11e Escadrille in September 1979. Other orders are from Ivory Coast (6), Morocco (24), Qatar (6), Nigeria (12), Egypt (30) and Togo (5).

De Havilland (Canada) DHC-4 Caribou Canada

Light tactical transport, in service

Powered by: Two 1,450hp Pratt & Whitney R-2000-7M2 piston-engines
Span: 95ft 7.5in (29.15m)
Length: 72ft 7in (22.13m)
Empty weight: 18,260lb (8,283kg)
Normal gross weight: 28,500lb (12,928kg)
Max speed: 216mph (347km/h) at 6,500ft (1,980m)
Range: 242 miles (290km) with max payload
Accommodation: Crew of three plus 32 combat troops or 26 paratroops or 22 litters and eight other persons

De Havilland Canada began design of this STOL tactical transport in 1955. The project gained US Army support in 1957 with a contract for five prototypes designated YAC-1; the Canadian Government ordered two, of which one was for RCAF evaluation as the CC-108.

The first Caribou flew on 30 July 1958 and the first YAC-1 in March 1959. Deliveries to the US Army began in October 1959 and the first of a continuing series of production orders was placed in 1960. The US Army AC-1s (later redesignated CV-2As) were delivered with a gross weight of 26,000lb (11,790kg); later aircraft (CV-2Bs) were to DHC-4A standard with a weight of 28,500lb.

A total of 159 Caribou was acquired by the US Army; 134 still in service in January 1967 were taken over by the USAF and redesignated C-7A. They are operated currently by a Tactical Airlift Group of the ANG assigned to MAC and by two squadrons of the AF Reserve. Four Caribou Mk 1A (DHC-4) ordered by the RCAF in August 1960 were allocated to UN forces in the Congo and five Mk 1B (DHC-4A) were purchased later, all with the CC-108 designation. Two CV-2As were transferred to the Indian Air Force in 1963 for evaluation, and 20 Caribou were subsequently purchased by India. Other air forces which bought Caribou, and continued to fly them in 1980, were those of Australia (26), Kenya (8), Zambia (5), Malaysia (17), Tanzania (12), Spain (12), Zaïre (2) and United Arab Emirates (3).

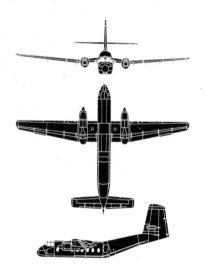

De Havilland (Canada) DHC-5 Buffalo

Canada

Assault transport, in production and service

Photo: DHC-5 of Togo Air Force
Data: DHC-5D
Powered by: Two 3,133shp General Electric CT64-820-4 turboprops
Span: 96ft 0in (29.26m)
Length: 79ft 0in (24.08m)
Empty weight: 25,050lb (11,362kg)
Gross weight: 49,200lb (22,316kg)
Max speed: 288mph (463km/h) at 10,000ft (3,050m)
Range: 690 miles (1,112km) with max payload
Accommodation: Crew of three; up to 41 troops or 35 paratroops or 24 litters and six other people

As the Caribou II, this design originated in a US Army requirement which was put out to industry in May 1962. De Havilland Aircraft of Canada, one of 25 companies invited to submit designs, had already sold three earlier types to the US Army in quantity — the Beaver, Otter and Caribou. The DHC-5, which was selected as winner of the design competition, was based on the Caribou wing and had the same general configuration, with a new, more capacious fuselage, a T-tail and T64 turboprop engines. The US Army ordered four DHC-5s for evaluation and development, originally with the designation YAC-2, this being changed later to YCV-7A and then to C-8A when the USAF took over US Army transports in January 1967. The first of these aircraft flew on 9 April 1964 and was delivered a year later. Late in 1964, the Canadian Armed Forces ordered 15 Buffaloes, of which most are now assigned to search and rescue duties. These are designated CC-115 and have a 20in (50cm) increase in overall length due to the nose radome, and more powerful engines. 24 similar aircraft were ordered for the Brazilian Air Force and 16 by Peru, deliveries taking place in 1971/72. The DHC-5D version, with uprated engines and higher operating weights, entered production in 1974 and first flew on 1 August 1975. Orders to date include eight for Kenya, seven for Zambia, six for Tanzania, five for United Arab Emirates, four for Sudan, three for Zaïre and two each for Mauritania, Ecuador, Togo and the Oman Police Air Wing.

EMBRAER EMB-111 and EMB-110 Bandeirante   Brazil

Twin-turboprop patrol aircraft (EMB-111) and light transport (EMB-110), in production and service

Photo: EMB-110C(N), Chile
Data and silhouette: EMB-111
Powered by: Two 750shp Pratt & Whitney (Canada) PT6A-34 turboprops
Span: 52ft 4.5in (15.96m)
Length: 48ft 8in (14.83m)
Gross weight: 15,430lb (7,000kg)
Cruising speed: 251mph (404km/h) at 10,000ft (3,050m)
Range: 1,693 miles (2,725km)
Armament: Provision for six air-to-surface rockets or three bombs or depth charges under wings
Accommodation: Crew of five or six

The EMB-111 is a shore-based maritime aircraft developed initially to meet a requirement of the Brazilian Air Force, which placed an order for 12 at the end of 1975. The design is a variant of the EMB-110 Bandeirante transport, from which it differs externally in having AIL AN/APS-128 search radar in a large nose radome, a podded searchlight in a nacelle on the starboard wing, wingtip tanks, and provision for rockets under the wings. The internal equipment is also extensively revised to suit the coastal surveillance role. The first EMB-111M for the FAB (with the military designation P-95) made its first flight in August 1977, and deliveries have been interspersed with six similar EMB-111Ns for Chile. One EMB-111 has also been ordered by the Force Aèrienne Gabonaise. The design of the EMB-110 itself was evolved initially by the aircraft department (PAR) of the official Aeronautical Technical Centre (CTA). Designated YC-95, the prototype first flew on 26 October 1968, and was followed by the slightly modified second prototype on 19 October 1969. These prototypes carried 7-10 passengers and had 550shp PT6A-20 engines; basic production aircraft have 12 passenger seats and 680shp PT6A-27 or 750shp PT6A-34 engines. By mid-1980, the Brazilian Air Force had ordered 116 Bandeirantes, of which 60 are the basic EMB-110 model (C-95); 40 are EMB-110K1 freighters (C-95A) with enlarged fuselage door, six are EMB-110B air survey versions (R-95) and three are EMB-110A navaid checking and calibration aircraft (EC-95). The Chilean Navy has acquired three EMB-110C(N)s and the Uruguayan Air Force has five EMB-110Cs. The Force Aèrienne Gabonaise has ordered three EMB-110P1 Bandeirante transports.

English Electric Canberra (and Martin B-57)

Three-seat tactical light bomber, reconnaissance aircraft, trainer and target, in service

Photo and silhouette: Canberra PR Mk 9
Data: Canberra B Mk 6
Powered by: Two 7,400lb (3,357kg) st Rolls-Royce Avon 109 turbojets
Span: 63ft 11.5in (19.51m)
Length: 65ft 6in (19.96m)
Gross weight: 55,000lb (24,950kg)
Max speed: 580mph (933km/h) at 30,000ft (9,145m)
Range: 3,790 miles (6,100km)
Armament: As bomber carries 6,000lb (2,720kg) of weapons internally. Later aircraft modified to carry up to 1,000lb (455kg) of bombs, rocket pods or guided weapons under each wing

About 100 Canberras remain in RAF service or in reserve, and others are in service with several foreign

air forces. Principal RAF service versions are the PR Mk 9 photographic reconnaissance aircraft used by one UK-based squadron; B Mk 2 and B Mk 6 bombers used for special duties and as trainers, and T Mk 4 trainers in service at the Canberra OCU. The E Mk 15 is a modification of the B Mk 6 for special duties and other modified variants are the T Mk 17 ECM trainer, the T Mk 19 radar target and the TT Mk 18 target tug. The T Mk 22 was the final British variant designated, for use as a special RN radar target. Among the users of exported Canberra versions, some of which are refurbished ex-RAF aircraft, are Zimbabwe, using a few B Mk 2s; Ethiopia, which flies a pair of similar B Mk 52s; Peru with B Mk 72s and Venezuela with B Mk 82s. Peru also has B(I) Mk 56s and B(I) Mk 78s (the final digit in these mark numbers corresponds with equivalent RAF variants); Venezuela has B(I) Mk 88 intruders. Also similar to the B(I) Mk 8 intruders are the B(I) Mk 12s of the SAAF, and the B(I) Mk 58s and B(I) Mk 12s of the Indian Air Force, while Argentina has B Mk 62s and India has B Mk 66s. Several of these air forces also operate reconnaissance and training variants — eg PR Mk 57s, T Mk 67s and T Mk 13s in India, PR Mk 82s and T Mk 84s in Venezuela, T Mk 74s in Peru, and T Mk 64s in Argentina. Three Mk 2s are used on special duties by the Luftwaffe. The RAAF uses Australian-built B Mk 20s and T Mk 21s for photo-reconnaissance and target-towing tasks. Under licence from the UK government, the Glenn L. Martin company put a version of the Canberra into production for the USAF. All but the initial B-57A/RB-57A variants featured a new cockpit arrangement with tandem seating, and versions up to B-57G were designated. Last of the USAF Canberras in service, until 1981, was a squadron of EB-57Bs and B-57Cs providing electronic warfare training in NORAD.

Fairchild A-10A Thunderbolt II

USA

Single-seat close support aircraft, in production and service

Powered by: Two 9,065lb (4,112kg) st General Electric TF34-GE-100 turbofans
Span: 57ft 6in (17.53m)
Length: 53ft 4in (16.26m)
Empty weight: 20,796lb (9,433kg)
Gross weight: 47,400lb (21,500kg)
Max combat speed: 449mph (723km/h), clean, at sea level
Combat radius: 288 miles (463km), with 2 hours in combat area (close air support)
Armament: One 30mm GAU-8/A multi-barrel gun and up to 16,000lb (7,257kg) external ordnance on 11 pylons

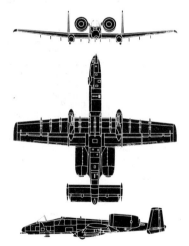

Designs submitted by Fairchild and Northrop in the USAF's A-X programme were chosen for prototype construction and a fly-off competition. The two prototypes of the Fairchild design, designated YA-10, first flew on 10 May and 21 July 1972, respectively and after intensive trials at Edwards AFB, the A-10 was declared winner on 18 January 1973. Competitive development of a new 30mm multi-barrel gun was also undertaken, and the General Electric GAU-8/A was chosen for the A-10 in August 1973, the first in-flight firing trials from the No 1 prototype taking place on 26 February 1974. A batch of six R & D A-10As was funded in the 1974 Defense Budget and the first of these flew on 15 February 1975. The total projected USAF requirement is put at 739, with funding for the initial production batch of 22 included in the FY75 budget, and additional batches each year subsequently. The first production A-10A flew on 21 October 1975 and deliveries began in the spring of 1976, to the 333rd TF Training Squadron at Davis-Monthan AFB. A year later, the first A-10As began to reach the first operational wing to form on the type (the 354th TFW) at Myrtle Beach AFB, South Carolina, with initial operational capability achieved in January 1978. Deployment of the six-squadron 81st Tactical Fighter Wing to bases in the UK began towards the end of 1978; eight-aircraft detachments from these bases are rotated to four forward operation locations (FOLs) in Germany. On 4 May 1979 Fairchild flew the prototype of a night/adverse-weather two-seat version of the A-10A, featuring multi-mode terrain-following radar, forward-looking IR and laser range finding. This version did not enter production but formed the basis for a two-seat combat-ready trainer, an order for 30 of which was placed by USAF in 1981.

FMA IA58 and IA66 Pucara

Argentina

Counter-insurgency attack aircraft, in production and service

Data, photo and silhouette: IA 58A
Powered by: Two 1,022shp Turboméca Astazou XVIG turboprops
Span: 47ft 6.75in (14.50m)
Length: 46ft 9in (14.25m)
Empty weight: 8,900lb (4,037kg)
Gross weight: 14,990lb (6,800kg)
Max speed: 310mph (500km/h)
Range: 1,890 miles (3,042km)
Accommodation: Two seats in tandem
Armament: Two 20mm Hispano cannon and four 7.62mm FN machine guns in fuselage. Three strong points under fuselage and wings for up to 3,300lb (1,500kg) of stores

The Pucará is the latest product of the Argentinian Military Aircraft Factory (the Fábrica Militar de Aviones) at Cordoba. It is a counter-insurgency and light tactical aircraft designed to meet the requirements of the Argentine Air Force, which is reported to have plans to acquire about 70 production examples. Flight testing of the design (originally named the Delfin) began with a full-scale unpowered prototype, with dummy engines and fixed undercarriage, which was first flown on 26 December 1967. This was followed by a powered prototype with 904shp Garrett-AiResearch TPE 331-U-303 engines, first flown on 20 August 1969, and a second prototype with 1,022shp Turboméca Astazou XVIG engines, first flown on 6 September 1970. Work on an initial production batch began in 1972 and the first of these flew on 8 November 1974, by which time the Argentine Air Force had placed a firm order for 30. Deliveries began in the first half of 1976 and the aircraft entered service with the II Escuadron de Exploracion y Ataque at Reconquista. A second batch of 30 IA 58s has now been ordered and the eventual Argentine Air Force requirement is about 100. The Uruguayan Air Force ordered six IA 58s in 1980. Early in 1979 the FMA flew the prototype of the IA 58B Pucará-B (the 25th Pucará-A converted) in which a pair of 30mm DEFA 533 cannon replace the 20mm Hispano guns in the forward fuselage, which is slightly deepened. The IA 66, under development in 1980, differs in having Garrett-AiResearch TPE 331-11 turboprops; also projected were a maritime surveillance variant and a dual control trainer.

43

Fokker F27 (Troopship and Maritime)   Netherlands

Short/medium-range military transport aircraft, in production and service

Photo: F27 Maritime, Peru
Data and silhouette: F27 Mk 400M Troopship
Powered by: Two 2,210shp Rolls-Royce Dart RDa7 Mk 532-7 turboprops
Span: 95ft 2in (29.00m)
Length: 77ft 3.5in (23.56m)
Empty weight: 23,430lb (10,628kg)
Gross weight: 45,000lb (20,410kg)
Normal cruising speed: 302mph (486km/h) at 20,000ft (6,100m)
Range: 1,285 miles (2,000km) with max payload
Accommodation: Crew of two or three and up to 45 troops, or freight

Although it is best-known as a 40/56-seat airliner, the F27 Friendship is also in service as a military transport. The Royal Netherlands Air Force has three more-or-less standard Friendship airliners and the

Philippine Air Force has one for VIP duties and nine for cargo-carrying and trooping. In addition, the RNAF has six F27M Troopships with accommodation for 45 paratroops, 13,800lb (6,260kg) of freight or 24 litter patients and 7 attendants in an air ambulance rôle. The Troopship (F27 Mk 400) has a large cargo door at the front on the port side and an enlarged rear cabin door, for parachuting, on each side. Three former RNAF examples have been transferred to the RNN as navigation trainers. Four were supplied to the Sudanese Air Force in 1965 and the Argentine Air Force has five Troopships and five Mk 600s, which lack some of the special features of the F27M. The Uruguayan Air Force acquired two F27 Mk 100s together with two Fairchild FH-227Bs and the Bolivian Air Force has six F27s. The Imperial Iranian Air Force purchased a total of 14 Troopships and six F27 Mk 600s, four of the Mk 400Ms being equipped to serve as target tugs. The Iranian Army had two F27s and the Navy had four. Nigeria bought two F27Ms, one F27 Mk 600 and one Troopship are in service in the Republic of the Ivory Coast, and in 1973 the Ghana Air Force bought three Troopships and two Srs 600. The Indonesian Air Force has eight F27Ms and six F27s bought by Air Algerie are also available for use by the Algerian Air Force. Burma has five F27s, Senegal has acquired six F27s, two serve with the Benin Force Armées Populaire and two with the Finnish Air Force. On 28 February 1976, Fokker-VFW flew the prototype of the F27 Maritime, a version equipped for maritime patrol duties, with Litton AN/APS 504(V)-2 radar in the fuselage. Two examples of the Maritime have been bought by the Peruvian Navy, three by the Spanish Air Force (designated D2), two by the Netherlands Navy (MLD) for operation in the Netherlands Antilles, one by Angola and three by the Philippine Air Force. The RNZAF has acquired three F27 Mk 100s from NAC and these have been converted for maritime patrol and navigation training.

GAF Mission Master and Search Master   Australia

STOL utility transport, in production and service

Data, photo and silhouette: Mission Master
Powered by: Two 400shp Allison 250-B17B turboprops
Span: 54ft 0in (16.46m)
Length: 41ft 2.25in (12.56m)
Empty weight: 4,666lb (2,116kg)
Gross weight: 8,500lb (3,855kg)
Normal cruising speed: 193mph (311km/h)
Range: 840 miles (1,352km)
Accommodation: Two pilots and up to 14 persons in cabin

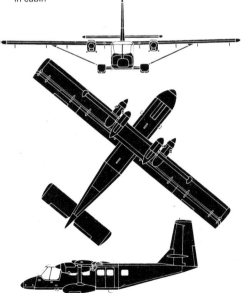

Design of a small utility transport with both military and civil applications began at the Government Aircraft Factories at Fishermen's Bend in 1965, this being the first full-scale design project of the GAF. Previously the Factories had built a number of European aircraft under licence, including the Canberra and Mirage, and had developed and produced the Jindivik target and the Ikara anti-submarine weapon. The transport design was designated Project N and evolved as a conventional high-wing aircraft with single fin and rudder, retractable undercarriage, and emphasis upon simple construction and ease of operation. Two prototypes were built, making their first flights respectively on 23 July and 5 December 1971, and these subsequently became known as Nomad 22s. During 1972, an initial production batch of 20 was ordered by the Australian government, of which 11 were delivered for service with the Australian Army Aviation Corps and six were to be supplied to the Indonesian Navy in the maritime patrol role, under the terms of Australian aid for Indonesia. By the beginning of 1978, production of 95 aircraft had been authorised in four versions. The basic civilian model is the N22B, and a lengthened 19-passenger civilian version is avilable as the N24A. The Mission Master is the standard military counterpart of the N22B for the Australian Army (11), Papua New Guinea (5) and the Philippines (12). The derivative for coastal surveillance duty is the Search Master, available in two versions: Search Master B has a Bendix RDR 1400 search radar in the nose while Search Master L has the Litton APS 504(V)-2 radar in an under-nose radome. The Indonesian Navy (TNI-AL) has ordered six of this variant and six L versions.

General Dynamics F-16 Fighting Falcon USA

**Single-seat fighter and two-seat operational
trainer, in production and service**

Data, photo and silhouette: F-16A
Powered by: One Pratt & Whitney F100-PW-100
turbofan, rated at approx 25,000lb (11,340kg) st
with afterburning
Span: 31ft 0in (9.45m)
Length: 47ft 7.75in (14.52m)
Empty weight: approx 14,000lb (6,350kg)
Max gross weight: 33,000lb (14,968kg)
Max speed: Above Mach 2
Radius of action: More than 575 miles (925km)
Armament: One internally-mounted M61A-1
20mm multi-barrel gun with 500 rounds of
ammunition. One advanced Sidewinder air-to-air
missile on each wingtip. Underwing attachments for
other stores; max external load, 15,200lb (6,895kg)

Two prototypes of this aircraft were ordered in April
1972, under the USAF's Lightweight Fighter (LWF)
programme, simultaneously with two prototypes of
the Northrop YF-17. The first YF-16 flew on
20 January 1974, followed by the second on 9 May
and in January 1975 the GD design was named
winner of what had become the Air Combat Fighter
(ACF) evaluation, with a first order for six single-seat
F-16As and two two-seat F-16Bs for 'full-scale
development'; the tandem-seat F-16B has the same
overall dimensions but reduced internal fuel to
accommodate the second seat. The first of these
F-16As flew on 8 December 1976 and the first
F-16B (fourth of the FSD batch) flew on 9 August
1977. The USAF has a requirement for a total of
1,388 F-16 Fighting Falcons (including 204 F-16Bs);
the first production aircraft flew on 7 August 1978
and service introduction began in January 1979 at
the 388th TF Wing, Hill AFB. In 1975, four NATO
nations adopted the F-16 as an F-104 replacement
and a licence-manufacturing programme was set up,
with final assembly by SABCA at Gosselies and
Fokker at Schiphol, where first flights were made on
11 December 1978 and 3 May 1979 respectively
(F-16Bs in each case). The European programme
embraces Belgium, 104 F-16A and 12 F-16B;
Denmark, 46 A and 12 B; Netherlands, 80 A and
22 B and Norway, 60 A and 12 B. Israel ordered 67
F-16A and 8 F-16B, deliveries of which began early
1980 and Egypt has ordered 60 F-16s including
two-seaters. An additional 22 were ordered by the
Netherlands early in 1981.

General Dynamics F-111

Two-seat tactical fighter (and jamming aircraft) in service

Photo: F-111C
Silhouette: F-111E
Data: EF-111A
Powered by: Two 18,500lb (8,400kg) st Pratt & Whitney TF30-P-3 afterburning turbofans
Span: 63ft 0in (19.20m) spread; 31ft 11.5in (9.74m) swept
Length: 77ft 1.5in (23.51m)
Empty weight: 53,418lb (24,230kg)
Max take-off weight: 87,478lb (39,680kg)
Max speed: 1,160mph (1,865km/h) (at combat weight)
Combat radius: Over 1,000 miles (1,610km/h) for close air support mission
Ferry range: 2,484 miles (3,998km)

Initial contracts for 18 F-111A (USAF) and five F-111B (USN), for development flying, were followed by production of several variants of this tactical fighter for the USAF. The F-111A first flew on 21 December 1964, and the variable-sweep wing was operated on the second flight on 6 January 1965. The first F-111A (a trials aircraft) was delivered for service in July 1967. The first operational unit was the 474th TFW, which received its first aircraft (the 31st F-111A) in October 1967. Production of the F-111A totalled 141 (excluding the trials aircraft), followed by 94 F-111Es which have revised intake geometry. The first of these swing-wing aircraft deployed to Europe were F-111Es assigned to the 20th TFW at Upper Heyford in September 1970, where they were still operating in 1980. These were followed by 96 F-111Ds, with uprated avionics, and 106 F-111Fs with TF30-P-100 turbofans to equip two more TAC Wings, the 27th and 366th respectively. The 366th TFW now flies the F-111As relinquished by the 474th TFW and the F-111Fs are flown by the 48th TFW in the UK. Two F-111Ks, intended for, but not delivered to the RAF, went to USAF as YF-111As; one development aircraft was flown as RF-111A, and the RAAF acquired 24 F-111C strike aircraft supplemented in 1980 by four ex-USAAF F-111As. Four of the F-111Cs have been modified for tactical reconnaissance duties with sensors in the weapon bay; first flight of this variant was made on 27 April 1979. Two F-111As were converted to EF-111A tactical jamming aircraft by Grumman, with pallet-mounted ALQ-99 jamming system in the weapons bay and a large fin-tip radome, and with all ordnance provision deleted. An aerodynamic prototype EF-111A flew on 10 March 1977, followed by a second prototype with full avionics on 17 May 1977. The USAF plans to acquire 40 similar EF-111A conversions from mid-1981 onwards.

General Dynamics FB-111A

USA

Two-seat strategic bomber, in service

Powered by: Two 20,350lb (9,230kg) st Pratt &
Whitney TF30-P-7 afterburning turbofans
Span: 70ft 0in (21.34m) spread; 33ft 11in
(10.34m) swept
Length: 73ft 6in (22.40m)
Gross weight: 100,000lb (45,360kg) (estimated)
Max speed: Mach 2.5 (1,650mph; 2,655km/h) at
36,000ft (11,000m)
Range: 4,100 miles (6,600km) with external fuel
Armament: External points for four 2,200lb
(1,000kg) Boeing AGM-69A SRAM short-range
attack missiles with two more in weapons bay.
Provision for up to 31,500lb (14,285kg) of
conventional weapons. Typical load comprises two
750lb bombs in internal weapon-bay and 36 in twin
clusters of three on six underwing attachments with
wings at 26° sweep (Only 20 such bombs can be
carried at full wing-sweep)

The FB-111A was derived from the original swing
wing F-111 (previous page) to provide Strategic Air
Command of the USAF with an advanced supersonic
bomber to supplement its B-52 force. Procurement
of as many as 253 FB-111As was planned originally,
but development hold-ups, cost escalation and
changes in the US strategic posture led to successive
reductions to a total production run of 76, completed
in 1971, to equip only two wings. The FB-111A
airframe is a hybrid, using the larger wing, with six
pylons, developed originally for the Navy's F-111B,
with the fuselage and intakes of the F-111E. It also
has a new avionics fit, higher gross weight, beefed-
up structure and landing gear, and uprated engines.
The FB-111A prototype was a conversion of the last
F-111A development airframe (No 18), first flown on
30 July 1967. Two other modified F-111As were
used in the development programme before the first
flight of the first production FB-111A on 13 July
1968 (fitted temporarily with TF30-P-3 engines).
The first SAC unit to equip with the new bomber was
the 340th Bomb Group at Carswell AFB, on
8 October 1969; this unit provides combat crew
training for the two two-squadron wings which are
equipped with the FB-111A — the 509th Bomb
Wing at Pease AFB, NH, and the 380th Strategic
Aerospace Wing at Plattsburgh, NY. Following
cancellation of the B-1, development of an improved
version of the FB-111 was suggested and a proposal
was studied to convert aircraft to the projected
FB-111H configuration with lengthened fuselage,
General Electric F101 engines, increased bomb-load
and other changes. In 1980, less radical proposals
were being studied to update the FB-111As to
FB-111B/C configurations.

Grumman A-6 Intruder

USA

Two-seat carrier-based strike and reconnaissance aircraft, in service

Data, photo and silhouette: A-6E
Powered by: Two 9,300lb (4,218kg) st Pratt & Whitney J52-P-8A or 8B turbojets
Span: 53ft 0in (16.15m)
Length: 54ft 7in (16.64m)
Empty weight: 25,630lb (11,625kg)
Max gross weight: 60,400lb (27,397kg)
Max speed: 643mph (1,035km/h) at sea level
Armament: Up to 17,280lb (7,838kg) of assorted stores on four underwing attachments and in a semi-recessed fuselage bay

US Navy and Marine Corps experience in Korea led to a new requirement for a long-range, all-weather low-altitude attack aircraft, able to carry a heavy load of conventional or nuclear weapons. A design competition was held in May 1957 and Grumman was named the winner at the end of that year. Features of the Grumman design, originally called A2F-1, included tilting tailpipes on the engines, to help shorten take-off distances, but production aircraft have a fixed downward tilt on the jet pipes. The US Navy ordered eight Intruders for trials and the first flew on 19 April 1960. Production of the A-6A followed, and this became the standard all-weather attack aircraft for Navy and Marine squadrons. Production totalled 482, of which 19 became A-6B carrying AGM-78A Standard ARM anti-radar missiles, and 12 became A-6C with FLIR (forward-looking infra-red) in a dorsal pod. A prototype KA-6D 'buddy' flight-refuelling tanker flew on 23 May 1966, and 62 A-6As were converted to this standard. Second major Intruder production variant was the A-6E, first flown on 27 February 1970, with Norden multi-mode navigation and attack radar. To equip 12 USN squadrons and five USMC squadrons, a total procurement of 318 A-6Es was planned, including A-6A conversions. Most new and converted A-6Es are in due course to have target recognition attack multisensor (TRAM) equipment, first flown on a test aircraft on 22 March 1974, and Harpoon missile capability. The TRAM-equipped A-6E version first flew with full avionics/sensor fit on 22 October 1974 and deployment with VA-165 aboard the USS *Constellation* began in 1977, without the undernose turret containing the detection and ranging set. The latter became available in late 1979.

Grumman E-2 Hawkeye

USA

Five-seat carrier-borne airborne early warning and fighter control aircraft, in production and service

Data, photo and silhouette: E-2C
Powered by: Two 4,910shp Allison T56-A-422/425 turboprops
Span: 80ft 7in (24.56m)
Length: 57ft 7in (17.55m)
Empty weight: 38,009lb (17.256kg)
Gross weight: 51,900lb (23,540kg)
Max speed: 348mph (560km/h)
Ferry range: 1,605 miles (2,583km) with full internal fuel
Armament: None

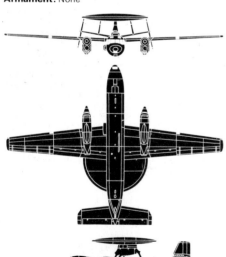

Like the E-1 Tracer which it replaced, the E-2 carries a large saucer-shaped radome above the fuselage, and a mass of electronic devices to process the information provided by the radar. The complete installation is called Airborne Tactical Data System — ATDS — and the information provided by it is transmitted to a Naval Tactical Data System. Taking information from a team of E-2s disposed around a Naval task force, the NTDS can assess and act upon the threat of attack from any direction.

An aerodynamic prototype of the E-2 flew on 21 October 1960, followed by the first with full electronic equipment on 19 April 1961. Deliveries began on 19 January 1964, and the first Hawkeye unit, VAW-11, became operational in 1966, followed by VAW-12, both squadrons providing detached flights on board operational aircraft carriers. Production of the E-2A ended in 1967 with a total of 59 built. A few became TE-2As with the ATDS removed and training equipment added. Between 1969 and 1971, the entire remaining E-2A force was modified to E-2B standard by installation of an updated general-purpose computer of increased capacity. The E-2C has a completely revised electronic system and improved engines. A prototype flew on 20 January 1971 and a second followed later in the year. The first production E-2C flew on 23 September 1972 and procurement of 86 is expected to be complete by 1985, to allow each operational USN carrier to keep one of its four E-2Cs airborne continuously for an extended operational period. From 1976, E-2Cs have been delivered with improved AN/APS-125 radar. A small number of TE-2C training versions is in service. Four E-2Cs have been delivered to Israel and Japan ordered in late 1979 the first four of a planned total of 15.

Grumman EA-6B Prowler

USA

Four-seat carrier-based electronic counter-measures aircraft, in production and service

Powered by: Two 9,300lb (4,218kg) st Pratt & Whitney J52-P-8A, -8B or -408 turbojets
Span: 53ft 0in (16.15m)
Length: 59ft 5in (18.11m)
Empty weight: 34,581lb (15,686kg)
Max gross weight: 65,000lb (29,483kg)
Max speed: 656mph (1,055km/h)
Range: 1,180miles (1,897km) with max load and reserves
Armament: Normally unarmed; external weapons attachment points retained as on A-6
Accommodation: Pilot, navigator and two radar operators

A version of the A-6 Intruder intended specifically for electronic countermeasures duties was developed soon after the basic A-6A had entered service in 1963. Designated EA-6A, this was selected for operation by the US Marine Corps and differed in having an extensive array of special electronic detection and jamming devices, carried internally, in pods on the fuselage and underwing strongpoints and in a new radome atop the fin. A prototype, converted from an A-6A, flew in 1963 and 27 production EA-6As were built (including six converted A-6As). The single remaining operational detachment will serve on USS *Midway* until the ship is retired in the mid-1980s.

To enhance the ECM capability of the aircraft, the EA-6B was developed, with a new front fuselage section incorporating two additional seats for radar/ECM operators. The avionic equipment was also revised and updated. First flight of a prototype was made on 25 May 1968 and production began to provide the US Navy with a new standard ECM (tactical jamming) aircraft to replace the EKA-3B. Procurement of a total of 96 EA-6Bs by the mid-eighties is planned, with current production aircraft being to ICAP (Increased Capability) standard with enhanced avionics. Named Prowler to avoid confusion with the Intruder attack versions of the A-6, the EA-6B entered service in 1971 and four aircraft detachments serve aboard USN aircraft carriers when at sea. A tanker version designated KA-6H has been proposed.

Grumman F-14 Tomcat

USA

Two-seat carrier-borne air superiority and general purpose fighter, in production and service

Data, photo and silhouette: F-14A
Powered by: Two 20,600lb (9,344kg) st Pratt & Whitney TF30-P-414 afterburning turbofans
Span: 64ft 1.5in (19.54m) spread; 38ft 2in (10.12m) swept
Length: 61ft 10.5in (18.86m)
Empty weight: 38,930lb (17,659kg)
Max gross weight: 74,348lb (33,724kg)
Max speed: Mach 2.34 (1,564mph/2,517km/h) at 40,000ft (12,190m)
Armament: One General Electric M61-A1 multi-barrel gun in port side of front fuselage. Four missile bays semi-recessed under fuselage for Sparrow air-to-air missiles, or four Phoenix missiles on pallets. Two underwing pick-ups for a combination of a fuel tank and two Sidewinder air-to-air missiles on each pylon; or a Sparrow or Phoenix plus one Sidewinder on each pylon

The US Navy issued a Request for Proposals for a new carrier-based air superiority fighter to five US aerospace companies on 21 June 1968. From the initial proposals, the Navy selected Grumman and McDonnell Douglas for final competition, as a result of which the Grumman G303 design was selected on 15 January 1969. Since that date, the company has received a series of contracts, the first two of which were each for six development aircraft; total procurement planned in 1980 was 491 (including the 12 RDT&E aircraft) Tomcats. The prototype F-14A first flew on 21 December 1970, but was lost on its second flight. Testing resumed on 24 May 1971, and seven more of the test aircraft flew during that year. Two prototypes of an F-14B version were flown, with more powerful YF401 engines; but problems with this engine led to planned procurement of 179 F-14Bs being dropped by the Navy. Initial F-14A deliveries were made to VF124 for training, and the first operational units were VF1 and VF2, which were serving on board the USS *Enterprise* by September 1974, followed by VF14 and VF32 on board the USS *John F. Kennedy* in 1975. Fourteen squadrons were to be equipped with Tomcats by the end of 1978. During 1974, the Iranian Imperial Air Force ordered 80 F-14As in two batches; the first of these flew on 5 December 1975 and deliveries began in 1976. They are believed to have been unused since the Iranian revolution of 1978.

It was announced in 1978 that F-14s fitted with reconnaissance pods will serve as interim reconnaissance aircraft until a definitive replacement for the RA-5C and RF-8G is available. The TARPS (Tactical Air Reconnaissance Pod System) for this variant carries two cameras and an IR sensor. Persistent problems with the TF30 engine led to a programme to modify the original P-412A version to P-414 standard and in 1981 an F-14A was to be test-flown with General Electric F101DFE engines to provide data for a possible alternative to the TF30, if required.

Grumman OV-1 Mohawk

USA

Two-seat observation aircraft, in service

Data, photo and silhouette: OV-1D
Powered by: Two 1,150eshp Lycoming T53-L-701 turboprops
Span: 48ft 0in (14.63m)
Length: 41ft 0in (12.50m)
Empty weight: 12,054lb (5,467kg)
Gross weight: 18,109lb (8,214kg)
Max speed: 308mph (496km/h) at 5,000ft (1,520m)
Range: 1,010 miles (1,625km) with external tanks
Armament: Six wing strong-points allow for pylon-mounted bombs, rockets, etc, if required

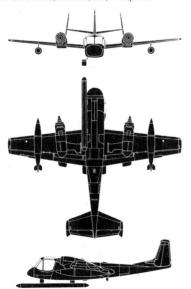

Designed originally to meet joint US Army and Marine Corps requirements, the Mohawk is now exclusively an Army aircraft, and was the first turboprop-engined type to into service with the US Army. The primary mission for which it was designed (as the Grumman G-134) was tactical observation and battlefield surveillance in direct support of Army operations, flying from unprepared fields and having a STOL performance. Initial contracts were for nine test aircraft designated YAO-1AF (later YOV-1A); the first of these flew on 14 April 1959. Production models were the OV-1A, primarily for photographic reconnaissance; the OV-1B with SLAR (side-looking airborne radar) in a long container under the fuselage, and the OV-1C with infra-red mapping gear. Deliveries to the Army began in 1961 and production of the three models totalled 64, 101 and 133 respectively. During 1968, four Mohawks were completed to OV-1D standard, with side-loading doors to accept pallets with SLAR or infrared or other sensors; this version also added a third photographic system, comprising a vertical, panoramic camera. Production of 37 OV-1Ds followed successful evaluation of the prototypes, and a programme to convert 108 OV-1Bs and OV-1Cs to OV-1D standard began in 1974.

Some OV-1C and OV-1D were permanently modified for electronic reconnaissance as RV-1C and RV-1D respectively. In addition, the Army studied a proposal to convert OV-1Bs to EV-1 electronic surveillance aircraft, with AN/ALQ-133 radar target locator system in pods on the centreline and under each wingtip. In 1980, the Army had 141 OV-1s and 26 RV-1s in its Active inventory and 60 OV-1s serving with the National Guard. Two EV-1s were delivered to Israel in 1976.

Grumman S-2 Tracker

USA

**Four-seat carrier-based anti-submarine attack
aircraft, in service**

Photo: CP-121
Data and silhouette: S-2E
Powered by: Two 1,525hp Wright R-1820-82WA
piston-engines
Span: 72ft 7in (22.13m)
Length: 43ft 6in (13.26m)
Empty weight: 18,750lb (8,505kg)
Gross weight: 29,150lb (13,222kg)
Max speed: 265mph (426km/h) at sea level
Ferry range: 1,300 miles (2,095km)
Armament: 60 echo-sounding depth charges in
fuselage; one Mk 101 or Mk 57 nuclear depth bomb
or similar store in bomb bay; 32 sonobuoys in
nacelles; four float lights; six underwing pylons for
5-inch rockets, torpedoes, etc

First flown on 4 December 1952, the S2F-1 (as the
Grumman G-89 was originally designated) went into
production for the US Navy for combined 'hunter-

killer' operations in the anti-submarine role. Of 755
S-2As built, over 100 were for export to Argentina,
Brazil, Italy, Japan, South Korea, the Netherlands,
Taiwan, Thailand and Uruguay, and were still serving
in 1980 with all these nations except the
Netherlands, in several cases having been
supplemented by S-2Es or S-2Fs.

The S2F-1T (later TS-2A) was used as a trainer.
The 60 S-2Cs (S2F-2s) had enlarged bomb-bays to
accommodate two homing torpedoes and most were
converted to US-2C utility aircraft. The S-2D
(originally S2F-3) had an 18in (45cm) front fuselage
extension, a 35in (89cm) greater span, a wider
cockpit and improved equipment. Production totalled
119, and deliveries began in May 1961. In October
1962, the S-2E succeeded the S-2D with more
advanced ASW equipment, and 245 were built.
Similar equipment added to early S-2As changed
their designation to S-2B and, with further
modifications, to S-2F. In 1972, Martin Marietta
produced a prototype YS-2G and kits for 49 more
S-2Gs to be converted by the USN, this version
having updated equipment for interim use until the
S-3A entered service. The Tracker was phased out of
first line USN service in 1976. Conversion
programmes produced the US-2A, US-2B, US-2C
and US-2D versions for target towing and utility
transport duty; the TS-2A and TS-2B trainers and
RS-2C photo-survey version. Few of these remained
in service in 1980. Production of the S-2E ended in
1968 with a batch of 14 for the RAN; 16 ex-USN
S-2Gs were acquired by the RAN in 1977 after 10
S-2Es were lost in a hangar fire. The Royal Canadian
Navy obtained 100 Trackers built by D. H. Canada, of
which 17 later went to the Netherlands; the first 43,
starting in January 1957, were CS2F-1s and the
final 57, starting in October 1958, were CS2F-2s,
with improved equipment. Redesignated CP-121, 20
were modified in 1979/80 for inshore surveillance
and fishery protection, with AN/APS-504 search
radar plus other new equipment.

HAL Ajeet and (HSA) Gnat

India

Light interceptor and close support fighter, in service

Data, photo and silhouette: Ajeet
Powered by: One 4,500lb (2,043kg) st Rolls-Royce Orpheus 701-01 turbojet
Span: 22ft 1in (6.73m)
Length: 29ft 8in (9.04m)
Empty weight: 5,086lb (2,307kg)
Gross weight: 9,195lb (4,170kg)
Max speed: 716mph (1,152km/h) at sea level
Combat radius: 127 miles (204km) with two 500lb bombs and underwing tanks

The Ajeet (Invincible) is a locally developed, improved version of the Gnat lightweight fighter, evolved by Hindustan Aeronautics during 1972–1974 to meet the specific requirements of the Indian Air Force. Prior to the appearance of the Ajeet, the first prototype of which flew on 5 March 1975, the IAF had received 213 Gnat 1s built under licence by HAL at Bangalore to the original design of W. E. W. Petter and with the assistance of the UK parent company, Folland Aircraft Ltd (later Hawker Siddeley Aviation). The IAF's eight squadrons of Gnats were progressively re-equipped in 1979/81, four converting to Ajeets and the others to MiG-21s. The Ajeet (originally Gnat Mk 2) was developed by HAL to improve on the Gnat's characteristics and overcome certain inherent shortcomings. The major differences comprise the use of a 'wet' wing and doubling the number of wing hardpoints to four, to allow a greater variety of weapons to be carried. There are also some equipment changes, similar to those applied to some Gnat 1s which, when modified, became Gnat 1As. The last two Indian Gnat 1s (Nos 214 and 215) served as Ajeet prototypes, and the first production Ajeet of about 80 flew on 30 September 1976. An Ajeet trainer, with fuselage lengthened by 4ft 7in (1.40m) and a raised rear cockpit for an instructor, was projected but not built and production of the Ajeet ended early in 1981, by which time four squadrons were equipped.

HAL HF-24 Marut

India

Single-seat fighter, in service

Data, photo and silhouette: Marut Mk 1
Powered by: Two 4,850lb (2,200kg) st Rolls-Royce
Orpheus 703 turbojets
Span: 29ft 6.25in (9.00m)
Length: 52ft 0.75in (15.87m)
Gross weight: 24,048lb (10,908kg)
Max speed: Mach 1.02 (673mph; 1,083km/h) at
40,000ft (12,200m)
Normal range: 750 miles (1,200km)
Armament: Four 30mm cannon in nose and
retractable pack of 48 air-to-air rockets in fuselage
aft of nose-wheel bay; four 1,000lb bombs or
rockets under wings

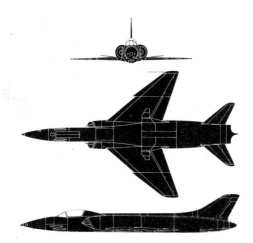

First supersonic fighter designed in any Asian
country outside of the Soviet Union, the HF-24
Marut (Wind Spirit) was developed initially under the
leadership of Professor Kurt Tank, whose earlier
products included the wartime Focke-Wulf Fw190
fighter. Design studies were started in 1956, to meet
an Indian Air Force requirement, and early research
work included flight testing of a full-scale wooden
glider version of the HF-24. The prototype HF-24
Mk 1 fighter flew for the first time on 17 June 1961.
It was followed by a second prototype and then by
the first of a production batch of 129 Mk 1s in March
1963. The initial batch of Mk1s was accepted
formally by the Indian Air Force on 10 May 1964,
and three squadrons, Nos 10, 31 and 220, have
been equipped with the type. In addition to the
single-seat Mk1s, HAL built 18 tandem two-seat
Mk1T trainers, the first prototype of which flew on
30 April 1970.

In an attempt to improve the performance of the
Marut, HAL projected a Mk II version with Adour
engines, but this was not built. In another
programme, HAL developed a reheat system for the
Orpheus engines, flying a prototype installation in a
Marut 1A in September 1966. Two more trials
aircraft with afterburners were designated Marut 1R,
but one of these crashed on 10 January 1970, and
further development was subsequently cancelled.

One HF-24 was sent to Egypt as a flying test-bed
for the Helwan E-300 afterburning turbojet and, as
the Mk 1BX, flew with this engine on 29 March
1967; but the E-300 was eventually abandoned.

Handley Page Victor K Mk 2

UK

Five-seat flight refuelling tanker, in service

Powered by: Four 20,600lb (9,344kg) st Rolls-Royce Conway RCo17 Mk 201 turbojets
Span: 117ft 0in (35.69m)
Length: 114ft 11in (35.0m)
Gross weight: 223,000lb (101,242kg)
Max speed: Over 600mph (966km/h) at 40,000ft (12,000m)
Max range: 4,600 miles (7,400km)
Armament: None

The first production Victor B Mk 1 bomber with Sapphire turbojets flew on 1 February 1956, and deliveries to the RAF began in 1958, production of 50 aircraft being sufficient to equip four squadrons. Late production aircraft were designated B Mk 1A, signifying equipment changes and the addition of ECM radar in the rear fuselage, and 24 were eventually converted to this standard. Subsequently, six were modified to B(K)1A two-point flight refuelling tankers and 24 others to K1 or K.1A three-point tankers. The B Mk 2 (first flown on 20 February 1959) had Rolls-Royce Conway turbojets and the wing span increased from 110ft (33.5m) to 120ft (36.6m). Deliveries to No 139 Squadron began late in 1961 and this was the first Victor unit to become operational with the Blue Steel missile in February 1964, 21 of the 34 production B2s being converted for this role. Another nine were modified for strategic reconnaissance duties as Victor SR Mk 2, for service with No 543 Squadron until 1974. They were then replaced by Vulcans and, together with B Mk 2s, were allotted for conversion to K Mk 2 tanker configuration by Hawker Siddeley. The first K Mk 2, with slightly reduced wing span and other modifications, plus three-point refuelling as in the K Mk 1/1A, flew on 1 March 1972 and the first delivery to the RAF was made on 8 May 1974, for service with No 232 OCU. A total of 24 K Mk 2s was delivered by mid-1977, to equip Nos 55 and 57 Squadrons. These still made up the RAF's sole tanker force in 1980, but were to be supplemented from 1982 onwards by a squadron of VC10 tankers.

Hawker Hunter

UK

Single-seat fighter and two-seat trainer, in service

Data: Hunter FGA Mk 9
Silhouette: Hunter F Mk 6
Photo: Hunter T Mk 8M
Powered by: One 10,000lb (4,540kg) st Rolls-Royce Avon 207 turbojet
Span: 33ft 8in (10.26m)
Length: 45ft 10.5in (13.98m)
Gross weight: 24,000lb (10,885kg)
Max speed: Mach 0.92 (710mph; 1,140km/h) at sea level
Range: 1,840 miles (2,965km) with external tanks
Armament: Four 30mm cannon in nose; underwing attachments for two 1,000lb bombs, or two packs each containing up to 37×2in rockets, or 12×3in rockets on inner pylons, plus up to 24×3in rockets outboard

As the Hawker P1067, the prototype Hunter (WB188) first flew on 20 July 1951. The Avon-powered F Mk 1 made its first flight on 16 May 1953, and aircraft of this mark equipped the first RAF squadron, No 43, in mid-1954. This version is no longer in service; nor are the Sapphire-powered F Mk 2 and 5. The Mk 1 was superseded in production by the F Mk 4, with Avon 115, more internal fuel and provision for underwing weapons or fuel tanks, and this mark saw service in Denmark (F Mk 51) and Peru (F Mk 52). It was followed by the F Mk 6 (prototype first flown 22 January 1954), with Avon 203, and export versions are still flying in India (FGA Mk 56), Switzerland (F Mk 58), Lebanon (F Mk 6 and 70) and Oman (F Mk 73 and FGA Mk 6). Final version in RAF service was the FGA Mk 9, a ground attack development of the Mk 6 with tail parachute and increased weapon load, a few examples of which remained in use in 1980. Versions of the Mk 9 also serve with the Zimbabwe, Chilean (FGA Mk 71) and Iraqi (FGA Mk 59) Air Forces. Singapore has over 30 FGA 74s, some modified as FGA 74Bs with additional wing and fuselage weapon pylons, and four FR 74As; the United Emirates Air Force operates 10 FGA Mk 76s and FR Mk 76As, and two two-seat T Mk 72As. FGA Mk 78s and T Mk 79 two-seaters were supplied to Qatar and in 1974 Kenya acquired six FGA Mk 9s.

Other side-by-side two-seat trainer versions of the Hunter include the RAF's T Mk 7 and Royal Navy's T Mk 8 and T Mk 8M, the latter with Blue Fox radar for Sea Harrier training. Two-seaters were also delivered to Peru (T Mk 62), India (T Mk 66), Lebanon (T Mk 66), Switzerland (T Mk 68), Iraq (T Mk 69), Chile (T Mk 72), Kuwait (T Mk 67), and Singapore (T Mk 75). In the mid-1970s, Switzerland added 52 F Mk 58As and eight T Mk 68s to about 90 already in service, to maintain nine front-line squadrons.

Hawker Siddeley Buccaneer

UK

Two-seat carrier-borne and land-based low-level strike aircraft, in service

Data, photo and silhouette: Buccaneer S MK 2B
Powered by: Two 11,100lb (5,035kg) st Rolls-Royce RB168 Spey Mk 101 turbofans
Span: 44ft 0in (13.41m)
Length: 63ft 5in (19.33m)
Max gross weight: 62,000lb (28,123kg)
Max speed: Mach 0.85 (646mph; 1,038km/h) at 200ft (60m)
Typical strike range: 2,300 miles (3,700km)
Armament: Internal weapons-bay, with rotating door, for nuclear or conventional (four 1,000lb) bombs, or camera pack; four underwing attachments for Bullpup or Martel missiles, 1,000lb bombs (three on each pylon) or rocket packs. Max weapon load 16,000lb (7,257kg)

Work on what was then known as the Blackburn B103 began in the early 1950s to meet the requirements of a Naval specification and the first of 20 pre-production aircraft flew on 30 April 1958.

A production order for 50 aircraft was placed in October 1959, and the final 10 aircraft were completed as Buccaneer S Mk 2s, with Speys replacing the 7,100lb (3,220kg) st Gyron Junior 101s in the first version. Orders for 74 more S Mk 2s were placed by the Royal Navy, and the type entered service with No 801 Squadron in October 1965.

In 1968, the RAF ordered 26 Buccaneer S Mk 2Bs, with revised equipment, a bomb-door fuel tank and provision for carrying Martel missiles, followed by a second contract for 17 in 1972, plus three for use as weapons trials aircraft at the RAE, West Freugh, and two as test-beds for Panavia Tornado equipment. About 60 ex-Navy aircraft were also converted to S Mk 2A (without Martel capability) or S Mk 2B for the RAF. The first RAF Buccaneer squadron, No 12, became operational in July 1970 and was joined subsequently in Strike Command by No 208. The first of two squadrons to fly the Buccaneer in Germany, No 15, formed in October 1970 and was followed by No 16. After HMS *Ark Royal* was retired, the aircraft operated by No 801 Squadron were used to form a fifth RAF unit, No 216 Squadron. Following an accident attributed to structural failure, all RAF Buccaneers were grounded for several months in 1980 and it was then announced that over one-third of the force of 65 aircraft would need extensive repair before being returned to service. The South African Air Force has eight Buccaneer S Mk 50s, this variant being fitted with an 8,000lb (3,630kg) st BS605 twin-chamber auxiliary rocket engine.

Hawker Siddeley Vulcan

UK

Five-seat medium bomber, in service

Data, photo and silhouette: Vulcan B Mk 2
Powered by: Four 20,000lb (9,072kg) st
Rolls-Royce Bristol Olympus 301 turbojets
Span: 111ft 0in (33.83m)
Length: 99ft 11in (30.45m)
Gross weight: Over 180,000lb (81,650kg)
Max cruising speed: Over Mach 0.94 (625mph;
1,005km/h) at 50,000ft (15,250m)
Combat radius: 1,725-2,875 miles
(2,780-4,630km)
Armament: No guns. Mk 2 can carry nuclear
free-fall weapons or 21 × 1,000lb high-explosive
bombs

The prototype Avro 698 (VX770) made its first flight on 30 August 1952, and was powered by Rolls-Royce Avons. The second prototype (VX777) flew on 3 September 1953, and had Olympus 100 engines and the later-standard visual bomb-aiming station under the nose. Production Vulcan B Mk 1s (45 built, commencing XA889) began to appear in February 1954, with Olympus 101, 102 or 104 engines. Deliveries to the RAF began in mid-1956, and Mk 1 and 1A (the latter having ECM radar in bulged tailcone) eventually equipped three operational squadrons of RAF Bomber Command. On 31 August 1957, VX777 flew as the aerodynamic test vehicle for the Mk 2, with enlarged and modified wing. The first production Mk 2 (XH533) flew in August 1958 and deliveries to the RAF began on 1 July 1960, the first squadron equipped being No 83. Following transfer of responsibility for Britain's nuclear deterrent to the Royal Navy's Polaris submarine force, the Vulcans of Strike Command were assigned primarily to the low-level penetration and strike role. Six squadrons were equipped with these Vulcans in 1980 (Nos 9, 35, 44, 50, 101 and 617), plus the OCU (No 230) and were scheduled to continue doing so until replaced by Tornado GR Mk 1s.

Conversion of some Vulcans for the strategic reconnaissance role began in 1973 and, with the designation SR Mk 2, these were issued to No 27 Squadron in 1974, to replace the Victors of No 543 Squadron. These also were continuing in service in 1981.

Ilyushin Il-28   USSR
(NATO code-names 'Beagle' and 'Mascot')

Four-seat tactical bomber, reconnaissance and ECM (electronic countermeasures) aircraft, in service

Photo: Il-28, East Germany
Powered by: Two 5,950lb (2,700kg) st Klimov VK-1 turbojets
Span: 64ft 0in (19.50m)
Length: 58ft 0in (17.68m)
Gross weight: 46,300lb (21,000kg)
Max speed: 560mph (900km/h) at 15,000ft (4,575km)
Range: 1,355 miles (2,180km) with max bomb-load
Armament: Two 23mm cannon in nose; two 23mm cannon in tail turret; 4,500lb (2,050kg) of bombs

Russia's counterpart to the Canberra (which it preceded chronologically), the Il-28 was first shown publicly on May Day, 1950, when it took part in fair numbers in the Aviation Day fly-past over Moscow. Several thousand were built and Il-28s served as light attack/reconnaissance aircraft in the air forces of Russia, Poland, Bulgaria, Czechoslovakia, Hungary, East Germany, Afghanistan, Algeria, Iraq, North Korea, Morocco, Nigeria, Syria, North Vietnam, South Yemen, Indonesia, Yemen and Egypt. Replacement of the bomber version with Su-7 fighter-bombers was completed in most of these countries by the early 1970s. Elsewhere, a few examples, adapted for electronic warfare and other support duties, remain in use. Finland has two which are used primarily for target-towing. Following the political break between China and the Soviet Union, the Il-28 was put into production at Harbin factory and according to US sources, some 400 were in service in 1979, including about 100 of the Il-28T torpedo-carrying version with the Chinese Navy. The Chinese designation is B-5 or Type 5 Bombing Aeroplane. An operational trainer version designated Il-28U (NATO code-name 'Mascot') has a second pilot's cockpit below and forward of the standard fighter-type canopy. China also has some examples of this version in service.

Ilyushin Il-38 (and Il-18)
(NATO code-names 'May' and 'Coot')

USSR

Maritime reconnaissance and anti-submarine aircraft, in service

Photo: 'Coot-A'
Data and silhouette: 'May'
Powered by: Four Ivchenko AI-20 turboprops
Span: 122ft 8.5in (37.4m)
Length: 129ft 10in (39.6m)
Weights: Probably similar to those of Il-18
Max cruising speed: 400mph (645km/h)
Max range: 4,500 miles (7,250km)

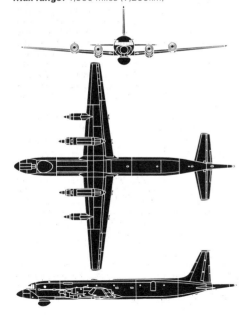

This Soviet maritime patrol aircraft bears the same relationship to the Il-18 as does the Lockheed P-3 Orion to the Electra transport. To fit it for its important role it has a MAD tail 'sting', an undernose radome, other ASW (anti-submarine warfare) electronics and weapon-carrying capability. The main cabin has few windows on each side. Concentration of equipment and weapons in the forward area changed the centre of gravity so much that the wing had to be moved forward and the rear fuselage lengthened considerably by comparison with the Il-18.

The Il-38 is the standard shore-based maritime patrol aircraft of the Soviet Naval Air Force, which was believed to have 60 or more in service in 1980. In the early 1970s, a few operated in the markings of the Egyptian Air Force but were thought to be flown by Soviet crews operating from bases in North Africa. Il-38s flown by Soviet Naval Aviation crews have also operated from bases in North Yemen. Three Il-38s were ordered by the Indian Navy in 1975, these being the first genuine export examples of the type; they entered service with INAS 315 late in 1977 and were to be followed later by sufficient additional aircraft to re-equip INAS 312, scheduled to continue flying Super Constellations until 1981.

During 1978, an electronic reconnaissance/ECM version of the basic Il-18 appeared in Soviet service and was given the NATO code-name 'Coot-A'. This utilised the Il-18 airframe in its original configuration, including cabin windows and without the MAD and forward radomes of the Il-38. Instead, it carried a long radome under the centre fuselage, presumed to carry SLAR and other sensor fairings and aerials.

Ilyushin Il-76
(NATO code-name 'Candid')

USSR

Medium/long-range strategic freighter, in production and service

Powered by: Four 26,455lb (12,000kg) st Soloviev D-30KP turbofans
Span: 165ft 8in (50.50m)
Length: 152ft 10.5in (46.59m)
Gross weight: 374,785lb (170,000kg)
Max payload: 88,185lb (40,000kg)
Cruising speed: 466-497mph (750-800km/h) at 29,500-39,350ft (9,000-12,000m)
Range: 3,100 miles (5,000km) with max payload
Accommodation: Basic flight crew of three
Armament: Gun turret at tail (not shown in illustrations)

This Soviet counterpart to the C-141A StarLifter was first flown on 25 March 1971, and the prototype was displayed only two months later at the Paris Air Show. Its nominal task was described as the transport of 40 tonnes of freight for a distance of 5,000km in under six hours, after take-off from short, unprepared airstrips. The entire accommodation is pressurised, and advanced mechanical handling systems are installed in the freight hold for loading and unloading containerised cargoes via the rear ramp-door. There is a large ground-mapping radar under the navigator's station in the glazed nose, and a computer is fitted for use with the automatic flight control and automatic landing approach systems. The main eight-wheel bogies of the undercarriage retract inward into large blister fairings under the fuselage; two more large blister fairings cover the actuating mechanism. During development the rear fuselage has been modified, to increase the depth of the aft clamshell loading doors and so permit the entry of wider loads.

Production was launched on a large scale for both Aeroflot and the Soviet Air Force, as a replacement for the An-12. Military versions differ from the commercial model in having a tail gun turret. In addition, development of a version of the Il-76 as a flight refuelling tanker for the 'Backfire' bomber force was comfirmed in 1976, and it is likely that this aircraft will serve as a replacement for the M-4 'Bisons' used hitherto in that role. During 1980, the Il-76 was reported to be the basis for development of a new Soviet AWACS aircraft, expected to replace the Tu-126 Moss in due course. A series of flights in 1975 showed that, under the conditions laid down for record attempts, the Il-76 could lift a payload of 154,590lb (70,121kg) and could reach an altitude of 38,960ft (11,875m) with this load. Speeds of up to 533mph (857km/h) were recorded over closed circuits, with similar payloads.

Israel Aircraft Industries Kfir

Israel

Single-seat close support and air superiority fighter, in production and service

Data, photo and silhouette: Kfir-C2
Powered by: One 11,870lb (5,385kg) st dry and 17,900lb (8,120kg) st with afterburning General Electric J79-GE-17 turbojet
Span: 26ft 11.5in (8.22m)
Length: 51ft 0.25in (15.55m)
Gross weight: 32,190lb (14,600kg)
Max speed: Mach 1.1 at 1,000ft (305m) and Mach 2.3 above 36,000ft (10,970m)
Radius of action: 323 miles (520km) for air superiority, 745 miles (1,200km) for ground attack

The Kfir (Young Lion) is an Israeli-developed derivative of the Dassault Mirage, a total of 75

examples of which (Mirage IIICJ and IIIBJ) had been acquired by the Heyl Ha'Avir (Israeli Air Force) from 1962 onwards. These were to have been followed, from 1967 onwards, by 50 Mirage 5J close-support versions, but delivery of these later aircraft was embargoed by France. To help fill the gap which this decision left in the Heyl Ha'Avir inventory, IAI set about building a version of the Mirage 5J in Israel, helped by production drawings procured clandestinely in France. Powered by an Atar 9C engine, the prototype Israeli-built fighter flew in September 1969, named Nesher (Eagle), and deliveries began in 1972. As many as 100 are believed to have been built, of which about 40 saw operational service during the Yom Kippur war of October 1973. In parallel with the Nesher programme, IAI undertook the marriage of a Mirage airframe with a US-supplied J79 engine. Under the code-name 'Black Curtain', a prototype installation in a French-built airframe flew on 19 October 1970, and a full Israeli-built prototype flew in September 1971. The name Kfir was adopted for the production version, which replaced the Nesher on the production lines in 1975, and is in service with the Heyl Ha'Avir in several versions. With different radar and equipment fits, early Kfirs were optimised either for air superiority or air-to-ground operations; subsequently, the Kfir-C2 appeared, featuring fixed canard surfaces above and aft of the engine intakes, and dogtooth extensions on the outer wing leading edges. These modifications improve the dogfighting characteristics of the Kfir-C2, which became the standard version with over 150 built by 1980. A two-seat variant was also developed, with tandem seating. An attempt to sell a batch of 26 Kfirs to Ecuador early in 1977 was blocked by the US government (involved because of the J79 engines). As an alternative to the Kfir for export, IAI has developed the Dagger, basically the Mirage 5 airframe with Atar engine, and 26 of these have been sold to the Argentine Air Force.

Kawasaki C-1

Japan

**Twin-turbofan troop and freight transport, in
production and service**

Powered by: Two 14,500lb (6,575kg) st Pratt &
Whitney (Mitsubishi) JT8D-M-9 turbofans
Span: 100ft 4.75in (30.60m)
Length: 95ft 1.75in (29.00m)
Empty weight: 51,410lb (23,320kg)
Max take-off weight: 99,210lb (45,000kg)
Max speed: 501mph (806km/h) at 25,000ft
(7,620m)
Range: 2,084 miles (3,353km) with 4,850lb
(2,200kg) payload
Accommodation: Crew of five, 60 troops, 45
paratroops, 36 litters and attendants, or 17,640lb
(8,000kg) of freight
Armament: None

This medium-size troop and cargo transport was
developed by Nihon Aeroplane Manufacturing
Company (NAMC) to replace the Air Self-Defence
Force's veteran fleet of Curtiss C-46s, the last of
which was retired in 1977. Design work began in
1966 and the first of two XC-1 prototypes made its
first flight on 12 November 1970, followed by the
second on 16 January 1971. Two C-1
pre-production aircraft were ordered in the 1971
Fiscal Year, with Kawasaki designated as prime
contractor for the programme; these were delivered
early in 1974. 11 production C-1s were ordered
initially, in the 1972 Fiscal Year, followed by 13
more in FY 1975, two in FY 1978 and one in FY
1979, to equip three squadrons of the Transport
Wing of the JASDF; production of about 12 more
was planned for future years. Delivery of the first 24
aircraft was completed by early 1978 and included
two C-1s with long-range tanks in the wing centre-
section. Kawasaki builds the front fuselage and wing
centre-section, and is responsible for final assembly
and flight testing. The outer wings are built by Fuji;
the centre and rear fuselage and tail unit by
Mitsubishi, the flaps, ailerons, engine pylons and
pods by Nihon Hikoki; the undercarriage by
Sumitomo; and the cargo loading system by Shin
Meiwa. Standard freight loads include a 2.5-ton
truck, 105mm howitzer, two 0.75-ton trucks, three
jeeps, or three pre-loaded freight pallets, each 7ft 4in
(2.24m) wide by 90ft 0in (2.74m) long. In 1980,
Japan's National Aerospace Laboratory was working
on a QSTOL research aircraft using a C-1 airframe
with four MITI/NAL FJR-710-600S turbojets and
upper surface blowing. Versions of the C-1 also were
planned for ECM, minelaying, flight refuelling tanker
and weather reconnaissance duties.

Kawasaki P-2J (and Lockheed P-2 Neptune)

Japan (USA)

Twelve-seat anti-submarine and maritime patrol bomber, in service

Data, photo and silhouette: P-2J
Powered by: Two 3,060ehp General Electric T64-IHI-10E turboprops and 3,417lb (1,550kg) st Ishikawajima Harima J3-IHI-7D auxiliary turbojets
Span: (over tip-tanks) 10ft 3.5in (30.87m)
Length: 95ft 10.75in (29.23)
Empty weight: 42,500lb (19,277kg)
Gross weight: 75,000lb (34,019kg)
Max cruising speed: 250mph (402km/h)
Max range: 2,765 miles (4,450km)
Armament: Attachments for 16 5in rockets under wings. Internal stowage for 8,000lb (3,630kg) of bombs, depth charges or torpedoes

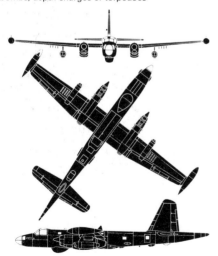

The P-2J was the final development of the Lockheed P-2 Neptune of which Kawasaki manufactured 42 for the Japanese Maritime Self-Defence Force in 1959-65. Work on the prototype P-2J began in 1965, after four years of design effort, and it flew for the first time on 21 July 1966. Although produced by conversion of a standard P-2H, only the wings and tail unit remained substantially unchanged, apart from an increase in rudder chord. The fuselage was lengthened by 50in (1.27m) forward of the wing to accommodate improved electronic equipment, almost up to the standard of that carried by the P-3 Orion. The undercarriage was redesigned to have twin-wheel main units. Biggest change of all was to the power plant, with the original piston-engines replaced by less powerful T64 turboprops built under licence by Ishikawajima-Harima; take-off performance was maintained by use of underwing jet engines, as on later models of the P-2 itself. Fuel capacity was increased, and an additional crew member, known as the combat co-ordinator, was carried. The first of an initial series of 46 production P-2Js flew on 8 August 1969, and was delivered to the JMSDF on 7 October that year. The first P-2J squadron had 10 aircraft in service by February 1971, and all 46 of the first series had been delivered by 31 March 1974. Further orders were placed in annual increments that brought the total delivered to 83; delivery of the last of these in February 1979 brought to an end production of the Lockheed P-2 family, a total of 1,182 having been built since 1945. Of the several nations that acquired P-2s, the Argentine was among the last still operating the Neptune in 1980

Lockheed C-5A Galaxy

USA

Heavy strategic transport, in service

Powered by: Four 41,000lb (18,600kg) st General Electric TF39-GE-1 turbofans
Span: 222ft 8.5in (67.88m)
Length: 247ft 10in (75.54m)
Operating weight empty: 354,000lb (140,516kg)
Gross weight: 769,000lb (348,810kg)
Max speed: 571mph (919km/h) at 25,000ft (7,600m)
Range: 6,529 miles (10,505km) with 112,600lb (51,074kg) payload
Armament: None

The design of the massive Lockheed C-5A began in 1963 when the Military Air Transport Service (now Military Airlift Command) issued to industry a requirement for an outsize logistics transport which could carry a 125,000lb (56,700kg) load for 8,000 miles (12,875km), and could operate from the same airfields as those used by the C-141 StarLifter. Development contracts went to Boeing, Douglas and Lockheed in May 1964, and to Pratt & Whitney and General Electric for engine development. During 1965, Lockheed's L500 design — the work of the company's Georgia Division — was selected, together with General Electric GE1/6 engines, to meet the requirement. An initial contract for 58 aircraft was placed with Lockheed, with first and second options for 57 and 85 more. First flight of the first C-5A was made on 30 June 1968; the first operational model (the ninth C-5A built) was delivered to MAC on 17 December 1969. Production plans were limited subsequently to a total of 81 aircraft, because of rising costs; these now equip MAC units based at Dover AFB and at Travis AFB, some manned by AF Reserve personnel. During development, a C-5A took off at the then world record weight of 798,200lb (362,064kg). In service, loads such as two M-48 tanks, each weighing 99,000lb (45,000kg), or three CH-47 Chinook helicopters, have been airlifted over trans-oceanic ranges. During 1978, Lockheed developed and tested a major wing modification programme designed to extend the fatigue life of the Galaxy, and it is expected that all 76 remaining C-5As will be modified in this way by Lockheed in 1983-1987. The prototype testing of the modified wing began on 14 August 1980.

Lockheed C-130 Hercules

USA

Multi-purpose transport, in production and service

Photo: C-130H-30, Indonesia
Data and silhouette: C-130H
Powered by: Four 4,508eshp Allison T56-A-15 turboprops
Span: 132ft 7in (40.41m)
Length: 97ft 9in (29.78m)
Empty weight: 75,621lb (34,300kg)
Max gross weight: 175,000lb (79,380kg)
Max cruising speed: 386mph (621km/h)
Range: 2,487-5,135 miles (4,002-8,264km)
Accommodation: Crew of four and 92 troops or 64 paratroops or 74 stretchers or freight.

First flight of the YC-130 Hercules was made on 23 August 1954 and delivery of the C-130A tactical transport began in December 1956. It was followed by the C-130B with higher weight and better range, production of the two versions totalling 461. The C-130E, first flown on 25 August 1961, was developed as an interim turbine transport for MAC, with more underwing fuel. On 8 December 1964, Lockheed flew the first of more than 70 HC-130Hs, with uprated T56-A-15 engines and special recovery

equipment on the nose; 20 of these became HC-130Ps with provision to air-refuel helicopters and to recover parachute-borne loads in mid-air. KC-130H tankers have been supplied to Israel and Spain. 15 HC-130Ns are similar to the HC-130H, with advanced direction-finding equipment. The current production C-130H, is basically an E with T56-A-15 engines instead of 4,050eshp T56-A-7s. The C-130K, similarly powered, was selected for the RAF; delivery began in 1967, and four squadrons were flying these Hercules C Mk 1s in 1980. Thirty of these are to be lengthened by 15ft (4.57m), to the standard of the commercial L-100-30 version, to increase capacity to 128 troops, 92 paratroops, 99 stretchers or seven (instead of five) cargo pallets. When converted, they are redesignated Hercules C Mk 3; the first flew on 3 December 1979. Four EC-130Gs and 14 improved EC-130Qs are operated by the US Navy for command communications, including worldwide relay of emergency action messages to ballistic missile submarines. Some Hercules were modified as AC-130A/H Gunships for the interdiction role in Vietnam and now fly with the Air Force Reserve. Special versions of the Hercules have included DC-130A/E/H drone carriers; 10 JC-130Bs and four JHC-130Hs for air-snatch satellite recovery; 12 C-130Ds with skis for Arctic operations. Also in service are 12 HC-130Bs for USCG search and rescue duties; the EC-130E for electronic surveillance duty with USAF; the MC-130E for covert electronic sensing; 19 weather reconnaissance WC-130B/E/Hs used by the USAF; 46 KC-130Fs and 16 KC-130R tankers, used by the Marine Corps; seven US Navy C-130Fs; and six LC-130R ski-planes (converted from C-130H) used by the Navy and NSF in the Antarctic. Orders totalled over 1,560 by 1980, for service with more than 40 foreign air forces, mostly in the C-130E and C-130H versions. Indonesia has three C-130H-30s with stretched fuselages and Malaysia has the C-130H-MP maritime patrol variant.

Lockheed C-141 StarLifter

USA

Long-range strategic freighter, in service.

Photo and silhouette: C-141A
Data: C-141B
Powered by: Four 21,000lb (9,525kg) st Pratt &
Whitney TF33-P-7 turbofans
Span: 159ft 11in (48.74m)
Length: 168ft 3.5in (51.29m)
Operating weight empty: 149,848lb (67,970kg)
Max take-off weight: 344,900lb (156,444kg)
Max cruising speed: 569mph (916km/h)
Range with max payload: 3,200 miles (5,148km)
Accommodation: Crew of four-six plus 154 troops,
123 paratroops, 80 stretchers and 16 sitting
casualties, or freight

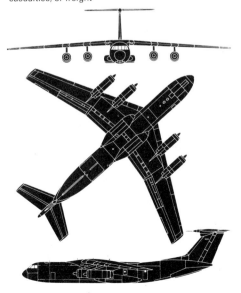

Lockheed won a hotly contested design competition
in March 1961 with this design, laid out to meet the
USAF's Specific Operational Requirement 182. The
requirement was for a jet freighter to modernise the
MAC fleet of piston-engined and turboprop
transports. On 16 March 1961, following selection
of the Lockheed design, procurement authorisation
was issued to allow production of the new freighter
to begin, and this was followed on 16 August by the
contract for the first five aircraft. The original
requirement was for 132 aircraft and later orders
brought the total built to 284 by the time production
ended late in 1967. The first of the evaluation
aircraft flew on 17 December 1963 and delivery of
operational aircraft to the USAF began in 1965. The
StarLifter is the flying element of the Logistics
Support System 476L, and is built round an 81ft
(24.7m) long cargo compartment, 10ft by 9ft
(3.12m by 2.77m) in cross-section, with straight-in
rear loading at truck-bed height and provision for
air-dropping. Some aircraft have been modified to
carry the Minuteman ICBM in a container, and have
structural strengthening for the 86,207lb (39,103kg)
weight of this load.

To increase the versatility of the StarLifter,
Lockheed developed, under USAF contract, the
C-141B configuration with fuselage lengthened by
23ft 4in (7.11m) and provision for in-flight refuelling.
A prototype YC-141B conversion first flew on
24 March 1977 and in June 1978 the USAF
contracted with Lockheed to convert all 270
StarLifters to this standard by 1983, increasing the
usable space inside each aircraft by 30%. The
prototype was brought up to full production standard
and resumed flight testing on 27 February 1980 and
production conversions began to come off the line at
Marietta, Georgia, later in the year.

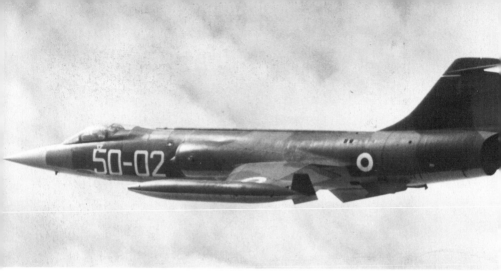

Lockheed F-104 Starfighter

USA

Single-seat all-weather tactical strike and reconnaissance fighter, in service

Silhouette: F-104G
Data and photo: F-104S
Powered by: One 17,900lb (8,120kg) st (with afterburning) General Electric J79-GE-19 turbojet
Span: 21ft 11in (6.68m) without tip-tanks
Length: 54ft 9in (16.69m)
Empty weight: 14,900lb (6,760kg)
Gross weight: 31,000lb (14,060kg)
Max speed: Mach 2.2 (1,450mph; 2,330km/h) at 36,000ft (11,000m)
Combat radius: 775miles (1,247km) with max fuel
Armament: One 20mm M61 Vulcan rotary-barrel cannon and up to 4,000lb (1,815kg) of external stores. Normally, two AIM-7 Sparrow and two AIM-9 Sidewinder air-to-air missiles for interceptor role.

Lockheed's Model 83 Starfighter was built in limited quantities for the USAF Tactical and Air Defense Commands after protracted development, following the first flight of the prototype on 7 February 1954. The single-seat F-104A and two-seat F-104B were used by ADC for North American air defence, and some were supplied to China and Pakistan; the F-104C and F-104D were TAC equivalents. A major re-design produced the F-104G multi-mission version with a 15,800lb (7,167kg) st (with afterburning) J79-GE-11A engine, which became the subject of an intra-European production programme, with assembly lines in Germany, Italy, Holland and Belgium, which produced 977 aircraft plus a further 50 ordered by the Luftwaffe late in 1968; similar versions were built in Canada (for the CAF as CF-104s, and export) and in Japan. Lockheed built another 179 F-104Gs, including one each for Italy and Belgium, 96 for Germany and 81 under USAF contract for supply under MAP to other nations. European nations which received F-104Gs from US and Canadian production comprised Denmark, Greece, Norway, Spain and Turkey. Lockheed also built the two-seat F-104DJ for Japan, F-104F for Germany and TF-104G for Germany, Belgium, Italy, Netherlands, Denmark and other European air forces. Final production version was the F-104S, with nine external stores points and provision for Sparrow missiles. The Italian Air Force ordered 205 of this version, and the first of two prototypes built by Lockheed flew in 1966. Production was initiated by Aeritalia at Turin, where the first production model was flown on 30 December 1968 and production was completed 10 years later. Deliveries were completed in 1976 of 40 F-104S Starfighters ordered in addition by the Turkish Air Force; earlier versions of the Starfighter remain in service with the air forces of several of those nations mentioned above.

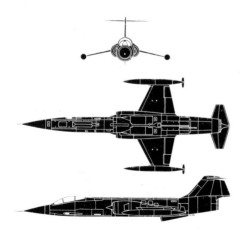

Lockheed P-3 Orion and CP-140 Aurora   USA

Shore-based anti-submarine reconnaissance aircraft, in production and service. Crew of ten

Silhouette: CP-140 Aurora
Data and photo: P-3C
Powered by: Four 4,910eshp Allison T56-A-14 turboprops
Span: 99ft 8in (30.37m)
Length: 116ft 10in (35.61m)
Empty weight: 61,491lb (27,890kg)
Gross weight: 142,000lb (64,410kg)
Max speed: 473mph (761km/h) at 15,000ft (4,570m)
Mission radius: 1,550 miles (2,494km) with 3 hours on station at 1,500ft (450m)
Armament: Torpedoes, mines, depth charges and bombs (including nuclear weapons) in internal weapons bay; wing-mounted weapons on 10 pylons. Max total weapons load 20,000lb (9,070kg)

The Orion was designed to the US Navy's Type Specification 146, calling for an anti-submarine aircraft derived from an existing production type. Thus, an Electra transport modified as an aerodynamic prototype of the Orion flew on 19 August 1958. An operational prototype, the YP3V-1, flew on 25 November 1959, and the first production P3V-1 on 15 April 1961. The designation was changed to P-3A in July 1962, and on 13 August Navy Squadron VP-8 formally accepted the first three P-3A Orions, with 4,500eshp T56-A-10W engines. After 157 P-3As had been built, production switched to the P-3B with 4,910eshp T56-A-14 engines; a total of 125 P-3Bs was built for the US Navy. In addition, the RAAF acquired 10 P-3Bs, the RNZAF five and the Royal Norwegian Air Force five (plus two P-3Cs later). Three P-3As were delivered to the Spanish Air Force. Current US Navy production version is the P-3C, with A-NEW data processing system, which flew for the first time on 18 September 1968; over 200 were to be acquired by the USN, and the RAAF ordered 10 for 1977/78 delivery. A version of the P-3C ordered by Canada in 1976 uses avionics similar to those in the S-3A and is called the CP-140 Aurora; the first of 18 flew at Burbank on 22 March 1979 and deliveries began in May 1980. The Dutch Navy is acquiring 13 P-3Cs and Japan planned to acquire 45 P-3Cs between 1978 and 1987, of which 42 will be built by Kawasaki. Six P-3Fs for Iran differ in having some equipment deleted, including MAD and active sonar. Four WP-3As equipped for weather reconnaissance are operated by the US Navy, as are 12 EP-3E special reconnaissance aircraft with radomes above and below the fuselage, converted from P-3As (10) and EP-3Bs (2). A single RP-3D is operated by the US Naval Oceanographic Office for mapping the Earth's magnetic field. Two WP-3Ds are used by the US National Oceanic and Atmospheric Administration.

Lockheed S-3A Viking

USA

Four-seat carrier-borne anti-submarine aircraft, in service

Powered by: Two 9,275lb (4,207kg) st General Electric TF34-GE-2 turbofans
Span: 68ft 8in (20.93m)
Length: 53ft 4in (16.26m)
Empty weight: 26,650lb (12,088kg)
Gross weight: 52,539lb (23,831kg)
Max speed: 518mph (834km/h)
Combat range: More than 2,300 miles (3,705km)
Armament: Torpedoes, depth charges, mines, missiles, rockets and special weapons in internal bomb-bays and under wings

This carrier-based anti-submarine aircraft was developed to replace the S-2 Tracker in service with the US Navy. Lockheed-California was awarded an initial $461million contract for the S-3A in August 1969, after a design competition, and flew the first of eight research and development aircraft ahead of schedule on 21 January 1972. All eight were flying by the spring of 1973, and delivery of production S-3As to the Fleet began officially on 20 February 1974. A total of 187 was built, to provide 12 squadrons, one on each USN multi-purpose carrier; the last S-3A was delivered in 1978.

The crew of the S-3A consists of a pilot, co-pilot, tactical operator and acoustic sensor operator. The co-pilot is responsible for non-acoustic sensors, such as radar and infra-red devices. Improved sonobuoys and MAD equipment enhance the capability of finding the quieter, deeper-diving submarines now in service. The fuselage will take a 50% expansion of the present electronics, and the basic design could be adapted easily to provide variants for other tasks. One S-3A was used as a flight refuelling tanker during the flight trials of the Viking, to extend the endurance of other trials aircraft, and a KS-3A version has been projected by Lockheed. The USN planned to procure a US-3A version for COD use, and a prototype flew on 2 July 1976; it is in Fleet service but no further production had been ordered up to 1981, and no funds have yet been made available for the projected ES-3A special electronics version.

Lockheed SR-71

Two-seat strategic reconnaissance aircraft, in service

Data, photo and silhouette: SR-71A
Powered by: Two 32,500lb (14,740kg) st (with afterburning) Pratt & Whitney J58 (JTIID-20B) turbojets
Span: 55ft 7in (16.95m)
Length: 107ft 5in (32.74m)
Empty weight: 60,000lb (27,240kg)
Gross weight: 170,000lb (77,110kg)
Max speed: More than Mach 3.0 (2,000mph; 3,220km/h)
Range: 2,982 miles (4,800km) at Mach 3.0 at 78,750ft (24,000m)
Armament: Unarmed

Developed in strict secrecy and with remarkable speed, the basic Lockheed A-11 flew for the first time on 26 April 1962, but was not revealed publicly until February 1964. The original requirement is believed to have been for a U-2 replacement, an aircraft capable of flying at sufficient altitude and speed to be virtually un-interceptable if used on long-range strategic reconnaissance flights. Between 12 and 20 are believed to have been built. Three A-11s were modified during 1964 for evaluation as YF-12As in the role of air defence fighters, carrying eight Hughes AIM-47A missiles in internal bays. The similar but longer SR-71A was first flown on 22 December 1964 and at least 27 were built to equip the 9th Strategic Reconnaissance Wing of SAC, which received its first SR-71s in January 1966. Since then, its aircraft have seen extensive worldwide use, as the fastest military aircraft ever put into service, able to photograph 100,000sq miles (259,000sq km) in one hour. Two SR-71Bs each had a raised rear cockpit and were used as trainers by the 9th Wing. When one crashed, it was replaced by one of the YF-12As converted for the training role and designated SR-71C. Before the fully-operational SR-71s entered service, an initial batch of A-11s is reported to have been used to launch GTD-21 reconnaissance drones on operational missions. The GTD-21, also built by Lockheed, was of similar wing configuration to the A-11, but had only a single engine.

World records set up by a YF-12A on 1 May 1965, included a speed of 2,070mph (3,331km/h) over a 15/25km course and a sustained height of 80,258ft (24,462m). These stood as absolute records until July 1976, when they were bettered by an SR-71A which reached an altitude of 85,069ft (25,929m) and a speed of 2,193mph (3,529km/h). Two important point-to-point records set up by a USAF SR-71A in 1974 comprised a New York to London transatlantic record of 1hr 55min 32sec, and a London to Los Angeles time of 3hr 47min 39sec at an average speed of 1,480mph (2,382km/h).

Lockheed U-2 and TR-1

USA

Single-seat strategic (and, TR1, tactical) reconnaissance aircraft, in production and service

Data, photo and silhouette: U-2R
Powered by: One 17,000lb (7,710kg) st Pratt & Whitney J75-P-13 turbojet
Span: 103ft 0in (31.39m)
Length: 63ft 0in (19.20m)
Max take-off weight: 29,000lb (13,154kg)
Max speed: 430mph (692km/h)
Operational ceiling: 90,000ft (27,430m)
Max range: Over 3,000 miles (4,830km)

The U-2 leapt into the limelight in 1960, when one was shot down by a surface-to-air missile while on a clandestine high-altitude reconnaissance mission over the Soviet Union. A product of Lockheed's 'Skunk Works', where the prototype first flew on 1 August 1955, the U-2 was designated in the USAF's 'Utility' category to cloak its real role of strategic reconnaissance. Although Soviet overflights ended in 1960, U-2s continued to be used for a variety of tasks associated with the collection of visual, electronic and other data in various parts of the world. The original production model was the U-2A with 11,200lb (5,080kg) st J57-P-37A turbojet; most of those built were later converted to the more powerful U-2B with J75-P-13, and a few of these were further modified to U-2Cs for ELINT duty. Production of these variants totalled 48, plus five U-2D trainers with a second seat in tandem. In 1968, production was resumed to build 12 single-seat U-2Rs (originally designated WU-2C) for continued service with SAC's 99th Strategic Reconnaissance Squadron, alongside the 1st SRS with SR-71s at Beale AFB. The U-2R has greatly increased wing span, longer fuselage and enhanced capability. One U-2C and one U-2D were converted to two-seat U-2CT conversion trainers for the U-2Rs. In 1979, USAF ordered production of the TR-1, similar to the U-2R but intended primarily for tactical reconnaissance duties in Europe and carrying new equipment and sensors. Procurement of 23 TR-1As and two two-seat TR-1Bs is planned, plus one ER-2A for earth resources reconnaissance.

McDonnell F-101 Voodoo

USA

Two-seat long-range interceptor fighter, in service

Photo: CF-101B
Data and silhouette: F-101B
Powered by: Two 14,880lb (6,750kg) st (with afterburning) Pratt & Whitney J57-P-55 turbojets
Span: 39ft 8in (12.09m)
Length: 67ft 5in (20.55m)
Gross weight: 46,500lb (21,100kg)
Max speed: Mach 1.85 (1,220mph; 1,963km/h) at 40,000ft (12,200m)
Max range: 1,550 miles (2,495km)
Armament: Two Genie missiles in internal weapon bay plus two Falcon missiles under fuselage

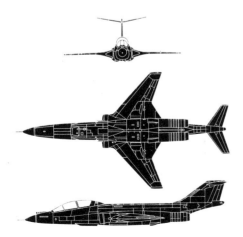

The Voodoo was derived from an earlier McDonnell design, the XF-88, only two prototypes of which were built. A production order for the developed design, the F-101, was placed in 1951 to provide Strategic Air Command with a single-seat escort fighter for its B-36s. This requirement was later dropped and production of the F-101 was continued for Tactical Air Command. The first flight was made on 29 September 1954 and three squadrons were equipped with F-101As (77 built) before the F-101C (47 built) succeeded it, with improved load-carrying ability. During 1967 and 1968, many of these aircraft were converted to reconnaissance fighters for ANG squadrons, with nose-mounted cameras, as RF-101Gs and RF-101Hs respectively. The RF-101A and RF-101C also carried cameras in a lengthened nose, production totals being 35 and 166 respectively. For service with Air Defense Command, the F-101B was developed as a two-seat long-range interceptor, with all-weather capability; this version first flew on 27 March 1957. Production totalled 480, including some with full dual control designated TF-101B. The Voodoo is out of service with the active USAF, but three ANG units fly F-101Bs within TAC as part of the air defences of the USA. 56 Voodoo two-seaters were supplied to the RCAF after servcie with ADC, plus ten with dual control, these being designated F-101F and TF-101F respectively by the USAF, and CF-101B and CF-101F by the Canadian Armed Forces. In the early 1970s, the 58 remaining CF-101B/F aircraft were exchanged for 66 refurbished aircraft of similar type with updated electronics and other refinements. These remain operational in four squadrons of the CAF under NORAD control.

McDonnell Douglas A-4 Skyhawk

USA

Single-seat carrier-based light attack bomber, in service

Data, photo and silhouette: A-4M
Powered by: One 11,200lb (5,080kg) st Pratt & Whitney J52-P-408A turbojet
Span: 27ft 6in (8.38m)
Length: 40ft 3.25in (12.27m)
Empty weight: 10,465lb (4,747kg)
Gross weight: 24,500lb (11,113kg)
Max speed: 645mph (1,038km/h) with 4,000lb (1,814kg) bombs
Range: 2,055 miles (3,307km) with external fuel
Armament: Two 20mm cannon in wings; fuselage crutch and four wing strong points carry maximum 10,000lb (4,535kg) load of assorted bombs, rockets or other stores

The prototype XA4D-1 flew on 22 June 1954, with a Wright J65-W-2 engine, and the first production version of the Skyhawk entered service in October 1956. By the time the designation changed to A-4 in 1962, the A-4E was in production. The TA-4E trainer, with lengthened fuselage for tandem seating and a J52-P-8A engine, flew on 30 June 1965; production models were redesignated TA-4F. On 31 August 1966, Douglas flew the prototype A-4F, and deliveries of 146 of this version began in June 1967, with a J52-P-8A turbojet; avionics in a saddle bay behind the pilot and other changes. The two-seat TA-4J is a simplified trainer for the US Navy with P-6 engine. A-4Cs modified to A-4F equipment standard, for service with USN Reserve carrier air wings, are designated A-4L. The A-4M, first flown on 10 April 1970, is a USMC derivative of the A-4F with J52-P-408A and other improvements. About 170 were procured to maintain a five-squadron force, these being the last Skyhawks produced. Production ended at a grand total of 2,960 with delivery of an A-4M to the Marine Corps on 27 February 1979. Also for the Marines, 23 TA-4Fs were converted to two-seat OA-4M forward air control versions in 1979/80. The RAN purchased 12 A-4Gs and 4 TA-4Gs; the RNZAF bought 10 A-4Ks and 4 TA-4Ks; Argentina acquired 75 A-4B Skyhawks, redesignated A-4Q (Navy, 15) and A-4P (Air Force, 60) after modification; and Singapore has 40 A-4Ss converted from A-4Bs, plus seven TA-4S tandem two-seat trainers. Kuwait bought 30 A-4KUs and six two-seat TA-4KUs. The A-4N Skyhawk II, with P-408A engine, uprated avionics and 30mm guns, first flown on 8 June 1972, was produced for Israel, following the delivery of substantial quantities of A-4Es, A-4Hs and TA-4Hs; the total number of Skyhawks supplied to Israel exceeded 350. In 1980, the US government agreed to supply 88 surplus A-4Cs and A-4Ls to Malaysia, and Israel sold 14 A-4Es and two TA-4Hs to Indonesia.

McDonnell Douglas F-4 Phantom II   USA

Two-seat multi-mission land and carrier-based fighter and fighter-bomber, in production (Japan only) and service

Silhouette and data: F-4E
Photo: Phantom FGR Mk 2
Powered by: Two 17,900lb (8,120kg) st (with afterburning) General Electric J79-GE-17 turbojets
Span: 38ft 5in (11.70m)
Length: 63ft 0in (19.20m)
Empty weight: 30,328lb (13,770kg)
Max gross weight: 61,795lb (28,055kg)
Max speed: Mach 2.15 (1,245kts; 2,304km/h) at 36,000ft (11,000m)
Max range: 1,613 miles (2,595km)
Armament: Basic armament of four Sparrow missiles on semi-submerged mountings under fuselage and two Sparrow or four Mitsubishi AAM-2 or Sidewinder missiles on two wing pylons. Alternative armament includes bombs exceeding 16,000lb (7,250kg) in weight, gun pods, rocket pods, etc

Development of the Phantom II began for the USN in September 1953 and the first XF4H-1 was flown on 27 May 1958. Trials in the ground attack rôle led to USAF adoption, and basic Navy and USAF versions

became the F-4B and F-4C respectively, plus RF-4B and RF-4C reconnaissance versions. Production totalled 696 F-4A/Bs, 46 RF-4Bs, 583 F-4Cs and 505 RF-4Cs; some F-4As have become TF-4As for land-based training duties and several F-4Bs have been converted as QF-4B drones. Later USAF versions are the F-4D (flown 8 December 1965; 825 built) with improved avionics, and F-4E with nose-mounted M61 gun. The Navy acquired one squadron of F-4Gs with improved avionics, followed by full production of F-4Js with J79-GE-10 engines and many improvements. The F-4K and F-4M are Spey-engined Phantom FG Mk 1 and FGR Mk 2 respectively; the RN received 24 Phantom FG Mk 1s, later transferred to the RAF, which received 28 FG Mk 1s and 118 FGR Mk 2s and in 1980 had seven squadrons assigned to air defence. Iran received 225 F-4D/Es and 32 RF-4Es, and delivery of 36 F-4Ds to South Korea began in mid-1969, followed by 37 F/RF-4Es. Israel received the first of 216 F-4Es and RF-4Es in the latter half of 1969. Germany received 88 RF-4E reconnaissance fighters and 175 F-4Fs (modified to have leading-edge slats, also retrofitted to all F-4Es); and Japan bought 154, including 14 RF-4EJs; all but two of the 140 F-4EJs are being assembled or licence-built by Mitsubishi, which flew its first example on 12 May 1972. Other operators of the F-4E and RF-4E include the Turkish and Greek Air Forces, which received 80 and 64 respectively. Spain has received 40 F-4Cs and 4 RF-4Cs (designated C12 and CR12) and during 1980, the USAF transferred 35 F-4Es to Egypt. The USN has updated 178 F-4Bs as F-4Ns and has a similar programme to update F-4Js to F-4S standard, while the USAF is acquiring 116 F-4G (Wild Weasel) electronic warfare conversions of F-4Es to equip four squadrons. Late in 1979 McDonnell Douglas delivered the 5,057th and last F-4 assembled and flown in the USA. In addition, Japan is building 138 and 16 sets of parts remained at St Louis unassembled.

McDonnell Douglas F-15 Eagle

USA

Single-seat and two-seat air superiority fighter, in production and service

Data, photo and silhouette: F-15A
Powered by: Two 25,000lb (11,340kg) st Pratt & Whitney F100-PW-100 afterburning turbofans
Span: 42ft 9.75in (13.05m)
Length: 63ft 9.75in (19.45m)
Gross weight: 56,000lb (25,401kg)
Max speed: More than Mach 2.5
Ferry range: more than 2,875 miles (4,630km); 3,450 miles (5,560km) with 'Fast Pack' flush-fitting lateral fuel tanks
Armament: One internally-mounted M61 20mm multi-barrel gun in fuselage. AIM-9L advanced Sidewinder air-to-air missiles on wing stations. Four AIM-7F advanced Sparrow air-to-air missiles on lower corners of air intake trunks. Provision for carrying electronic warfare pods on outboard wing stations. Max external weapon load 12,000lb (5,443kg)

When Russia's Mig-25 was first shown in public in 1967, the USAF began the urgent development of an air superiority fighter capable of fighter sweep, escort and combat air patrol duties in areas where the Soviet fighter might be met. McDonnell Douglas was selected to design and build the new aircraft, as the F-15, in December 1969, and received an initial order for 20 aircraft for development testing.

The first single-seat F-15A, named Eagle, flew for the first time on 27 July 1972, and was subsequently joined in the flight test programme by 17 more F-15As and two F-15B (originally TF-15A) two-seat trainers, with full combat capability. Production of the first 30 aircraft for Tactical Air Command was authorised in 1973. Subsequent annual increments brought the total on order for the USAF to 639 by 1980, out of a planned procurement of 729 Eagles for 19 squadrons. Deliveries to TAC began on 15 November 1974, when the first F-15B was delivered to the 555th Squadron, 58th TF Training Wing; the 1st TF Wing at Langley AFB subsequently became the first fully equipped with Eagles, followed by the 49th TFW at Holloman AFB, the 36th TFW in Germany and the 32nd TFS in Holland. The F-15A and F-15B have now been superseded by the F-15C and D respectively, with improved radar, more internal fuel and ability to carry Fast Pack (Fuel and Sensor Tactical Package) pallets on the sides of the air intake trunks. The first F-15C flew on 26 February 1979. McDonnell Douglas has supplied 35 F-15s to Israel and Saudi Arabia is to receive 47 F-15Cs and 15 F-15Ds from early 1982. Japan plans to acquire 88 F-15CJs and 12 F-15DJs by 1987, all but two to be built by Mitsubishi. The first of two F-15CJ prototypes flew in the USA on 4 June 1980. Also in 1980, McDonnell Douglas demonstrated an Advanced Wild Weasel configuration on the F-15, and flew an all-weather interdiction version known as the Strike Eagle, with synthetic aperture radar and up to 24,000lb (10,885kg) of external stores.

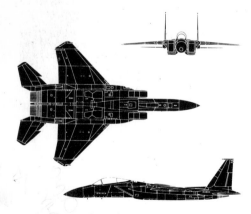

McDonnell Douglas F-18, A-18 and CF-18 Hornet   USA

Single-seat carrier-borne multi-mission fighter, in production

Powered by: Two 16,000lb (7,264kg) st General Electric F404-GE-400 turbofan engines
Span: 37ft 6in (11.43m)
Length: 56ft 0in (17.07m)
Take-off weight: 33,585lb (15,234kg) (fighter mission)
47,000lb (21,319kg) (attack mission)
Max speed: Over Mach 1.8
Combat radius: Over 460 miles (740km) with internal fuel for fighter mission; over 633 miles (1,019km) for attack mission
Armament: Seven weapon stations under wings and fuselage, plus wing-tip missile shoes, with combined capacity for 18,000lb (8,165kg) of ordnance

The F-18, in production by McDonnell Douglas at its St Louis plant under contract to the US Navy and in collaboration with Northrop, is the outcome of a competitive evaluation by the USN of the two fighter prototypes produced for USAF evaluation in 1964 by General Dynamics and Northrop. Although the General Dynamics F-16 had meanwhile gained USAF backing, it was the Northrop YF-17 that provided the basis for the USN selection and around which a full-scale development programme was launched in January 1976, with McDonnell Douglas the prime contractor in collaboration with Northrop. The designation F-18 was adopted to avoid the impression that the Navy was buying a USAF cast-off, and McDonnell Douglas influence subsequently led to an overall scaling up of the original design, with more fuel capacity in the fuselage, radar in the nose and greater wing area. The first of 11 FSD (full-scale development) F-18s, including two two-seat TF-18s, was flown at St Louis on 18 November 1978, at which time the USN planned to procure 811 Hornets for its own and Marine Corps squadrons. This quantity was later increased to 1,377. The Hornet is intended to replace Navy and Marine Corps F-4s in the fighter rôle (F-18A) and USN A-7s in the attack role (A-18A); about 150 will be TF-18A two-seaters. In April 1980 the Canadian Armed Forces adopted the land-based CF-18 to meet its New Fighter Aircraft requirement and ordered 113 CF-18As and 24 two-seat CF-18Bs for delivery from October 1982.

McDonnell Douglas KC-10A Extender USA

Advanced tanker/transport aircraft, in production

Powered by: Three 52,500lb st (23,814kg) General Electric F103-GE-100 turbofans
Span: 165ft 4in (50.42m)
Length: 181ft 7in (55.35m)
Operating weight empty: 244,471lb (110,892kg) (cargo)
240,245lb (108,975kg) (tanker)
Gross weight: 590,000lb (267,624kg)
Max cruising speed: 595mph (957km/h)
Max range: 4,375 miles (7,037km) (cargo)

The KC-10A Extender is a military variant of the commercial DC-10 Srs 30 airliner, adopted by the USAF to meet its Advanced Tanker/Cargo Aircraft (ATCA) requirement to complement its large fleet of KC-135A tankers. The requirement was for an aircraft of greatly increased payload/range performance, capable of supporting the deployment of air and ground forces to bases far distant from continental USA. The DC-10 was selected as the basis for ATCA after competitive evaluation with a version of the Boeing 747 and initial orders were placed against a planned total fleet of about 40 (subject to funding constraints). The Extender is basically a Srs 30CF airframe, with the cargo floor and forward fuselage side cargo door of the commercial version. Fuel capacity is enhanced by installation of seven extra fuel tanks in the fuselage under the cabin floor, leaving the cabin itself free to accommodate cargo and up to 80 passengers. Total fuel capacity, including the standard wing tanks, is 356,000lb (161,500kg) and refuelling of other aircraft is effected through an advanced version of the flying-boom, using 'fly-by-wire' controls. A boom operator's station is located under the rear fuselage. The first KC-10A made its initial flight on 12 July 1980 and the Extenders were to enter service at Barksdale AFB in 1982.

Mikoyan/Gurevich MiG-17, (NATO code-name 'Fresco' Chinese designation F-4 and F-5)

USSR

Single-seat fighter, in service

Silhouette: 'Fresco-D'
Data and photo: 'Fresco-C'
Powered by: One 6,990lb (3,170kg) st (with afterburning) Klimov VK-1A turbojet
Span: 31ft 0in (9.45m)
Length: 36ft 4in (11.10m)
Gross weight: 12,500lb (5,670kg) (clean)
Max speed: 700mph (1,125km/h) at sea level
Max range: 750miles (1,205km) with external tanks and bombs
Armament: Three 23mm NR-23 cannon; four eight-rocket pods or two 550lb (250kg) bombs

The MiG-17 was developed from the pioneer Soviet

swept-wing MiG-15, which it began to supersede in production in 1953. The design was considerably refined, with a thinner wing section, increased wing sweep and lengthened rear fuselage; but the MiG-17 remained subsonic in level flight. The initial production model, known to NATO as 'Fresco-A', had a 5,950lb (2,700kg) st VK-1 turbojet, without afterburner, narrow dive-brakes at the tail like the MiG-15 and an armament of one 37mm and two 23mm cannon. In 'Fresco-B', the dive-brakes were enlarged and moved to just aft of the wing trailing-edge. The next version, 'Fresco-C', retained the larger brakes but had them repositioned at the tail; it also introduced an afterburner, an additional 23mm cannon in place of the 37mm gun, and underwing armament. 'Fresco-D' was a limited all-weather fighter version of the 'C' with radar in a central bullet in its air intake, and sometimes carried four air-to-air missiles instead of cannon. 'Fresco-E' was similar but without afterburner. 'Fresco-C' was built in Czechoslovakia (as the S-104) and in Poland (as LiM-5) as well as in Russia. Many remain in service, especially with air forces in Asia and Africa which receive aid from the USSR and China. Reported Soviet designations are Mig-17P for 'Fresco-B', Mig-17F for 'Fresco-C', MiG-17PF for 'Fresco-D' and MiG-17PFU for 'Fresco-E'. In 1956, the first Mig-17F built under licence in China was completed at Shenyang. This version received the designation F-4, being followed by the Mig-17PF as the F-5. Many hundreds were built and were still in large-scale service in 1980; a few had also been supplied to Tanzania and Albania. As the FT-5, China also developed a two-seat training variant of the basic design, with a cockpit similar to that of the original Mig-15UTI, and this variant is in service with the Pakistan Air Force.

Mikoyan MiG-19
(NATO code-name 'Farmer'
Chinese designation F-6)

USSR

Single-seat fighter, in service

Silhouette: MiG-19S
Data and photo: F-6 (MiG-19PF)
Powered by: Two 7,165lb (3,250kg) st (with afterburning) Klimov RD-9B turbojets
Span: 29ft 6.5in (9.00m)
Length: 48ft 10.5in (14.90m)
Empty weight: 12,700lb (5,760kg)
Gross weight: 19,180lb (8,700kg)
Max speed: 902mph (1,450km/h) at 33,000ft (10,000m)
Combat radius: 426 miles (685km) with external tanks
Armament: Three 30mm cannon and underwing pylons for two fuel tanks and either two 500lb (or 250kg) bombs, two 212mm rockets or two pods, each containing eight air-to-air rockets

With the MiG-19, Mikoyan finally achieved supersonic performance in level flight. He retained the basic layout of the MiG-15 and 17, but mounted two small-diameter turbojets side-by-side in the rear

fuselage, more than doubling the thrust of the earlier types. The initial version ('Farmer-A') entered service early in 1955, armed with one 37mm and two 23mm cannon, plus underwing rockets, missiles and drop tanks. 'Farmer-B' was similar, but with radar in a bullet radome in the air intake for limited all-weather operations. The most widely-used version ('Farmer-C') introduced an underfuselage air-brake, supplementing the original air-brakes on the sides of the rear fuselage, and was fitted with three improved cannon of 30mm calibre. 'Farmer-D' is the limited all-weather counterpart of the 'C', with radar in a nose bullet and only two guns. Some 'Farmer-Ds' are armed with four underwing missiles (code-name 'Alkali') and no guns. Soviet designations are MiG-19S for early 'Farmer-Cs' with Klimov AM-5 turbojets, MiG-19SF for later RD-9B-powered 'Farmer-Cs', MiG-19PF for 'Farmer-D' and MiG-19PM for the 'D' with 'Alkali' missiles. Before its break with the USSR, China concluded a licence agreement for the MiG-19 and put both 'Farmer-C' and 'D' versions into production at Shenyang under the designation F-6. Manufacture got underway only slowly, but was still continuing in 1980 at the rate of almost two a week to replace the many hundreds of F-2 (MiG-15bis) and F-4 and F-5 (MiG-17) fighters still in service with the Chinese Air Force and Naval air component. Some F-6s have fuselage cameras for the tactical reconnaissance role. The Pakistan Air Force has received 150 Chinese-built F-6s, Tanzania has received eight, Bangladesh was presented with 30, Albania has 36 and Egypt received 40 in 1979. According to some reports, Zambia, Sudan and Somalia have received 12 F-6s each. A two-seat version of the F-6 has also been developed in China and is designated FT-6; examples are also in service in Egypt and Pakistan.

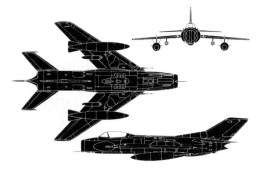

Mikoyan MiG-21
(NATO code-names 'Fishbed' and 'Mongol'
Chinese designation F-7)

USSR

Single-seat lightweight fighter and two-seat trainer, in production and service

Silhouette: 'Fishbed-K' with reconnaissance pod
Data: MiG-21MF
Powered by: One 14,550lb (6,600kg) st (with afterburning) Tumansky R-13-300 turbojet
Span: 23ft 5.5in (7.15m)
Length: 51ft 8.5in (15.76m)
Gross weight: 20,725lb (9,400kg)
Max speed: Mach 2.1 (1,385mph; 2,230km/h) at 36,000ft (11,000m)
Armament: One twin-barrel 23mm cannon. Four under-wing pylons for K-13A ('Atoll') and/or 'Advanced Atoll' missiles, packs of 16 rockets or drop tanks

First seen in prototype form in the 1956 Aviation Day fly-past over Moscow, the MiG-21 is the most widely used fighter in the world, serving with some 35 air forces. The original MiG-21F is a short-range clear-weather fighter, with armament of one 30mm gun and two rocket pods or 'Atoll' infra-red homing missiles. With a wider-chord fin and optional underbelly twin-barrel 23mm gun pack it became 'Fishbed-E'. The MiG-21PF ('Fishbed-D') introduced a lengthened nose of larger diameter, housing more effective radar to give limited all-weather capability. Cannon armament is deleted, the pitot boom repositioned above the nose, and the R-11 turbojet uprated from the former 12,676lb (5,750kg) st to 13,120lb (5,950kg). Late MiG-21PFs and subsequent versions also have provision for flap-blowing (SPS) to reduce landing speed. A wider-chord fin, improved radar, optional underbelly gun pack, 13,668lb (6,200kg) st R-11-300 engine, but no SPS, identifies the MiG-21FL. The MiG-21PFM ('Fishbed-F') differs from the late-model PF in having the broader fin, a sideways-hinged canopy instead of the original one-piece windscreen/canopy, and the same radar as the FL, and was built in both the Soviet Union and Czechoslovakia. MiG-21PFMA ('Fishbed-J') was the first of a new multi-role family, with two additional underwing pylons, able to carry, among other things, new 'Advanced Atoll' radar-homing missiles. The dorsal spine fairing is deepened back to the fin, and late PFMAs can have the 23mm gun buried inside the fuselage with only the barrels visible, so that an underbelly drop tank can also be carried. Variants are the MiG-21MF ('Fishbed-J'),

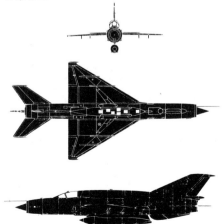

Top: MiG-21RF 'Fishbed-H'

83

Above: MiG-21

Below: MiG-21MF 'Fishbed-J'

with more powerful R-13-300 engine; Mig-21SMT ('Fishbed-K'), with the deep dorsal spine extended rearward as far as the parachute brake housing, and optional wingtip ECM pods; and the MiG-21M, similar to the PFMA but built by HAL. The MiG-21R and RF ('Fishbed-H') are reconnaissance versions of the PFMA and MF respectively, with external pod for cameras and infra-red sensors, and wingtip ECM pods. 'Fishbed-L' is the first variant of the third-generation MiG-21bis, with updated electronics, wider and deeper dorsal fairing and generally improved construction standards. It has been followed by 'Fishbed-N', now standard in the Soviet Air Force, with 16,535lb (7,500kg) st Tumansky R-25 engine and further-enhanced electronics. Tandem two-seat training versions of the MiG-21 have the NATO code-name 'Mongol', the 'Mongol-B' being the two-seat counterpart of the MiG-21MF. The early MiG-21F variant was built also in Czechoslovakia and in China a version of the MiG-21F was built as the F-7, without help from the Soviet Union. Hindustan Aeronautics in India has built or assembled over 200 MiG-21s of several different versions.

Mikoyan MiG-23
(NATO code-name 'Flogger-A', 'B', 'C', 'E' and 'G')

USSR

Single-seat variable-geometry tactical fighter, in production and service

Photo: 'Flogger-E'
Silhouette: 'Flogger-B'
Data: 'Flogger-F'
Powered by: One Tumansky R-29 turbofan rated at 23,350lb (11,500kg) st with afterburning
Span: 46ft 9in (14.25m) spread; 26ft 9.5in (8.17m) swept (estimated)
Length: 55ft 1.5in (16.80m) (estimated)
Max gross weight: 44,312lb (20,100kg)
Max speed: Mach 2.3 (1,520mph; 2,450km/h) at 36,000ft (11,000m) with external stores
Combat radius: 600 miles (960km)
Armament: One 23mm GSh-23 twin-barrel cannon in belly. One pylon under centre fuselage, one under each air intake trunk, and one under each fixed inboard wing panel for air-to-air missiles (NATO 'Apex' and 'Aphid') or other stores

The prototype of this 'swing-wing' tactical fighter, allocated the code-name 'Flogger-A' by NATO, made its first public appearance in the 1967 Aviation Day display at Domodedovo Airport, Moscow, but did not land there. The commentator announced that it could fly at supersonic speed at ground level and Mach 2 at medium and high altitudes. Deliveries to the Soviet Air Force were reported to be under way in 1971. When photographs became available, it was clear that the basic single-seat MiG-23MF ('Flogger-B') differed considerably from the prototype, with the tail surfaces moved farther aft (except for the ventral fin), and a fixed section inboard of the leading-edge flap on each pivoted outer wing panel. The lower half of the ventral fin is hinged to fold sideways during take-off and landing, to provide ground clearance. The tandem two-seat MiG-23U ('Flogger-C') dual-role trainer/combat version differs from the MiG-23S in having an additional, slightly raised rear seat, with separate canopy, periscopic sight, and deepened fairing behind it; most examples also have a smaller radome. An export model, delivered to Cuba, Ethiopia, Egypt, Iraq, Libya and Syria is equipped to a lower standard, and is known as 'Flogger-E', usually with an armament of AA-2 'Atoll' AAMs. With its primary role switched from air defence to ground attack, 'Flogger-F' (MiG-23BM) has an R-29B turbofan and an entirely new nose section housing laser target marking equipment. 'Flogger-G' appeared in 1971 and is an improved air-to-air version with a smaller dorsal fin; it is one of the MiG-23 versions supplied to Warpac air forces, together with 'Flogger-F'. 'Flogger-D' is the MiG-27, separately described. In 1982, India will start to take delivery of 70 MiG-23BN ground attack aircraft and 15 two-seaters; all but a few of these are to be assembled by HAL and 80 MiG-23S fighters are expected to be obtained by India later.

Mikoyan MiG-25
(NATO code-name 'Foxbat')

USSR

Single-seat interceptor and reconnaissance aircraft, in production and service

Photo: 'Foxbat-B'
Data and silhouette: 'Foxbat-A'
Powered by: Two 24,250lb (11,000kg) st Tumansky R-31 afterburning turbojets
Span: 45ft 9in (13.95m)
Length: 73ft 2in (22.30m)
Gross weight: 79,800lb (36,200kg)
Max speed: Mach 2.8 with underwing missiles
Max combat radius: 805 miles (1,300km)
Armament: Four air-to-air missiles (NATO 'Acrid', 'Apex' or 'Aphid' on underwing pylons

The existence of a new Soviet aircraft designated E-266 was revealed in April 1965, when an aircraft of this type set a 1,000km closed-circuit speed record of 1,441.5mph (2,320km/h) carrying a 2,000kg payload. Four examples of the E-266 took part in the Aviation Day flypast over Moscow in July 1967, but the service designation Mig-25 was not confirmed until several years later. By that time, even more spectacular records had been set, including a still-unbeaten speed record of 1,852.62mph (2,981km/h) around a 500km closed circuit. A reconnaissance version ('Foxbat-B'), equipped with five cameras and side-looking airborne radar, was soon identified, in addition to the basic interceptor ('Foxbat-A'). Four 'Bs' were ferried to Egypt on board An-22 transports in 1971, subsequently making flights off the coast of Israel and over Israeli-occupied Sinai at speeds in excess of Mach 3, which made them impossible to intercept. When carrying missiles, 'Foxbat-A' is limited to Mach 2.8, whereas 'Foxbat-B' can attain Mach 3.2 at height. The wing of the 'B' also lacks the compound sweep of that on 'Foxbat-A' and has a span of only 44ft (13.40m). Other versions in service are 'Foxbat-D', a reconnaissance variant with larger SLAR but no cameras, and the tandem-cockpit MiG-25U ('Foxbat-C') two-seat trainer. The latest E-266M, with uprated (30,865lb; 14,000kg st) engines, has set an absolute height record of 123,523ft (37,650m) and climbed to 114,829ft (35,000m) in 4min 11.3sec. Over 400 MiG-25s are believed to be in service with the Soviet air forces and there have been sightings of MiG-25s in service with the Algerian and Libyan Air Forces. During 1979, the Mig-25 entered service with the Syrian Air Force, and eight have been ordered by the Indian Air Force for reconnaissance duties.

Mikoyan MiG-27
(NATO code-name 'Flogger-D')

USSR

Single-seat variable-geometry ground attack aircraft, in production and service

Data: Estimated
Powered by: One Tumansky turbojet, believed to give about 18,000lb (8,150kg) st with afterburning
Span: 46ft 9in (14.25m) spread, 26ft 9.5in (8.17m) swept
Length: 51ft 0in (15.55m)
Gross weight: 39,130lb (17,750kg)
Max speed: Mach 1.6
Max ferry range: 1,550 miles (2,500km) with three external fuel tanks
Armament: One six-barrel 23mm cannon. Five underfuselage and underwing attachments for 4,200lb (1,900kg) of external stores, including tactical nuclear weapons and 'Kerry' air-to-surface guided missiles

Although much of the airframe of the MiG-27 is similar to that of the MiG-23, this aircraft has been optimised for high-speed attack, with heavy armament, at tree-top height. Instead of housing a large search radar, its nose slopes down sharply for optimum forward vision, and houses both electronics for low-level navigation and specialised target-seeking aids such as a laser range-finder and marked target seeker. A Gatling-type gun adds to the attack potential of its external weapons. The cockpit is heavily armoured for protection against ground fire. The variable-geometry air intakes and nozzle of the Mig-23 have given way to the fixed intakes and nozzle more appropriate to an aircraft intended to fly at just below the speed of sound at sea level. The engine, different from that of the Mig-23, may be related to the Tumansky R-31 fitted in the Mig-25 'Foxbat' and was substituted for the R-29 in order to obtain better endurance at low altitude. Significantly, although the 'Flogger-F' export ground attack aircraft resembles the MiG-27 outwardly, it is basically a Mig-23, with only the nose shape and low-pressure tyres of the Soviet Air Force's 'Flogger-D'. The Mig-27 is in service with the tactical aviation component of the Soviet air forces, Frontavaya Aviatsiya (FA) but up to the end of 1980 had not been exported.

Mitsubishi F-1 and T-2

Japan

Single-seat close-support fighter, in production and service

Powered by: Two 7,070lb (3,207kg) st Ishikawajima-Harima TF40-IHI-801A (licence-built Rolls-Royce/Tuboméca Adour) afterburning turbofans
Span: 25ft 10.25in (7.88m)
Length: 58ft 6.75in (17.85m)
Empty weight: 14,017lb (6,358kg)
Gross weight: 30,146lb (13,674kg)
Max speed: Mach 1.6 (1,056mph; 1,700km/h) at 36,000ft (11,000m)
Combat radius: 173 miles (278km) with four Sidewinders and internal fuel only; 346 miles (556km) with two ASM-1s and an external tank
Armament: One JM61 multi-barrel 20mm cannon. One underfuselage and four underwing attachments for twelve 500lb bombs, two ASM-1 air-to-ship missiles, rockets or external fuel tanks. Two or four Sidewinder class air-to-air missiles on wingtips

The basic airframe, engines and systems of this efficient little fighter are similar to those of the Mitsubishi T-2 supersonic trainer. The two F-1 prototypes were, in fact, conversions of the third and second production T-2s, making their first flights in single-seat form on 3 and 7 June 1975, respectively. Unlike the production F-1, the prototypes retained the rear cockpit and canopy of the T-2, but carried fire control equipment and test instrumentation instead of a second crew member. Only other external difference by comparison with the trainer was the installation of a passive warning radar antenna at the tip of the tail-fin. The initial production contract, for 18 F-1s, was placed in March 1976; eight more were ordered a year later. The first production aircraft flew on 16 June 1977, and the JASDF plans to acquire a total of 77 to equip three squadrons. The first squadron was formed in the spring of 1978, when deliveries began to the 3rd Squadron, JASDF, at Misawa AB in northern Japan. This squadron is a unit of the 3rd Air Wing, together with the 8th Squadron, which was receiving its F-1s during 1980. Next to equip was to be one of the squadrons of the 8th Air Wing. Each Squadron has an establishment of 18 aircraft. The T-2 from which the F-1 is derived, originated in 1967 as Japan's first indigenous supersonic design. The prototype XT-2 flew on 20 July 1971 and production, after a second prototype and two pre-production examples, has totalled 32 T-2 advanced trainers and 44 T-2A combat trainers.

Myasishchev M-4
(NATO code-name 'Bison')

USSR

Four-jet long-range reconnaissance-bomber, in service

Photo and silhouette: 'Bison-C'
Data: 'Bison-B' estimated
Powered by: Four 19,180lb (8,700kg) st Mikulin AM-3D turbojets
Span: 165ft 7.5in (50.48m)
Length: 154ft 10in (47.20m)
Loaded weight: 350,000lb (158,750kg)
Max speed: 560mph (900km/h) at 36,000ft (11,000m)
Unrefuelled range: 7,000 miles (11,265km) at 520mph (837km/h) with 10,000lb (4,535kg) of bombs

This huge bomber, which was designed by V. M. Myasishchev, was described for many years as Russia's answer to the American B-52 Stratofortress. It was designed for the same task of carrying thermonuclear weapons over intercontinental ranges, with, the help of flight refuelling in extreme cases. But it was probably contemporary with rather than an 'answer' to, the B-52, because it first put in an appearance over Moscow in May 1954, only two years after the first flight of the prototype Stratofortress.

In contrast with the B-52's four pairs of podded turbojets, the M-4 has only four engines in a buried wing-root installation. Its service ceiling is believed to be little more than 45,000ft (13,700m), which explains the heavy defensive armament. On the original bomber version ('Bison-A'), of which more than 40 are in service as flight refuelling tankers, this included 10 23mm cannon in twin-gun turrets in the tail, above the fuselage fore and aft of the wing and under the fuselage fore and aft of the bomb-bays. A modified version ('Bison-B'), with refuelling probe on a 'solid' nose and new electronic equipment, appeared in the maritime reconnaissance role in 1964. A further maritime development ('Bison-C') had a large radar in a lengthened nose, and appears to be the definitive variant. A testbed version was powered by 28,660lb (13,000kg) st D-15 turbojets when used to set a series of payload-to-height records in 1959. Armament on the later versions is reduced to six 23mm guns. A few continue to serve in the offensive role, but 'Bisons' are most important in the role of flight-refuelling tankers, with hose-and-droque reels in the fuselage, to serve 'Backfire' and 'Bear' aircraft of the Soviet long-range Aviation force.

Nancheng A-5 (Kiang 5)
(NATO code-name 'Fantan')

China

Ground-attack fighter, in production and service

Powered by: Two 7,165lb (3,250kg) st with afterburning Shenyang-built WP-6A turbojets
Span: 33ft 5in (10.20m)
Length: 50ft 0in (15.25m)
Gross weight: About 17,500lb (7,950kg)
Max speed: About Mach 1.35 (900mph/1,450km/h) at 33,000ft (10,000m)
Combat radius: About 230 miles (370km) with full bomb load, all low-altitude mission

The Kiang 5, or Attack aeroplane 5, is a Chinese development of the MiG-19, which was put into production at the Shenyang factory more than 20 years ago under the terms of a licensing agreement between the Chinese and Soviet governments. Large numbers of MiG-19s were built as Chien Chi 6, or fighter aeroplane 6, and Chinese technicians put in hand the development of a version to meet indigenous requirements for a ground attack aeroplane. While this design effort was going on — at first under the designation F-6bis — Chinese/Soivet relations deteriorated to the point of a complete break, leaving the new project to continue without any Soviet input. For the ground attack rôle, the F-6bis, alias A-5, was designed to have a small internal weapons bay in the centre fuselage; to make this possible, it became necessary to redesign the air intakes and to adopt lateral intakes in place of the MiG-19's straight-through arrangement. This in turn made it possible to relocate various items of equipment from the fuselage to the nose. To supplement the internal weapon load of four 551lb (250kg) bombs, two more such bombs can be carried externally under the fuselage and there are four wing strong points, two of which normally carry 167 Imp gal (760litre) drop tanks while the inner pylons carry rocket pods. The Kiang 5 is believed to have been in production for at least 10 years and it is in service in substantial numbers with the Air Force of the People's Liberation Army.

North American F-86 Sabre

USA

Single-seat tactical fighter and fighter-bomber, in service

Photo: Sabre 5, US Army
Data and silhouette: F-86F
Powered by: One 5,970lb (2,708kg) st General Electric J47-GE-27 turbojet
Span: 39ft 1in (11.91m)
Length: 37ft 6.5in (11.44m)
Empty weight: 11,125lb (5,046kg)
Max gross weight: 20,610lb (9,350kg)
Max speed: 687mph (1,105km/h) at sea level
Range: 925 miles (1,488km) at 530mph (853km/h)
Armament: Six 0.50in machine guns, plus two Sidewinder missiles, two 1,000lb bombs or eight rockets

The Sabre first flew on 1 October 1947, and was produced as the USAF's first sweptwing fighter. It was widely used in the Korean War and was licence built in Australia, Canada, Italy and Japan. North American built more than 6,000 of the F-86A, D, E, F, H and K versions. Of these, the F-86A, E, F and H were day fighters and fighter-bombers. The F-86D was an all-weather interceptor with radar in a nose radome above the air intake and an afterburning engine. The F-86K, built by Fiat in Italy, was similar, for service with NATO air forces in Europe; and the F-86L, of which 981 were completed, was a conversion of the D with more advanced electronics. Although no longer operational with the USAF, versions of the Sabre still serve with a handful of air forces, of which the Chinese Nationalist Air Force was the largest user in 1980. Other air forces still using the F-86 included South Korea, Portugal, Yugoslavia, Venezuela, Argentina, Ethiopia, and Tunisia. In the USA, Sperry has a continuing programme to convert F-86Fs to QF-86F drones for US Navy use.

Canadair built 1,815 Sabres under licence between 1950 and 1958, for the RCAF, RAF and foreign air forces. The last version built was the Sabre Mk 6 with Orenda 14 turbojet.

A version of the F-86 with Rolls-Royce Avon engine was ordered by the RAAF from the Commonwealth Aircraft Corporation in 1951, and a prototype flew on 3 August 1953. This was followed by 111 production aircraft known as Sabre 30, 31 and 32. They were superseded in the RAAF by Mirage IIIs, but sufficient Avon-Sabre 32s to equip a single fighter-bomber squadron transferred to the Indonesian Air Force, with which they continued to serve in 1980.

North American F-100 Super Sabre

USA

Interceptor and fighter-bomber, in service

Photo: F-100D (Turkey)
Data and silhouette: F-100D
Powered by: One 17,000lb (7,710kg) st Pratt &
Whitney J57-P-21A afterburning turbojet
Span: 38ft 9in (11.81m)
Length: 54ft 3in (16.53m)
Empty weight: 21,000lb (9,525kg)
Gross weight: 34,832lb (15,800kg)
Max speed: Mach 1.3 (864mph; 1,390km/h) at
36,000ft (11,000m)
Range: 1,500 miles (2,410km) with two external
tanks
Accommodation: Pilot only
Armament: Four 20mm cannon in fuselage; six
underwing pick-up points for bombs, rockets, air-to-
air or air-to-surface missiles, etc

First of the USAF's 'Century Series' of fighters (so
called because the 'F' designations were 100 and
above), the Super Sabre began life, as the name
suggests, as a development of the F-86 Sabre. An
official contract was placed in November 1951 and
the prototype YF-100A flew on 25 May 1953. The
first production model F-100A flew on 29 October
1953, and three aircraft were delivered to the USAF
in the following month. The three principal variants
were the F-100A interceptor, the F-100C fighter-
bomber with a strengthened wing and the F-100D,
also a fighter-bomber, with improved equipment and
other changes. The F-100F was a two-seater with
lengthened fuselage, capable of use as a trainer or an
operational fighter. F-100s played a prominent part
in the war in Vietnam in its early years and several
hundred served with 11 Air National Guard units
assigned to USAF Tactical Air Command until
replaced with F-4s, A-7s, F-105s and A-10s by the
end of FY 1979. Examples of all production variants
were supplied under MDAP to other NATO nations,
including Denmark and Turkey, which continue to
operate the type in 1980. Others still serve with the
Nationalist Chinese Air Force, in Taiwan. During
1980, the USAF inaugurated a programme to
convert F-100s to QF-100 target drones, using a
more advanced Sperry flight control system than
that applied to the QF-102A Delta Dagger. An initial
batch of nine QF-100s was to be converted by
Sperry for development purposes, followed by 72
production conversions for service from 1983.

Northrop F-5 and F-5E/F Tiger II USA

Lightweight fighter, in production and service

Silhouette: F-5A
Data and photo: F-5E Tiger II
Powered by: Two 5,000lb (2,267kg) st General Electric J85-GE-21A afterburning turbojets
Span: 26ft 8in (8.13m)
Length: 48ft 2in (14.68m)
Empty weight: 9,683lb (4,392kg)
Gross weight: 24,664lb (11,187kg)
Max speed: Mach 1.64 (1,082mph; 1,742km/h) at 36,000ft (11,000m)
Max range: 1,784 miles (2,871km)
Accommodation: Pilot only
Armament: Two 20mm cannon in nose. One Sidewinder air-to-air missile on each wingtip; five pylons under fuselage and wings for assorted stores up to a total of 7,000lb (3,175kg)

The F-5 was the outcome of a project begun by Northrop in 1954 to develop a low-cost lightweight supersonic fighter. Construction of three N-156Fs

began in May 1958, and the first of these flew on 30 July 1959. Production contracts were placed by the Department of Defense for N-156s to be supplied as the F-5A and RF-5A (single-seat) and F-5B (two-seat), mainly under mutual aid programmes, to Greece, Turkey, Morocco, Nationalist China, the Philippines, Thailand, South Vietnam, Iran, Ethiopia, Libya, Pakistan and South Korea. The Royal Norwegian AF ordered 108, including F-5Gs, camera-equipped RF-5Gs and F-5Bs for training. Spain acquired 36 SF-5As and 34 SF-5Bs assembled by CASA and operated by the Spanish Air Force as A9s and AR9s respectively. Canadair built 89 CF-5A single-seaters and 44 two-seat CF-5Ds for the Canadian Armed Forces (now designated CF-116A and CF-116D), plus 75 NF-5As and 30 NF-5Bs for the RNethAF. Eighteen of the CF-5As and two CF-5Ds were transferred to Venezuela. Following flight trials of a YF-5B-21 prototype, with uprated engines, manoeuvring flaps and other improvements, the USAF ordered a production version for supply to America's allies under the designation F-5E Tiger II. The first F-5E flew on 11 August 1972. Deliveries have been made to many countries, including South Korea, Kenya, Singapore, Thailand, Jordan, Saudi Arabia, Chile, Brazil, Malaysia, Iran, Kenya, Morocco, Sudan and North Yemen, and F-5Es are built under licence in Taiwan and Switzerland for the airforces of these countries. Delivery of the 1,000th Tiger II was made in August 1979, the total including RF-5E camera-carrying reconnaissance-fighters (first flown 29 January 1979) and two-seat F-5Fs (first flown 25 September 1974). The USAF bought 112 F-5Es as 'aggressors' to simulate hostile aircraft in air combat training; the US Navy has 10 F-5Es and three F-5Fs. The F-5G, under development in 1981, has a single General Electric F404-GE-100 engine and other new features.

Panavia Tornado

UK/Germany/Italy

Two-seat multi-role combat aircraft, in production and service

Data and silhouette: Tornado GR Mk 1
Powered by: Two 16,000lb (7,264kg) st Turbo-Union RB199-34R Mk 101 afterburning turbofans
Span: 45ft 7.25in (13.90m) spread, 28ft 2.5in (8.60m) swept
Length: 54ft 9.5in (16.70m)
Max take-off weight: Over 58,000lb (26,332kg)
Max speed: Approx Mach 2.2 (1,452mph 2,336km/h) at 36,000ft (11,000m)
Armament: Guided and semi-active homing air-to-air missiles, 'scatter-weapons', and many types of nuclear and conventional air-to-surface weapons, according to version, on seven pylons under the fuselage and wings. Built-in armament comprises two 27mm Mauser cannon

Panavia Aircraft GmbH was set up in Munich in March 1969 to design and build a multi-rôle combat aircraft (MRCA) for service with the air forces of Great Britain, West Germany and Italy. Shareholders are British Aerospace (42%), Messerschmitt-Bolkow-Blohm (42%) and Aeritalia (16%). A second company, named Turbo-Union, was established by Rolls-Royce (40%), MTU (40%) and Fiat (20%) to supply engines for the MRCA, which is a compact swing-wing aircraft able to fulfil six major duties; close air support/battlefield interdiction, interdictor strike, air superiority, interception, naval strike, and reconnaissance. Nine prototypes were completed initially, four of them assembled in the UK, three in Germany and two in Italy. First to fly, on 4 August 1974, was the P-01 aircraft assembled by MBB. P-09, the ninth and last prototype, flew on 5 February 1977 in Italy and on the same day the first of six pre-series aircraft, P-11 flew in Germany. The RAF will eventually receive 220 interdictor/strike Tornado GR Mk 1s (including 68 with dual control, designated GR Mk 1(T)) to replace Vulcans and Buccaneers for overland strike, maritime strike and reconnaissance. The German Air Force and Navy will receive 212 and 112 respectively (47 and 10 trainers) and 100 Italian Air Force Tornadoes (12 with dual control) will replace F-104Gs and G91Rs for air superiority, ground attack and reconnaissance duties. The first production Tornado GR Mk 1 flew in Britain on 10 July 1979 followed by the first from

Top left: Two GR1s flanking a German Tornado

Top right: Italian IDS Tornado

Centre right: German Navy Tornado

Bottom right: Tornado F2

the German assembly line on 27 July. Deliveries began on 1 July 1980 to equip the Tri-national Tornado Training Establishment at RAF Cottesmore, where the first training course began in January 1981. The RAF also plans to acquire 165 Tornado F Mk 2 air defence fighters; this version has the fuselage lengthened by 53.5in (1.36m) to carry more fuel and a larger nose radar, and to carry four Sky Flash missiles semi-recessed under the fuselage, in addition to two Sidewinders on the inboard wing pylons that carry drop tanks. The first of three prototype F Mk 2s flew on 27 October 1979, the second on 18 July 1980 and the third on 18 November 1980.

Republic F-105 Thunderchief

USA

Single-seat long-range tactical fighter-bomber, in service

Photo: F-105F
Silhouette: F-105G
Data: F-105D
Powered by: One 26,500lb (12,030kg) st Pratt & Whitney J75-P-19W afterburning turbojet
Span: 34ft 11.25in (10.65m)
Length: 67ft 0.25in (20.43m)
Empty weight: 27,500lb (12,475kg)
Gross weight: 52,838lb (23,967kg)
Max speed: Mach 2.1 (1,385mph; 2,230km/h) at 36,000ft (11,000m)
Max range: Over 2,000 miles (3,220km)
Armament: One General Electric 20mm Vulcan multi-barrel gun, plus more than 14,000lb (6,350kg) of stores under fuselage and wings

Development of the F-105 was started in 1951. Two prototypes, designated YF-105A, had J57-P-25 turbojets, and the first of these flew on 22 October 1955. A switch to the more powerful J75-P-3 or -5 engine changed the designation to F-105B on the next 75 aircraft, these being the first to feature the Thunderchief's unique swept-forward air intakes. Three trials aircraft were laid down in the reconnaissance rôle as RF-105Bs, but this version was not developed. Principal production version was the F-105D (600 built) with many improvements. A proposed two-seat version, the F-105E, was dropped, but 143 F-105Fs were ordered in 1962 for use as operational trainers. These had a 31-inch longer fuselage, second cockpit with dual controls, and taller fin; the first F-105F flew on 11 June 1963. The F-105D and F-105F played a major part in the air war in Vietnam. Continuous updating enabled them to carry the latest missiles and equipment, including advanced electronic countermeasures devices. About 30 F-105Ds were modified to have the T-Stick II bombing system, including electronics in a 'saddle-back' fairing above the fuselage; the first of these flew with the new equipment on 9 August 1969. F-105Gs were Fs converted for the suppression of surface-to-air missile sites in Vietnam, with an ECM pod mounted on each of the lower sides of the fuselage, and four Shrike or two Standard ARM anti-radar missiles, and were known as Wild Weasels. In 1980, the AF Reserve had one squadron of F-105Bs, one of F-105Ds and one mixed F-105D/F unit. Four Air National Guard squadrons also were flying Thunderchiefs, one with F-105Bs, two with F-105Ds and one with F-105G Wild Weasels.

Rockwell International OV-10 Bronco

USA

Observation and COIN aircraft, in service

Data, photo and silhouette: OV-10A
Powered by: Two 715eshp Garrett AiResearch
T76-G-416/417 turboprops
Span: 40ft 0in (12.19m)
Length: 41ft 7in (12.67m)
Empty weight: 6,969lb (3,161kg)
Gross weight: 14,466lb (6,563kg)
Max speed: 281mph (452km/h) clean at sea level
Combat radius: 228 miles (367km) with max
weapon load, no loiter
Armament: Four 0.30in machine guns in sponsons,
which also carry a maximum of 2,400lb external
ordnance; provision for one Sidewinder AAM under
each wing, and for 1,200lb load under fuselage. Max
weapon load 3,600lb (1,633kg)

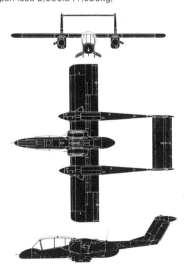

The North American NA300 won a design
competition for a light multi-purpose counter-
insurgency aircraft against entries from eight other
companies. Seven prototypes were ordered, under
the designation YOV-10A; and the first of these flew
on 16 July 1965. These early aircraft had 660shp
T76-GE-6/8 (handed) engines, span of 30ft (9.14m),
max weight of 12,364lb (5,608kg) and 'straight'
sponsons. The sixth YOV-10A was modified in 1967
to production configuration with a 10ft (3.1m)
increase in wing span, uprated engines, anhedral on
the sponsons and a number of smaller modifications.
The first production contracts were placed in October
1966 and deliveries began early in 1968. The USAF
acquired 157 OV-10As for forward air control and
secondary ground support duties; the US Marine
Corps received 114 similar aircraft, of which 18 were
loaned to the US Navy, for light armed
reconnaissance, helicopter escort and forward air
control duties in Vietnam. Production for the US
services ended in April 1969, but the Thai Air Force
ordered 32 OV-10Cs, while the Federal German
Government ordered 24 OV-10Bs for target towing
duties. One of the latter temporarily had a General
Electric J85 auxiliary turbojet mounted above the
fuselage to boost max speed to 393mph (632km/h),
and was redesignated OV-10B(Z). Further exports
comprised 16 OV-10Es to Venezuela, 16 OV-10Fs to
Indonesia and 24 OV-10Gs to South Korea. Morocco
received six ex-USAF OV-10As in 1980/81 and
further supplies of eight to Thailand and 16 to the
Philippines were arranged. Two YOV-10Ds
(converted OV-10As) were armed night observation
gunships for the US Marines (first flight 9 June
1970) and provided the basis for 18 slightly different
OV-10D conversions of OV-10As made in 1979/80.
They have night sensors in a lengthened nose and
1,040shp T76-G-420/421 engines but lack the
ventral gun turret of the YOV-10Ds.

Saab-35 Draken

Sweden

Single-seat fighter, reconnaissance aircraft and two-seat trainer, in service

Silhouette: J35F
Data and photo: Saab-35XD
Powered by: One 17,650lb (8,000kg) st Volvo Flygmotor RM6C (Avon 300-series) afterburning turbojet
Span: 30ft 10in (9.40m)
Length: 50ft 4in (15.35m)
Normal gross weight: 33.070lb (15,000kg)
Max speed: Mach 2 (1,320mph; 2,125km/h) at 36,000ft (11,000m)
Armament: Two 30mm cannon (optional). Racks under fuselage and wings for four Sidewinder air-to-air missiles, 9,000lb (4,080kg) of bombs, or rockets

Like the earlier Lansen, the Draken was designed to operate from auxiliary airstrips formed by sections of Sweden's main roads. The large area of its 'double delta' wing helps to give it short take-off and landing runs. The first of three prototypes flew on 25 October 1955, with an imported Avon. The first production J35A interceptor for the Swedish Air Force flew on 15 February 1958, with a 15,200lb (6,895kg) st Swedish-built R.M.6B (200-series Avon) and this version entered service in 1960. It was followed by the J35B (first flown on 29 November 1959) with a more advanced fire-control system for collision-course tactics. This version entered service in 1961, but most J35As and Bs were converted subsequently to J35D standard with 17,200lb (7,800kg) st RM6C engine, an improved autopilot and extra fuel. The prototype J35D flew on 27 December 1960, and this became operational in 1964. Some J35As were also converted into SK35C two-seat dual-control trainers, to supplement new production. The S35E is a reconnaissance version with cameras in its nose. Final production version for the Swedish Air Force was the J35F, basically similar to the D but with improved fire-control system and armament of one 30mm gun and two or four Falcon air-to-air missiles. More than 250 Lansens were still serving in Swedish Air Force all-weather fighter squadrons, plus two reconnaissance squadrons in 1980. First export customer for the Draken was Denmark, which took delivery of 51 Saab-35XDs, with greatly increased weapon load and range, including 20 F-35 fighter-bombers, 20 RF-35 reconnaissance/fighters and 11 TF-35 trainer/fighters. They were followed by six Saab-35BS Drakens (S=Suomi or Finland) supplied to Finland and 12 Saab-35Xs assembled by Valmet for the Finnish Air Force, to which were later added six ex-Swedish Air Force J35Fs and three two-seat S35Cs. Overload take-off weight of these export single-seaters, with nine 1,000lb bombs, is 35,275lb (16,000kg).

Saab-37 Viggen

Sweden

Single-seat multi-mission combat aircraft and two-seat trainer, in production and service

Photo and silhouette: JA37
Data: AJ37
Powered by: One 25,970lb (11,780kg) st Volvo Flygmotor RM8A (P&W JT8D-22) afterburning turbofan
Span: 34ft 9.25in (10.60m)
Length: 53ft 5.75in (16.30m)
Normal gross weight: approx 35,275lb (16,000kg)
Max speed: Mach 2 (1,320mph; 2,125km/h) at 36,000ft (11,000m)
Combat radius: 310-620 miles (500-1,000km)
Armament: Three attachments under fuselage and two under each wing, for RB04 or RB05 air-to-surface missiles, or alternative 30mm gun packs, bombs, rockets or mines

The Viggen is a multi-mission combat aircraft intended to replace the whole range of Lansens and J35 and S35E Drakens in service with the Swedish Air Force for attack, interception, and reconnaissance duties. Having pioneered the double-delta configuration with the Draken, Saab turned to another advanced aerodynamic shape for the Viggen, which uses a foreplane fitted with flaps, in combination with a main delta wing. This, together with a high thrust-to-weight ratio, gives it STOL capability and it is able to operate from roads and runways only 550yd (500m) long. The first of seven prototypes flew on 8 February 1967, and all were completed by 2 July 1970, when the SK37 tandem two-seat trainer version made its first flight. The initial production contracts, announced in 1967-68, were for a total of 175 of the AJ37 single-seat attack version, which has secondary interception capability, SK37 trainer, and SF/SH37 armed reconnaissance aircraft for overland and maritime operations respectively. The first production AJ37 flew on 23 February 1971, and deliveries to F7 Wing of the Swedish Air Force at Sätenäs began in June 1971. Two squadrons of this Wing and one squadron of F15 were equipped with AJ37s by early 1978. Following the first flight of an SF37 Viggen on 21 May 1973, deliveries to F21 Wing began in April 1977. The SH37 Viggen, first flown on 10 December 1973, already equipped one squadron of F13 and was being delivered to F17 in 1977. The prototype of the SK37 two-seat trainer flew on 2 July 1970 and production deliveries began in June 1972. Meanwhile, preliminary design work had begun in 1968 on the JA37 (*Jakt Viggen*) optimised for the intercept role. The first of four AJ37s converted to JA37 prototype flew on 4 June 1974; the first production JA37, of a total procurement of 149, flew on 4 November 1977 and deliveries to F13 at Norrkoping began in 1979.

Saab-105

Sweden

Two-seat basic trainer and light attack aircraft, in service

Silhouette: SK60C
Data and photo: Saab-105Ö
Powered by: Two 2,850lb (1,293kg) st General Electric J85-GE-17B turbojets
Span: 31ft 2in (9.50m)
Length: 35ft 5in (10.80m)
Empty weight: 6,173lb (2,800kg)
Max gross weight: 14,330lb (6,500kg)
Max speed: 603mph (970km/h) at sea level
Range: 1,820 miles (2,930km) at 43,000ft (13,100m) with external tanks
Armament: Six underwing attachments for up to 4,410lb (2,000kg) of Minigun or 30mm gun packs, rockets, rocket packs, bombs, Sidewinder missiles, or reconnaissance packs

Although it is operated mainly as a two-seater in its military roles, the Saab-105 is a multi-purpose light twin-jet aircraft capable of accommodating two more people on rear seats behind the crew. It was developed as a private venture, the first of two prototypes flying for the first time on 29 June 1963. Early in the following year, Saab received a Royal Swedish Air Board contract for 130 production models, each powered by two 1,640lb (743kg) st Turboméca Aubisque turbofans. Subsequently a further 20 were ordered. The first production model flew on 27 August 1965, and deliveries of the basic SK60A trainer to the Swedish Air Force began in the spring of 1966. Some were returned to Saab to be fitted with attachments for weapons and a gunsight, in which form they are designated SK60B; although still used mainly for training, they are now capable of quick conversion to attack configuration. In addition, a small number of the As that were modified to B standard were fitted with a permanent panoramic reconnaissance camera installation in the nose, whilst full attack capability is retained; the prototype of this version, the SK60C, flew on 18 January 1967. The Austrian Air Force acquired 40 Saab-105Ös (developed from the prototype Saab-105XT) with General Electric J85 turbojets, higher performance and much increased weapon load. The first of these flew on 17 February 1970 and deliveries began soon afterwards. The Saab-105G was a further development with increased armament, more advanced avionics and refined controls. It first flew on 26 May 1972, but did not go into production.

SEPECAT Jaguar

UK/France

Single-seat light tactical support aircraft, in production and service

Photo: Jaguar GR Mk 1, India
Data and silhouette: Jaguar GR Mk 1
Powered by: Two 8,400lb (3,811kg) st Rolls-Royce/Turboméca Adour 804 afterburning turbofans
Span: 28ft 6in (8.69m)
Length: 55ft 2.5in (16.83m)
Max gross weight: 34,000lb (15,500kg)
Max speed: Mach 1.6 (1,055mph; 1,698km/h) at 36,000ft (11,000m)
Max range: 2,190 miles (3,524km) with external tanks
Armament: Two 30mm Aden guns in lower fuselage. One attachment under fuselage and four under wings for up to 10,000lb (4,500kg) of stores (Martel missiles, 1,000lb bombs, napalm tanks, rocket pods, reconnaissance packs, etc)

Development of the Jaguar began in 1965, and the first of the two prototypes of the Jaguar E was first flown on 8 September 1968. It was followed by the first Jaguar A on 29 March 1969. The British single-seat prototype flew on 12 October 1969. The first production Jaguar E (of 40 built) flew on 2 November 1971, and deliveries of this version began in 1972, followed by 160 Jaguar A. The RAF took delivery of 165 Ss, designated Jaguar GR Mk 1 in service, and the first of these flew on 11 October 1972. The full production standard includes a laser rangefinder and marked target seeker in the nose and an electronic countermeasures pack near the tip of the fin. Two of the eight RAF squadrons operate Jaguars in a reconnaissance rôle, with an external camera/sensor pack. In addition, 37 Jaguar B (designated T Mk 2) two-seaters were delivered for operational conversion and continuation training. All British and French Jaguars were built with 7,305lb (3,313kg) st Adour 102 engines; RAF aircraft are being converted to have uprated Adour 104s. Jaguar Internationals have been delivered to Ecuador (12) and Oman (20 single-seat and four two-seat); these have the Adour 804 engines and provision for night sensors and dog-fight missiles on overwing pylons. On 6 October 1978 the Indian government signed an agreement to buy Jaguar Internationals with provision to assemble the aircraft under licence in India also. The first phase of Indian procurement comprised 16 ex-RAF GR Mk 1s and two T Mk 2s on loan; the first of these arrived in India in mid-1979 and all had been delivered by mid-1980. Delivery began in 1981 of 40 more which are being built in the UK and will be followed by a second, larger, batch, possibly to be assembled in India.

Shin Meiwa PS-1 and US-1   Japan

Four-turboprop STOL anti-submarine flying-boat, in production and service

Data, photo and silhouette: PS-1
Powered by: Four 3,060eshp Ishikawajima-Harima (General Electric) T64-IHI-10 turboprops
Span: 108ft 9in (33.15m)
Length: 109ft 9.25in (33.46m)
Empty weight: 58,000lb (26,300kg)
Gross weight: 94,800lb (43,000kg)
Max speed: 340mph (547km/h) at 5,000ft (1,525m)
Ferry range: 2,948 miles (4,744km) at 196mph (315km/h)
Accommodation: Crew of 10, comprising two pilots, a flight engineer, two sonar operators, navigator, MAD operator, radio and radar operators, and a tactical co-ordinator
Armament: Two underwing pods, between each pair of engine nacelles, each contain two homing torpedoes; six 5in rockets on attachments under wingtips; four 330lb anti-submarine bombs in weapon-bay

The big PS-1 flying-boat is a rarity at a time when most anti-submarine aircraft are land-based or carrier-borne. It has many novel features, including a built-in tricycle beaching gear which enables it to move on the ground under its own power. A 1,400shp General Electric T58-IHI-10 shaft-turbine is housed in the upper centre portion of the hull to provide compressed air for the 'blown' flaps and tail surfaces which help to give the PS-1 STOL capability. It will take off from a calm sea in 820ft (250m) and land in 590ft (180m). It has been designed to operate in winds of up to 25kts and waves 10ft (3m) high. The PS-1 is designed to alight and take off repeatedly, to dip its large sonar deep into the sea, while searching for submarines. Other operational equipment includes a searchlight, search radar in the nose, magnetic anomaly detector (MAD), sono-buoys and electronic countermeasures installation. The prototype, known as the PX-S, flew on 5 October 1967, and was followed by a second on 14 June 1968. They were delivered to a Maritime Self-Defence Force test squadron in 1968, and have been followed by 23 production aircraft, most of them operated by No 31 Squadron of the JMSDF. A US-1 amphibious search and rescue model has also been developed for use by No 71 SAR Squadron. The first of seven ordered so far made its first flight on 16 October 1974. Basically similar to the PS-1, the US-1 has a retractable tricycle undercarriage capable of use for conventional take-off and landing ashore, and a slightly less powerful (1,250shp) T58 engine for its STOL system. It is equipped normally to carry a crew of nine, and 12 survivors on stretchers. Alternatively, it could be equipped to carry 36 stretchers or 69 passengers.

Soko/CIAR Orao/IAR-93

Yugoslavia/Romania

Single-seat ground attack fighter, under development

Data, photo and silhouette: Prototypes
Powered by: Two 4,000lb (1,814kg) st Rolls-Royce Viper Mk 632-41 turbojets
Span: 24ft 9.75in (7.56m)
Length: 42ft 3.75in (12.90m)
Empty weight: 9,480lb (4,300lb)
Gross weight: 19,840lb (9,000kg)
Max speed: Mach 0.95 (627mph; 1,009km/h) at 36,000ft (11,000m)
Service ceiling: 45,925ft (14,000m)
Combat radius: 124-248 miles (200-400km) with 4,410lb (2,000kg) external stores, depending on altitude flown
Armament: Two 30mm cannon. One under-fuselage and four underwing attachments for 4,410lb (2,000kg) of external stores

Identified originally as the 'Jurom' (*Ju*goslavia-*Rom*ania), this Jaguar-like tactical fighter has been developed jointly by Yugoslavia and Romania in a programme intended to make these two nations less dependent on combat aircraft provided by the super-powers. It is known as the Orao (Eagle) in Yugoslavia, and as the IAR-93 in Romania. Design and manufacture are being shared by the industries of these countries, with the engines and much of the equipment coming from western Europe. The first prototype is believed to have flown in August 1974, followed by two more prototypes and nine pre-production aircraft. The second prototype is a tandem two-seater (the fuselage length remaining unchanged) representative of the planned operational conversion trainer. Non-afterburning Vipers have been fitted initially, but press reports have suggested that production Orao/IAR-93s may have Rolls-Royce-developed afterburners to give each turbojet a maximum output of 5,950lb (2,700kg) st. This would increase the gross weight to 22,700lb (10,300kg), permitting a 50% greater weapon load. Max speed at altitude would increase to about Mach 1.6, with Mach 1.0 attainable at low altitude. The Romanian and Yugoslav Air Forces are expected to obtain only 25 Orao/IAR-93s each, including a proportion of two-seaters, earlier plans for large-scale production having been abandoned because of the protracted development programme.

Soko J-1 and RJ-1 Jastreb

Yugoslavia

Single-seat light attack aircraft, in production and service

Data, photo and silhouette: J-1 Jastreb
Powered by: One 3,000lb (1,360kg) st Rolls-Royce Viper 531 turbojet
Span: 38ft 4in (11.68m) with wingtip tanks
Length: 35ft 8.5in (10.88m)
Empty weight: 6,217lb (2,820kg)
Gross weight: 11,245lb (5,100kg)
Max speed: 510mph (820km/h) at 20,000ft (6,100m)
Max range: 945 miles (1,520km)
Armament: Three 0.50in Colt-Browning machine guns in nose; eight underwing attachments for two bombs of up to 550lb each, and 57mm or 127mm rockets

The Jastreb is a light attack version of the Galeb two-seat basic trainer described on a later page, with modified wings, more powerful engine and heavier armament provisions. Its electrical system has been augmented to make the aircraft independent of ground supply for engine starting. Optional equipment includes assisted take-off rockets. Two prototypes were flying by early 1968, when the type was already in production for the Yugoslav Air Force and available for export. Four Jastrebs were supplied to Zambia in 1971.

New versions are the export J-1-E with updated equipment, first flown in 1975, of which several have already been ordered; and the tandem two-seat TJ-1 Jastreb Trainer, with full operational capability, of which deliveries to the Yugoslav Air Force and export customers began in January 1975.

There are specialised tactical reconnaissance versions of both the J-1 and J-1-E, designated RJ-1 and RJ-1-E respectively. The RJ-1 for the Yugoslav Air Force has one camera in the fuselage and two further cameras in the noses of the wingtip tanks. The RJ-1-E can be supplied with three Vinten 360/140A cameras in similar locations for daylight reconnaissance, or a single Vinten 1025/527 camera at the fuselage station for night operations, with flash bombs or high-explosive bombs on the underwing attachments.

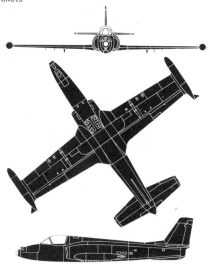

Sukhoi Su-7B
(NATO code-names 'Fitter-A' and 'Moujik')

USSR

Single-seat ground-attack fighter, in service

Photo: Su-7BM
Data and silhouette: Su-7B
Powered by: One 22,050lb (10,000kg) st Lyulka AL-7F-1 (TRD 31) afterburning turbojet
Span: 29ft 3.5in (8.93m)
Length: 57ft 0in (17.37m)
Max gross weight: 29,750lb (13,500kg)
Max speed: Mach 1.6 (1,055mph; 1,700km/h) at 36,000ft (11,000m); 530mph (850km/h) at sea level without afterburning
Max range: 900 miles (1,450km)
Armament: Two 30mm cannon in wing roots; attchments under wings for bombs (usually two 750kg and two 500kg) or rocket pods. External load reduced to 2,200lb (1,000kg) when two underbelly fuel tanks are carried

This sweptwing fighter was for many years standard equipment in Soviet ground attack squadrons, although its importance in the Frontal Aviation first line units was declining by 1980. Su-7s were also supplied to the Afghan, Algerian, Cuban, Czech, Peruvian, Polish, East German, Hungarian, North Korean, North Vietnamese, Egyptian, Iraqi, Romanian, Syrian and Indian air forces. The fuselage, power plant and tail unit appear to be almost identical with those of the delta-wing Su-11, with the same provision for carrying two external fuel tanks under the centre-fuselage. The Su-7 was one of four single-seat fighter aircraft seen for the first time, in prototype form, at the 1956 Tushino display, the others being the MiG-21, the Su-9 and a sweptwing counterpart of the MiG-21 which was allocated the NATO code-name 'Faceplate'. It seems probable that the Su-7 and 'Faceplate' were evaluated in competition to find a new fighter for close-support duties, and that the Sukhoi design was chosen, as 'Faceplate' did not enter service. When first seen, the Su-7 had its pitot boom mounted centrally above the air intake; but later versions have the boom offset to starboard. Very large area-increasing wing-flaps are fitted, extending from the root to more than mid-span. Wing sweep is approximately 60°, with fences at about mid-span and just inboard of the tip of each wing. Major variants are the Su-7B and the Su-7BM which can be identified by the bulged doors which enclose the low-pressure nosewheel tyre when the undercarriage is retracted. A tandem two-seat version, the Su-7U, is used for training and has the NATO code-name 'Moujik'.

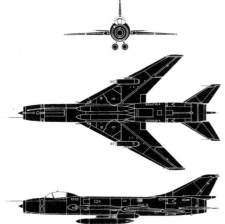

Sukhoi Su-9 and Su-11
(NATO code-names 'Fishpot' and 'Maiden')

USSR

Single-seat all-weather fighter, in service

Photo: Su-9
Data (estimated) and silhouette: Su-11
Powered by: One 22,050lb (10,000kg) st Lyulka
AL-7F-1 afterburning turbojet
Span: 27ft 8in (8.43m)
Length: 56ft 0in (17.00m)
Gross weight: 30,000lb (13,600kg)
Max speed: Mach 1.8 (1,190mph; 1,915km/h) at
36,000ft (11,000m)
Armament: Two 'Anab' infra-red and/or radar
homing air-to-air missiles under wings. No guns

In its prototype form, as seen in the 1956 Soviet
Aviation Day display in Moscow, this delta-wing
all-weather fighter had a small conical radome above
its air intake and was allocated the NATO code-name
'Fishpot-A'. On initial production aircraft
('Fishpot-B'), the radome forms a centre-body in the
circular air intake. The resulting fighter bears a
superficial resemblance to the MiG-21, but is
considerably heavier and has a much more powerful
(Lyulka AL-7F) engine, rated at 19,840lb (9,000kg)
st with afterburning. It is a generally cleaner design,
with a more sturdy-looking undercarriage and with
no cut-out at the roots of the tailplane trailing-edge.
   'Fishpot-B' probably has a better all-weather
capability than the MiG-21. It is normally seen with a
pair of external fuel tanks side-by-side under the
centre-fuselage. A developed version, first seen at
Tushino in 1961, has a new forward fuselage of
longer and less-tapered form, with enlarged
centrebody, and uprated engine; this is now known
to be designated Su-11 ('Fishpot-C'). Both versions
are in large-scale service, together with operational
trainers (NATO 'Maiden') with tandem cockpits like
those of the Su-7 trainer.
   Up to the present, the Su-9 and Su-11 have been
identified in service only with the Soviet Air Force. At
one time making up nearly 25% of its 2,600-strong
interceptor force. The process of re-equipping front-
line IAP-VO Strany (home defence) units with
MiG-23s had begun by 1979 and the Su-9/Su-11 is
now likely to be obsolescent.

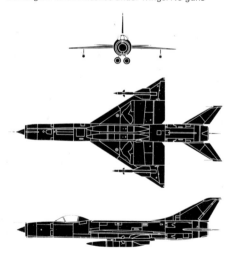

Sukhoi Su-15
(NATO code-name 'Flagon')

USSR

Single-seat interceptor, in production and service

Data (estimated), photo and silhouette:
'Flagon-F'
Powered by: Two 15,875lb (7,200kg) st Tumansky R-13F2-300 turbojets with afterburning
Span: 34ft 6in (10.53m)
Length: 68ft 0in (20.50m)
Gross weight: 35,275lb (16,000kg)
Max speed: Mach 2.5 (1,650mph; 2,655km/h) at 36,000ft (11,000m)
Combat radius: 450 miles (725km)
Armament: One radar-homing 'Anab' missile and one infra-red homing 'Anab' on underwing pylons. No guns

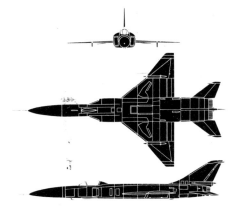

One of several types of Soviet aircraft making their first public appearance at the Domodedovo flying display in July 1967 was this high-performance interceptor, a product of the Sukhoi design bureau and now known to be designated Su-15. In addition to a single black-painted example, probably a prototype, in which Vladimir Ilyushin performed aerobatics, nine fighters of the same type appeared in formation, suggesting that the Su-15 had reached squadron service. Some carried an 'Anab' air-to-air missile beneath each wing. The initial production fighter (NATO code-name 'Flagon-A'), built in small numbers, had wings and tail surfaces almost identical to those of the Su-11. Also at Domodedovo in 1967 was a variant known as 'Flagon-B', which had STOL performance through the addition of lift-jets amidships. 'Flagon-B', which was a development aircraft rather than a service type, had extended wing-tips with reduced sweepback on the leading-edge of the outer panels. In other respects, it appeared to be a standard 'Flagon-A'.

The first major production version, 'Flagon-D', also has wings of compound sweep, produced by reducing the sweepback at the tips via a narrow unswept section. This increases the span to about 34ft 6in (10.53m). 'Flagon-C' is similar, but has two seats in tandem and is probably a trainer with combat capability. Speed and range improvements came with the installation of new and more powerful engines in 'Flagon-E'. Wings and conical radome were unchanged from the 'D', but the electronics were uprated, and this became the major production version from 1973. The later 'Flagon-F' differs in having an ogival radome. The 'Flagon' is the most important type of home defence fighter in service with IAP-VO Strany in 1981, with more than 1,000 believed to be in service.

Sukhoi Su-17, Su-20 and Su-22 (NATO code-name 'Fitter-C' and 'D')

USSR

Single-seat ground-attack fighter, in production and service

Photo: Su-20 'Fitter-F'
Silhouette: Su-17M 'Fitter-D'
Data (estimated): Su-17
Powered by: One 25,000lb (11,350kg) st Lyulka AL-21F-3 afterburning turbojet
Span: 45ft 11.25in (14.00m) spread; 34ft 9.5in (10.60m) swept
Length: 61ft 6.25in (18.75m)
Empty weight: 22,050lb (10,000kg)
Max gross weight: 41,887lb (19,000kg)
Max speed: Mach 2.17 (1,430mph; 2,300km/h) at 36,000ft (11,000m); Mach 1.05 at sea level
Combat radius: 224-391 miles (360-630km) with 4,410lb (2,000kg) of external stores
Armament: Two 30mm NR-30 cannon in wing roots. Max weapon load 11,023lb (5,000kg)

The prototype of this ground-attack fighter is believed to have been the first variable-geometry aircraft test-flown in the Soivet Union. When it appeared at the 1967 Aviation Day display at Domodedovo Airport it was regarded as a test-bed,

built to evaluate the merits of a swing-wing as economically as possible. It differed from the standard Su-7 only in having the outer 13ft (4.0m) of each wing pivoted, with one very large fence and two smaller ones near the tip of each inner, fixed panel. There was a full-span leading-edge slat on each outer panel. The NATO reporting name assigned to this prototype was 'Fitter-B'.

Photographs taken at Domodedovo suggested that this prototype had weapon attachments built into the bottom of its two large wing fences. The significance of these was made clear when one or two squadrons of similar aircraft were discovered to be in front-line service with the Soviet Air Force in 1972. Since then, several hundred have been delivered to Soviet tactical squadrons, all differing from the prototype in having a second nose-probe, a dorsal spine fairing between the cockpit canopy and fin, and a total of eight weapon attachments under the wings and fuselage. The basic Soviet Air Force Su-17 is powered by a Lyulka AL-21F-3 afterburning turbojet, and has more advanced equipment than the Su-20 now in service with most of Warpac forces and exported to Egypt, Algeria, Iraq, Libya and Syria. Both are known to NATO as 'Fitter-C'. A Soviet Air Force variant is 'Fitter-D', identified by a small, flat radome under its nose and laser marked target seeker in the bottom of its intake centre-body. During 1977, some of the Middle East-users of the Sukhoi fighter received examples of the Su-22 'Fitter-F', featuring an enlarged dorsal fin and enlarged diameter rear fuselage. A tandem two-seat operational training variant was identified as 'Fitter-E', and Peru has received four of the latter in addition to 48 'Fitter-Fs'. Latest versions of the basic type are the 'Fitter-H' and two-seat 'Fitter-G', featuring a deepened forward fuselage, taller fin and rudder and provision to carry two 'Atoll' IR homing AAMs.

Sukhoi Su-24 (NATO code-name 'Fencer')

USSR

Two-seat variable-geometry attack aircraft, in production and service

Data and silhouette: Provisional
Powered by: Two afterburning turbojets, each probably rated at about 25,000lb (11,340kg) st
Span: 56ft 3in (17.15m) spread, 31ft 3in (9.53m) swept
Length: 69ft 10in (21.29m)
Gross weight: About 85,000lb (38,500kg)
Max speed: Mach 2.5 (1,650mph; 2,655km/h) at 36,000ft (11.000m)
Combat radius: 200 miles (322km) at low altitude
Armament: One six-barrel Gatling-type 23mm cannon. Six underwing and underfuselage attachments for up to 18,000lb (8,165kg) of bombs, guided weapons, fuel tanks, etc

Nothing was known publicly about this Soviet counterpart of the F-111 and Tornado until 1974, when Admiral Thomas H. Moorer, then Chairman of the US Joint Chiefs of Staff, referred to it as 'the first modern Soviet fighter to be developed specifically as a fighter-bomber for the ground attack mission'. One year later, Su-24s were already based in western Russia, probably with an operational evaluation unit; but no good clear photographs of the type became available until the spring of 1981, one of the first being shown above. The silhouette is based on these first published photographs and show that the layout of the Su-24 is fairly conventional, with side-by-side seating for the crew of two, and a vertical tail unit of typical Sukhoi form. The air intake trunks probably derive from Su-15 technology, and the turbojets may well be similar to the Lyulka AL21F-3s of the Soviet Air Force's Su-17. Wing sweep is believed to be about 23 degrees spread, 70 degrees fully swept; an interesting feature is the first known Soviet use of pivoting weapon pylons under the variable-geometry outer panels. At least 250 Su-24s were operational in 1979, each able to carry about five times the weapon load five times as far as the aircraft they replaced. Such range would enable them to attack targets anywhere in England from bases in East Germany, although the Fencer had not been deployed on a large scale outside of the Soviet Union up to the end of 1980.

Transall C-160

France/Germany

Twin-turboprop medium-range transport, in production and service

Photo: C-160D
Powered by: Two 6,100shp Rolls-Royce Tyne RTy20 Mk 22 turboprops
Span: 131ft 3in (40.0m)
Length: 106ft 3.5in (32.40m)
Empty weight: 63,400lb (28,758kg)
Gross weight: 108,250lb (49,100kg)
Max speed: 333mph (536km/h) at 15,000ft (4,500m)
Range: 2,832 miles (4,558km) with 8ton payload
Accommodation: Crew of four, 93 troops, 61-81 paratroops, 62 litters or 35,270lb (16,000kg) freight
Armament: None

The Transall (Transporter Allianz) C-160 resulted from design collaboration between French and

German companies which, in January 1959, undertook the joint production of a medium transport to meet the requirements of the Armée de l'Air and Luftwaffe, with possible commercial applications also. The Rolls-Royce Tyne engines were built by a British/French/Belgian/German consortium, and equipment included a Smiths flight control system which was intended to be used as the basis of an automatic landing system. Operation from semi-prepared surfaces was one of the original requirements of the design, and there was provision (never utilised) for fitting two auxilary turbojets under the outer wings.

The first of three flying prototypes was assembled in France by Nord-Aviation (now part of Aérospatiale) and flew or 25 February 1963. The second, assembled in Germany by VFW (later VFW-Fokker), flew on 25 May 1963. The third, assembled in Germany by Hamburger Flugzeugbau (now part of Messerschmitt/Bölkow-Blohm), flew on 19 February 1964. Nord began flight testing the first of six C-160A pre-production aircraft, with a 20-inch longer fuselage, on 21 May 1965. The first production C-160s were completed in 1967. Subsequent deliveries totalled 52 C-160Fs for France, 108 similar C-160Ds to replace the Luftwaffe's Noratlas, and nine C-160Zs for the South African Air Force. 20 of the C-160Ds were transferred to the Turkish Air Force (as C-160T) and four C-160Fs were modified into C-160Ps for the French night mail service. Production ended in October 1972, but was restarted in 1977 to meet an Armée de l'Air requirement for 25 additional aircraft. Four of these were funded in 1978, with 10 to follow in FY 1979 and the rest in FY 1980. The new-batch aircraft, which will be assembled only in France, do not have the forward cargo loading door; their avionics are updated, provision is made for in-flight refuelling and other small changes have been made. The first flight of a new-production Transall was made on 9 April 1981.

Tupolev Tu-16
(NATO code-name 'Badger')

USSR

Twin-jet medium bomber, in service

Silhouette: 'Badger-G'
Photo: 'Badger-E'
Data: Estimated
Powered by: Two 20,950lb (9,500kg) st Mikulin AM-3M turbojets
Span: 108ft 0.5in (32.93m)
Length: 114ft 2in (34.80m)
Gross weight: 150,000lb (68,000kg)
Max speed: 587mph (945km/h) at 35,000ft (10,700m)
Range: 3,975 miles (6,400km) at 480mph (770km/h) with 3tons of bombs
Accommodation: Crew of six
Armament: 'Badger-A' has seven 23mm cannon, in pairs in dorsal, ventral and tail turrets and singly on starboard side of nose, plus nine tons of bombs in bomb-bay. 'Badger-G' is similar except that two rocket-powered 'Kelt' air-to-surface anti-shipping missiles are carried under wings. 'Badger-C' has a large nose radome, precluding fitment of the nose cannon, and carries a 'Kipper' air-to-surface missile under the fuselage.

First seen in a Moscow fly-past in 1954, the Tu-16 has been a standard Soviet medium-range reconnaissance-bomber ever since. It is the aircraft from which the Tu-104 airliner was evolved, by way of the Tu-16D. Some 2,000 appear to have been built, of which about 300 are still in service with the Soviet Long-Range Aviation force, supported by a few Tu-16 flight refuelling tankers, and more than 100 reconnaissance and ECM variants. The Naval Air Fleet has nearly 300 Tu-16 missile-carriers, 80 tankers and 70 reconnaissance/ECM models. Nine of the basic 'Badger-As' were supplied to the Iraqi Air Force, and more than 80 are operational with the Chinese Air Force, mostly built in China with the designation B-6. Indonesia received about 24 early 'Badgers', with provision to carry a 'Kennel' missile under each wing; these are no longer in use.

The Soviet Naval Air Fleet uses several versions of 'Badger' as long-range reconnaissance-bombers. Of these 'Badger-C' was first shown in the 1961 Aviation Day flypast over Moscow, and has a large radome built into its nose, plus provision for carrying a 'Kipper' anti-shipping missile. 'Badger-D' (with nose radome) has under-fuselage electronic blisters. 'Badger-E' has a glazed nose and windows in its bomb-bay doors for a battery of reconnaissance cameras; while 'Badger F' has electronic sensor pods on underwing pylons. 'Badger-G' carries two rocket-powered 'Kelt' missiles under its wings. Further variants for electronic warfare are 'Badger-H', which is primarily a chaff dispenser; 'Badger-J' which is a specialised ECM jamming aircraft and 'Badger-K' which is an electronic reconnaissance variant. Most examples are flown by Soviet naval crews, but some were supplied to Egypt and were used operationally against Israeli targets in the 1973 Yom Kippur war. All versions can refuel in flight from other 'Badgers', using a unique wingtip-to-wingtip hose technique.

Tupolev Tu-22M (NATO code-name 'Backfire')   USSR

Supersonic variable-geometry strategic bomber, in production and service

Photo and silhouette: 'Backfire-B'
Data: (estimated) 'Backfire-B'
Powered by: Two afterburning turbofans, probably related to the 44,090lb (20,000kg) st Kuznetsov NK-144s used in the Tu-144 supersonic airliner
Span: 113ft 0in (34.45m) spread, 86ft 0in (26.21m) swept
Length: 132ft 0in (40.23m)
Gross weight: 270,000lb (122,550kg)
Max speed: At least Mach 2.0 (1,320mph 2,124km/h) at high altitude. Mach 0.9 (680mph; 1,094km/h) at low altitude
Max combat radius: 3,570 miles (5,745m)
Armament: Single gun in radar-directed tail mounting. Nominal weapon load of 20,800lb (9,435kg), including 'Kitchen' or 'Kingfish' missile and the complete range of Soviet nuclear and conventional free-fall weapons

Failure of the Tu-105 to fulfil its planned role as a supersonic strategic bomber, through inadequate range, required the Tupolev design bureau to try again, and the existence of a Soviet variable-geometry (swing-wing) medium bomber was acknowledged in the West by 1969. Apprehension was allayed a little when reports indicated that the original version of the bomber (known to NATO as Backfire-A) also seemed unlikely to achieve its intended range. However, this was soon remedied by redesign, including an extension of the wing span and deletion of the large main landing gear pods on the inner wings. It was soon apparent that, even without flight refuelling or staging from bases in the Arctic, the redesigned 'Backfire-B' could attack virtually anywhere in the continental USA on a one-way mission, with recovery in a third country such as Cuba. Using Arctic staging and refuelling, it could achieve similar coverage and return to its base in the USSR. The nuclear-warhead 'Kingfish' missile developed for 'Backfire' and carried semi-recessed in the fuselage is equally formidable, with a range of 375 miles (600km) at high supersonic speed.

Up to twelve pre-production 'Backfires' appear to have followed the prototypes. Production of 'Backfire-A' was then limited to sufficient aircraft for a single Soviet Air Force squadron. By early 1978, more than 100 'Backfire-Bs' were operational with the Air Force and Naval Air Fleet, with production thought to be continuing at the rate of 36 per year towards an eventual force of at least 250, and perhaps as many as 400 aircraft. The 'Backfire' was at first thought to be the Tu-26, but Soviet sources attribute to it the designation Tu-22M.

Tupolev Tu-28P (NATO code-name 'Fiddler') USSR

Two-seat all-weather fighter, in service

Data: Estimated
Powered by: Two unidentified turbojets with afterburners; rating about 27,000lb (12,250kg) st each
Span: 65ft 0in (20.00m)
Length: 85ft 0in (26.00m)
Gross weight: About 100,000lb (45,000kg)
Max speed: Mach 1.75 (1,150mph; 1,850km/h) at 36,000ft (11,000m)
Range: 3,100 miles (4,990km)
Armament: Four large infra-red and/or radar-homing air-to-air missiles (NATO code-name 'Ash') under wings

This very large long-range interceptor was first seen at the 1961 Tushino air display. Its evolution can be traced back to the Tu-16 ('Badger') through the Tu-98 ('Backfin') prototypes which were produced in 1955 to provide a long-range all-weather interceptor capable of defending the USSR against British and American strategic bombers. The examples of 'Fiddler' seen in 1961 each carried two 'Ash' missiles, but three Tu-28Ps displayed in 1967 each carried four of these missiles and dispensed with the large ventral fairing and ventral fins of the earlier versions.

According to the US Secretary of Defense in 1974, Tu-28Ps, MiG-25s, Su-15s and Yak-28Ps made up about 50% of the Soviet Union's 2,500-strong interceptor fighter force at that time. However, there is reason to believe that the number of Tu-28Ps in first-line service has never exceeded 150. Unconfirmed reports have suggested that these may have been replaced by an interceptor conversion of the Tu-105. The design bureau designation for the 'Fiddler' is Tu-128; the Tu-28P Service designation is not confirmed.

Tupolev Tu-95 and Tu-142 (NATO code-name 'Bear')

USSR

Four-turboprop long-range bomber, in service.

Data: 'Bear-F' estimated
Photo and silhouette: 'Bear-D'
Powered by: Four 14,795shp Kuznetsov NK-12MV turboprops
Span: 167ft 8in (51.10m)
Length: 162ft 5in (49.50m)
Gross weight: 414,470lb (188,00kg)
Max speed: 500mph (805km/h) at 41,000ft (12,500m)
Range: 7,800 miles (12,550km) with 11ton of bombs
Armament: Six 23mm cannon, in pairs in dorsal, ventral and tail turrets. 'Bear-A' carries up to 25,000lb (11,340kg) of bombs in internal bay. 'Bear-B/C' have nose radome and carry 'Kangaroo' air-to-surface missile under fuselage. Some 'Bears' also carry 'Kitchen' missile.

The Tu-95 (NATO 'Bear-A') was first seen in the 1955 Aviation Day display, when seven flew over Moscow escorted by MiG-17 fighters. Four NK-12MV turboprops made it the fastest propeller-driven aircraft in service, with a cruising speed matching that of the twin-jet Tu-16 and a greater range and bomb carrying capacity than the Myasishchev M-4. By 1961, a modernisation programme was under way, based on the employment of a long-range jet-powered air-to-surface missile (code-name 'Kangaroo'). The updated aircraft (redesignated 'Bear-B' by NATO) took part in the Tushino air display that year, and about 100 continue in service with the Soviet strategic bomber force. Others, in Naval service, have been seen frequently, minus missile, on long-range reconnaissance flights to photograph NATO fleet movements at sea, and on electronic intelligence missions; these are believed to have the design bureau designation Tu-142. 'Bear-B' has a wide nose radome, instead of glazing, and a flight refuelling probe. Another maritime reconnaissance version is 'Bear-C' with streamlined blister fairings on both sides of its rear fuselage. 'Bear-D', first seen in 1967, has an under-nose radome like that of the Canadair Argus and a huge under-belly radome; it is able to seek and pinpoint targets for anti-shipping missiles launched from other aircraft or ships. 'Bear-E' is generally similar to the A but carries reconnaissance cameras on its bomb-bay. 'Bear-F' has enlarged fairings at the rear of its undercarriage pods, longer front fuselage, under-belly radar like that of 'Bear-D' but further forward, a second stores bay in the rear fuselage, and only two (tail) guns. 'Bear-G', first seen in 1979, has a lengthened front fuselage.

Tupolev Tu-105 (NATO code-name 'Blinder')   USSR

Twin-jet supersonic bomber, in service

Photo and silhouette: 'Blinder-B'
Powered by: Two unidentified turbojets with
afterburners, rated at about 27,000lb (12,250kg) st
each
Span: 90ft 11.5in (27.70m)
Length: 132ft 11.5in (40.53m)
Gross weight: 185,000lb (83,900kg)
Max speed: Mach 1.4 (920mph; 1,480km/h) at
40,000ft (12,000m)
Max range: 1,400 miles (2,250km)
Accommodation: Crew of three
Armament: 'Blinder-B' carries 'Kitchen' missile
semi-recessed in fuselage undersurface, radar-
controlled tail gun

This rear-engined bomber was first shown at the
1961 Tushino air display, prior to which time it was
unknown to the West. Ten examples flew overhead
on that occasion; of these, nine appeared to be
reconnaissance-bombers, with a fairly small internal
weapon-bay and a pointed nose radome. The tenth
carried a 'Kitchen' (NATO code-name) air-to-surface
missile under its belly and was fitted with a
considerably larger radome. In both cases there were
large windows in the bottom of the fuselage,
immediately aft of the radome, for visual bomb-
aiming or cameras. The designation Tu-22
subsequently became widely used for this aircraft,
but remains unconfirmed. The design bureau
designation (distinct from the Service designation) is
Tu-105.
   At the 1967 air display over Domodedovo, a
total of 22 Tu-105s appeared, most of them carrying
'Kitchen' missiles. All had flight refuelling probes and
the wider radome of the single example seen
previously. This version is now identified as
'Blinder-B', while the version carrying internally-
housed free-fall weapons is 'Blinder-A'. A total of
about 140 of the two models remain operational
with the Soviet Air Force, and 12 have been supplied
to Libya. A third version, 'Blinder-C' can be identified
by the six windows for reconnaissance cameras in its
bomb-bay doors. There is also a trainer version
('Blinder-D') with an extra pilot's cockpit above and
to the rear of the standard position. Of the 250
Tu-22s thought to have been built, about 65 were
transferred to the Naval Air Force, which continues
to use about 50 'Blinder-Cs' as shore-based attack
bombers and reconnaissance aircraft; an ECM
version has also been reported.

Tupolev Tu-126 (NATO code-name 'Moss') USSR

Airborne early warning and fighter control aircraft, in service

Powered by: Four 14,795shp Kuznetsov NK-12MV turboprops
Span: 168ft (41.20m)
Length: 181ft 1in (55.20m)
Armament: None

This AWACS (airborne warning and control system) aircraft caused quite a stir when it was first seen in a Soviet documentary film in 1968, because the USAF was at that time only beginning to consider development of a similar machine based on the Boeing 707 transport (now in service as the E-3 Sentry). 'Moss' is based on the Tu-114 transport, which was itself evolved from the Tu-95 bomber, and has a similar power plant of four Kuznetsov NK-12MV turboprop engines, driving contra-rotating propellers. Changes centre mainly on the fuselage, which has only a few windows in the electronics-packed cabin and a great number of added excrescences, including a flight refuelling nose-probe, ventral tail-fin and many external antennae and fairings. The 36ft (11m) diameter rotating 'saucer' radome above the fuselage is intended to detect incoming attack aircraft over long ranges, so that 'Moss' can direct interceptor fighters towards them. It might also assist Soviet attack aircraft, by helping them to elude fighters sent up to intercept them, although it is said to operate effectively only over water, where there is no ground 'clutter' to affect its radar picture.

Aircraft of this type have been encountered frequently during NATO exercises. The Tu-126's specification should be similar to that of the Tu-114, which has a gross weight of 376,990lb (171,000kg), maximum speed of 540mph (870km/h) and maximum range of 5,560 miles (8,950km). It is believed that no more than 20 examples of the Tu-126 were produced. They probably will be replaced by an AWACS version of the Il-76 'Candid'.

Vought A-7 Corsair II

USA

Single-seat light attack aircraft, in production and service

Photo: A-7E
Data and silhouette: A-7D
Powered by: One 14,250lb (6,465kg) st Allison TF41-A-1 (Rolls-Royce Spey) turbofan
Span: 38ft 9in (11.80m)
Length: 46ft 1.5in (14.06m)
Empty weight: 19,781lb (8,972kg)
Gross weight: 42,000lb (19,050kg)
Max speed: 698mph (1,123km/h) at sea level
Max ferry range: 2,871 miles (4,621km)
Armament: One M-61 20mm multi-barrel cannon in fuselage. Two fuselage and six wing strong-points for external load of more than 15,000lb (6,805kg) of missiles, bombs, rockets, gun packs or fuel tanks

Winner of a 1963 design contest for a light-weight attack aircraft for the US Navy, the A-7A Corsair II was derived from the F-8 Crusader fighter. An initial

contract for three prototypes was placed in March 1964 and the first of these aircraft flew on 27 September 1965. Deliveries to a Corsair II training unit began in October 1966 and the first operational unit, VA-147, was commissioned in February 1967: it was deployed to the Vietnam theatre in December 1967. LTV Aerospace built 199 A-7As with TF30-P-6 engines; in 1980, the US government agreed to sell 20 of these to the Portuguese Air Force, refurbished as A-7Ps. The first A-7B (196 built) flew on 6 February 1968, with a 12,200lb (5,534kg) st TF30-P-8 engine. In October 1966 the USAF ordered the A-7D, with more advanced avionics and an Allison TF41 (Rolls-Royce Spey) engine. The first Spey-powered A-7D flew on 26 September 1968, following earlier trials with two A-7D airframes powered by TF30 engines. Deliveries began in December 1968, and 459 were built. The US Navy's A-7E also has more advanced avionics and features of the A-7D. The first 67 had TF30-P-8 engines (first flown 25 November 1968) and were retrospectively designated A-7C to avoid confusion with subsequent A-7Es (596 produced) which have a 15,000lb (6,805kg) st TF41-A-2. The YA-7E (originally YA-7H, first flown 29 August 1972) was a private-venture tandem two-seat training/combat conversion of an A-7E, with an overall length of 48ft 2in (14,68m). The US Navy ordered 65 similar trainers as TA-7Cs, converted from A-7Bs and A-7Cs, and the first of these flew on 17 December 1976. Similar TA-7Ds were ordered in 1978 for ANG use the designation was subsequently changed to A-7K to indicate that full combat capability was retained and the first example was completed late in 1980, being a converted A-7D with TF41-A-1 engine. Thirty A-7Ks were on order by April 1981. Sixty A-7Hs for Greece are similar to A-7Es; the first flew on 6 May 1975 and deliveries were completed by mid-1977. One A-7H was converted to TA-7H two-seat configuration in 1979, and five new-production TA-7Hs followed in 1980.

Vought F-8 Crusader

USA

Single-seat carrier-based day fighter, in service

Photo: F-8H Philippines
Data and silhouette: F-8E
Powered by: One 18,000lb (8,165kg) st Pratt & Whitney J57-P-20 turbojet
Span: 35ft 8in (10.87m)
Length: 54ft 6in (16.61m)
Max gross weight: 34,000lb (15,420kg)
Max speed: Nearly Mach 2
Armament: Four 20mm cannon. Four Sidewinder missiles on fuselage; wing racks for 2,000lb bombs or two Bullpup A or B missiles or 24 Zuni air-to-ground rockets

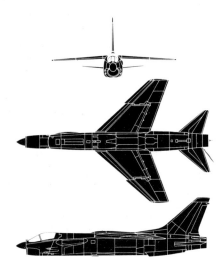

The Crusader was winner of a 1953 design competition for a deck-landing supersonic fighter. An unusual feature of the design was the high wing position, adopted to permit the wing incidence to be increased for low approach speeds without high angles of incidence on the fuselage. The original designation for the Crusader series was F8U, changed to F-8 in 1962. First flight of the prototype was on 25 March 1955 and deliveries of the F-8A (with 16,000lb; 7,257kg st J57-P-12) for VF-32 Squadron began in March 1957. Later As had a J57-P-4A of 16,200lb (7,327kg) st. The F-8B was similar with J57-P-4A and improved radar; production of these first two models totalled 318 and 130 respectively, plus 144 camera-equipped RF-8As. Distinguished by two ventral fins, the F-8C introduced the 16,900lb (7,665kg) st J57-P-16 and first flew on 20 August 1958. Production totalled 187 before the F-8D appeared. First flown on 16 February 1960, this introduced the P-20 engine and limited all-weather capability; 152 were built. With higher-performance radar and a three-inch longer nose radome, the F-8E prototype first flew on 30 June 1961 and this version went into service in February 1962. Production ended in mid-1964 when 286 F-8Es had been built. The French Navy purchased 42 F-8E(FN)s with provision for Matra 530 missiles; the first of these flew on 26 June 1964, and they still equip two Flottilles. In post-production modification and modernisation programmes, 73 RF-8As became RF-8Gs, and 89 F-8Ds and 136 F-8Es were updated to F-8H and F-8J respectively, with attack capability and other improvements. Subsequently, 87 F-8Cs were modified to F-8K and 61 F-8Bs to F-8L. Surviving F-8As are now designated TF-8A. By 1977, the F-8s were out of active USN service, but several squadrons of RF-8Gs were still operational, and the USN Reserves flew two squadrons of F-8Js and two of RF-8Gs. The Philippine Air Force acquired 35 ex-USN F-8H Crusaders, delivered in 1978.

Yakovlev Yak-28, Yak-28P and Yak-28U (NATO code-names 'Brewer', 'Firebar' and 'Maestro')

USSR

Two-seat multi-purpose tactical aircraft, all weather fighter and trainer, in service

Data (estimated), photo and silhouette: Yak-28P
Powered by: Two 13,120lb (5,950kg) st Tumansky R-11 turbojets, with afterburning on current aircraft
Span: 42ft 6in (12.95m)
Length: 71ft 0.5in (21.65m)
Gross weight: 35,000lb (15,875kg)
Max speed: Mach 1.1 (733mph; 1,180km/h) at 36,000ft (11,000m)
Combat radius: 575 miles (925km)
Armament: Two 'Anab' air-to-air missiles under wings, with alternative infra-red or semi-active radar homing heads

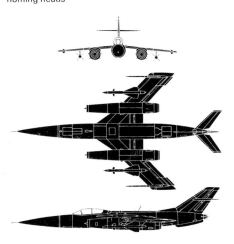

These successors to the long-retired Yak-25/27 were first seen at the 1961 Tushino display and can be identified by their shoulder-mounted wing, compared with the mid-wing of the Yak-25/27 series. They have extended wingtips and pointed balancer wheel fairings, as on the Yak-26 ('Mangrove') but the entire wing leading-edge inboard of the nacelle on each side is extended forward. Another major change is that the undercarriage of the Yak-28 series has two twin-wheeled units in tandem, with the rear unit much farther aft than on the earlier designs. The engine nacelles have intake centre-bodies.

The Yak-28P ('Firebar') is a tandem two-seat all-weather fighter with pointed radome and underwing armament of two 'Anab' air-to-air guided missiles. A new and longer radome has been fitted retrospectively to some aircraft and a substantial number remain in service for home defence duties in 1980.

The basic Yak-28 ('Brewer-A to C') was a multi-purpose tactical aircraft, with glazed nose, and could be regarded as a 'third generation' counterpart of 'Mangrove'. It had one or two 30mm cannon submerged in the sides of the fuselage, an internal weapon-bay and, usually, an underfuselage radar fairing. Few remain in service in the offensive role. 'Brewer-D' has cameras in the weapon-bay. 'Brewer-E' has an ECM pack protruding from its weapon-bay and a rocket pod under each outer wing. A further variant, the Yak-28U ('Maestro'), is a dual-control training version of 'Firebar', with an additional blister canopy forward of, and lower than, the rear canopy, and a much larger nose-probe.

Yakovlev Yak-36 (NATO code-name 'Forger')   USSR

Single-seat VTOL carrier-based combat aircraft in production and service

Data, photo and silhouette: 'Forger-A'
Powered by: One propulsion turbojet rated at about 17,000lb (7,170kg) st. Two lift-jets, each rated at about 5,600lb (2,540kg) st
Span: 23ft 0in (7.00m)
Length: 49ft 3in (15.00m)
Gross weight: 22,050lb (10,000kg)
Max speed: Mach 1.3 at 36,000ft (11,000m)
Radius of action: About 340 miles (550km) clean
Armament: Four underwing pylons for about 2,000lb (907kg) of gun pods and rocket packs

Alexander Yakovlev's first thoughts on V/STOL combat aircraft design were revealed at the 1967 Soviet Aviation Day display at Domodedovo Airport, Moscow. A pair of rather ungainly 'fighters' were sent to the airport, one of which took part in the flying programme; NATO allocated the code-name 'Freehand' to the type, but nobody expected the aircraft to enter squadron service, even when one of the small batch of four or five development models was used for experimental operations from a platform installed on the helicopter cruiser *Moskva*.

Reports of a more refined Yakovlev design were confirmed when the first of the Soviet Navy's new 40,000ton carrier/cruisers, the *Kiev*, entered the Mediterranean in July 1976, for a working-up cruise that took her on through the North Atlantic to Murmansk. En route, considerable flying was done by her complement of about a dozen Ka-25 ASW helicopters and a similar number of completely new VTOL fixed-wing aircraft which were designated Yak-36. Most were single-seaters (NATO 'Forger-A'); but they were accompanied by a much-lengthened tandem two-seat training version, which received the NATO code-name of 'Forger-B'. Take-off was seen to be made with the two vectored-thrust nozzles of the propulsion turbojet rotated about 10 degrees forward of vertical, and with the two lift-jets (inclined about 10 degrees rearward; immediately aft of the cockpit) switched on. Handling was precise; but short take-off (STO) techniques, as used by the Harrier to achieve better weapon loads, could not be made by an aircraft with the Yak-36 engine arrangement. The aircraft on *Kiev* were assumed to be from a development squadron; similar, or possibly the same, Yak-36s were subsequently seen aboard the *Minsk*, with different fuselage numbers.

120

Aeritalia/Aermacchi AMX   Italy

In association with Aermacchi, Aeritalia began project design work in 1977 on a new single-engined, single-seat subsonic close air support/strike aircraft to meet Italian Air Force requirements. At one period, attempts were made to combine this requirement with that of the Swedish Air Force, bringing Saab into design partnership, but this plan did not come to fruition. Instead, during 1980, negotiations were resumed between Italy and Brazil with a view to EMBRAER becoming a partner in AMX development (as had been proposed at the outset of the project) with ultimate production of about 100 in Brazil to provide a replacement for the EMB-312 Xavante (Aermacchi MB 326). The Italian Air Force requirement is for about 200. The AMX, as projected in 1980, was intended to be powered by an 11,030lb (5,000kg) st Rolls-Royce Spey 807 turbofan but few details other than the external appearance (as shown here) had been released. The development programme provides for construction of six prototypes, with first flight in 1983 and entry into service in 1986. **Data:** Span 29ft 1.75in (8.88m). Length 44ft 1in (13.44m).

Aeritalia/Aermacchi AM3C   Italy

The three-seat AM3 was developed as a potential replacement for the L-19s and other observation aircraft in service with the Italian Army. It was a joint product of the Aermacchi and Aeritalia companies and utilised the basic wing of the Aermacchi-Lockheed AL60. The prototype flew for the first time on 12 May 1967, powered by a 340hp Continental GTSIO-520-C engine, and was followed by a second on 22 August 1968; both were subsequently re-engined with the Piaggio-Lycoming GSO-480-B1B6. A hard-point under each wing, immediately outboard of the bracing strut pick-up point, enables the AM3 to be used for light tactical support duties, carrying a wide variety of armament, including two AS11 or AS12 wire-guided missiles, two 250lb bombs, 12 2.75in rockets, two Minigun pods and 3,000 rounds of ammunition or two pods each containing a pair of 7.62mm machine guns and 2,000 rounds. The principal customer was the South African Air Force, which acquired 40 AM3Cs and named them Bosboks; delivery was completed in December 1974. The only other customer for the type was the Rwanda Air Force, which bought three, but these were later returned to the manufacturer. **Data:** Span 41ft 5.5in (12.64m). Length 29ft 5.5in (8.98m). Gross weight 3,860lb (1,750kg). Max speed 173mph (278km/h). Range 615 miles (990km).

Aermacchi/Lockheed AL60C5 (Trojan)　　Italy

This all-metal utility aircraft was designed and built in prototype form (first flight 15 September 1959) by Lockheed-Georgia. Production was then entrusted to two Lockheed associates — Lockheed-Azcarate SA in Mexico and Aermacchi in Italy. The version built in Mexico is no longer in service. The air force of the Central African Empire has 10 AL60C5/F5 Conestogas, built by Aermacchi, with tailwheel undercarriage and 400hp Lycoming IO-720-A1A engine. A similar variant is used by the Mauritanian Islamic Air Force (1) and by the Zimbabwe Air Force as the Trojan (10). **Data** (AL60C5): Span 39ft 4in (11.99m). Length 28ft 10.5in (8.80m). Gross weight 4,500lb (2,041kg). Max speed 156mph (251km/h). Range 645 miles (1,037km).

Aero L-29 Delfin　　Czechoslovakia
(NATO code-name 'Maya')

The prototype of this tandem two-seat basic trainer flew for the first time on 5 April 1959, with a Bristol Siddeley Viper turbojet, but production machines have a locally designed M-701 VC-150 or S-50 engine of 1,960lb (890kg) st. The L-29 was designed to replace piston-engined trainers in service with the Czech Air Force and, after evaluation in competition with jet trainers built in other countries, was also chosen as the standard basic trainer of the Soviet Air Force. Other nations which have received L-29s include Bulgaria, East Germany, Egypt, Guinea, Hungary, Nigeria, Romania, Syria and Uganda, and more than 3,500 had been delivered by the time production ended in 1974. Two underwing attachments can be used to carry external fuel tanks, 100kg bombs, 7.62mm machine gun pods or up to eight rockets. The L-29A Akrobat single-seater for specialised aerobatics did not enter series production. **Data** (L-29): Span 33ft 9in (10.29m). Length 35ft 5.5in (10.81m). Gross weight 7,804lb (3,540kg). Max speed 407mph (655km/h). Range 555 miles (894km). **Photo:** L-29 of Hungarian Air Force.

Aero L-39 Albatros   Czechoslovakia

Powered by a 3,192lb (1,722kg) st Ivchenko AI-25-TL engine built in Czechoslovakia as the Walter Titan, the L-39 is a subsonic trainer with capability for development in the light strike role, carrying bombs, rocket-pods or air-to-air missiles on up to four underwing pylons. The first flight was made on 4 November 1968 and four more prototypes had joined the flight test programme by mid-1970. An initial production batch of 10 was put in hand in 1971 and full production deliveries began in 1974, initially to the Czech and Soviet Air Forces. The L-39C was chosen as the standard advanced flying and armaments trainer for the principal Warsaw Pact nations except Poland, which uses the home-produced TS-11 Iskra in this role. Exports have also been made to Iraq, Libya and Afghanistan, these being of the L-39ZO version with an optional gun pod on the fuselage centreline and four wing hardpoints. The similarly-armed L-39Z is a single-seat light strike version. **Data:** Span 31ft 0.5in (9.46m). Length 40ft 5in (12.32m). Gross weight 10,141lb (4,600kg). Max speed 435mph (700km/h) at sea level. Range 565 miles (910km) without tip tanks. **Photo:** L-39, Iraqi Air Force.

Aerospace Airtrainer CT4   New Zealand

This primary trainer was designed more than 25 years ago in its basic form, and won a design competition for two-seat light aircraft organised by the Royal Aero Club of Great Britain. Its designer was an Australian, Henry Millicer, and it eventually went into production as the Airtourer, first by Victa Ltd in Australia and then by NZAI in New Zealand. Four Airtourer T6/24s were delivered to the RNZAF in 1970. The Airtrainer CT4, first flown on 23 February 1972, was derived from the Airtourer by way of the four-seat Aircruiser. It is aerodynamically similar, but with completely new structure, and is powered by a 210hp Continental IO-360-D engine. Provision is made for bombs, or rocket pods or gun pods, beneath the wings. Deliveries totalled 19 for the RNZAF (CT4B version), 24 for the Royal Thai Air Force and 37 for the RAAF. **Data:** Span 26ft (7.92m). Length 23ft 2in (7.06m). Gross weight 2,350lb (1,066kg). Max speed 188mph (303km/h). Endurance about 5hr. **Photo:** CT4, RAAF.

Aérospatiale Caravelle   France

The Caravelle, one of the earliest of commercial jet transports, has found its way into limited military service in common with most of its contemporaries. Principal user in 1980 was the Armée de l'Air, which had one Caravelle III for VIP use attached to the *Groupe des Liaisons Aeriennes Ministerielles* (GLAM) at Villacoublay and three Caravelle 11Rs (ex-Air Zaire and Iberia) to equip the Escadron de transport d'outre-mer 82 (Etom 82) 'Maine', providing transport support in Tahiti. Other Caravelles are used as VIP or Presidential transports in some of the ex-French African territories. The Caravelle III is powered by two Rolls-Royce Avon 533R turbojets. **Data:** Span 112ft 6in (34.30m). Length 105ft 0in

(32.01m). Gross weight 101,413lb (46,000kg). Max cruising speed 500mph (805km/h). Range with max payload 1,430 miles (2,300km).

Aérospatiale N262/Frégate   France

The original N262 was developed by Nord-Aviation as a 26/29-seat transport powered by two Turboméca Bastan turboprops. Layout is conventional, with a pressurised cabin and fairings to house the main undercarriage when it is retracted. Many N262s were sold for commercial operation, and in June 1967 the French Navy ordered 15 of the Srs A version, with 1,065eshp Bastan VIC engines, for use as aircrew trainers and light transports. It subsequently acquired six more, including five previously operated by the French Air Force. The latter had six Srs A transports and 24 Frégates, with 1,145eshp Bastan VIIs, for training and liaison duties, taking

delivery of the first of these in November 1968. Another Frégate was sold to the Congo Air Force. **Data** (Frégate): Span 74ft 1.75in (22.60m). Length 63ft 3in (19.28m). Gross weight 23,810lb (10,800kg). Max speed 260mph (418km/h). Range 1,135 miles (1,825km) at 247mph (397km/h). **Photo:** N262 Srs A.

Aérospatiale SE313B   Alouette II Artouste,   France
SA315 Lama and SA318C Alouette II Astazou

The five-seat SE313B, with 360hp Turboméca Artouste IIC turboshaft, first flew on 12 March 1955. The total of 1,305 built included about 363 for the French Services and others for military and civilian customers in 33 different counties, including 267 for the West German Services and 17 for the British Army (as Alouette AH Mk 2). Also included in the total were some SA318C Alouette IIs with 360hp (derated) Turboméca Astazou IIA turboshafts, giving higher performance. The SA315B Lama combines the airframe of the Alouette II with a 550shp (derated) Artouste IIIB and dynamic components of the Alouette III. Production totalled 302 by early 1980; among the military users are the air forces of Argentina, Chile, Bolivia and Ecuador. The Indian Air Force acquired 40, followed by 100 manufactured in India by HAL with the local name of Cheetah. The first HAL-built SA315 was delivered in November 1972. The SA315B is also assembled by Helibras in Brazil with the local name Gaviao. **Data** (SA318C): Rotor diameter 33ft 5.5in (10.20m). Length 31ft 11.75in (9.75m). Gross weight 3,630lb (1,650kg). Max speed 127mph (205km/h). Range 447 miles (720km). **Photo:** SA315 Cheetah.

Aérospatiale SA316/319 Alouette III   France

The Alouette III, a larger and more powerful development of the Alouette II, is available for military use as a tactical troop transport or assault helicopter, and can carry a variety of armament. The basic version, with 570shp Artouste IIIB engine, first flew on 28 February 1959, and serves as the SA316A and SA316B, the latter having a strengthened transmission and increased weights. By the beginning of 1978 production totalled 1,362, including 218 for French military and civil operators, and exports to 70 countries. Sixty were built in Switzerland and 130 are in production in Romania. In addition, some 240 Alouette IIIs have been built in India by HAL with the name Chetak; some serve with the Indian Navy carrying Mk 44 torpedoes and a few have been presented by India to the Royal Nepal Army. The SA319 variant has a 600shp Astazou XIV engine, gross weight of 4,960lb (2,250kg), max speed of 137mph (220km/h), and max range of 375 miles (600km). **Data** (SA316): Rotor diameter 36ft 1.75in (11.02m). Length 32ft 10.75in (10.03m). Empty weight 2,474lb (1,122kg). Gross weight 4,850lb (2,200kg). Max speed 130mph (210km/h) at sea level. Max range 335 miles (540km). **Photo:** SA316, Denmark.

Aérospatiale SA321 Super Frelon
France

The first of two prototypes of the Super Frelon, largest helicopter yet built in France, flew on 7 December 1962, with 1,320hp Turmo engines, and subsequently set a helicopter speed record of 217.77mph (350.47km/h) over a 15/25km course which stood until 1971. The second prototype was representative of the naval anti-submarine version, with crew of four, sonar, search radar in the stabilising floats and provision for other special equipment and weapons. Four pre-production Super Frelons followed the prototypes, with 1,500hp engines; the first of these flew on 31 January 1964. Orders include 24 SA321G anti-submarine versions for the French Navy, operated by Flottille 32F, 16 SA321L

transports for the South African Air Force, 12 SA321K transports for the Israeli Defence Force, 10 for Iraq, 16 for the Imperial Iranian Army, and nine transports for Libya. During 1974, deliveries began of 13 SA321J utility versions of the Super Frelon ordered by the Chinese People's Republic, and sales totalled 99 by the end of 1979. **Data:** Rotor diameter 62ft 0in (18.90m). Fuselage length 65ft 10.75in (20.08m). Empty weight (Naval version) 14,600lb (6,625kg). Gross weight 28,660lb (13,000kg). Max speed 171mph (275km/h) at sea level. Endurance 4hr. **Photo:** SA321 of the Aéronavale.

Aérospatiale (Westland) SA330 Puma
France/UK

Development of the SA330 to meet a French Army requirement for a 'hélicoptère de manoeuvre' was authorised in June 1963, with a contract for two prototypes and six pre-production aircraft. The first of these flew on 15 April 1965. The SA330 became one of three helicopters in the joint Anglo-French programme agreed early in 1968, with Westland becoming responsible for production of certain components and for assembly of 40 Pumas ordered by the RAF. The first British production SA330E Puma HC Mk 1 flew on 25 November 1970. Deliveries of French-built SA330Bs began in 1969 and the first French army unit became operational in June 1970. The first RAF unit, No 33 Squadron, formed on the type a year later; a second squadron, No 230, equipped with the Puma subsequently and production of an additional eight Pumas for the RAF was initiated in 1979. French army orders total 140 and

the French Air Force has acquired about 10. Military users of the export model SA330C (Turmo IVA) and SA330H (Turmo IVC) include Algeria, Chile, Portugal, South Africa, Belgium (Police air arm), Kuwait, Morocco, Pakistan, Zaire, Ivory Coast, Congo Republic, Nigeria, Spain (as HT19), Lebanon, Zimbabwe, Argentina, Indonesia and United Arab Emirates. The SA330F and SA330G are civil versions and the SA330J and SA330L are respectively civil and military variants with Turmo IVC engines, composite rotor blades and increased take-off weight. Over 500 Pumas have been built. **Data:** Rotor diameter 49ft 2.5in (15.00m). Fuselage length 46ft 1.5in (14.06m). Empty weight 7,795lb (3,536kg). Gross weight 15,430lb (7,000kg). Cruising speed 159mph (257km/h) at sea level. Max range 360 miles (580km) with standard fuel. **Photo:** Puma HC Mk 1.

Aérospatiale (Westland) SA341/342 Gazelle France/UK

The five-seat SA341 was conceived as a modernised development of the Alouette II, utilising the same transmission system and a 590shp Astazou III engine. The SA340-01 prototype, fitted initially with an Alouette II tail rotor, flew on 7 April 1967, and was followed by a second prototype and four pre-production SA341s. British variants, assembled by Westland, are the Gazelle AH Mk 1 (184 for the Army and Marines), HT Mk 2 (36 for the Navy), HT Mk 3 (24 for the RAF) and HCC Mk 4 (a single RAF communications version). The SA341H export model is licence-built in Yugoslavia. To meet Middle Eastern requirements, Aérospatiale developed the uprated SA342 during 1973, with an 870shp Astazou XIVH engine to improve take-off and climb under 'hot and high' conditions. Deliveries of the SA 342K military export model to Kuwait began in 1974; others have gone to Egypt and Libya. The French Army ordered in December 1978 140 of the SA342M armed version, with gyro-stabilised sight above the cabin and provision for four Euromissile HOT air-to-surface missiles; these supplement 110 SA341Fs modified to carry four HOTs each. Production of all models totalled 751 by January 1978. **Data** (SA342): Rotor diameter 34ft 5.5in (10.50m). Length 31ft 3.25in (9.53m). Gross weight 4,190lb (1,900kg). Max speed 192mph (310km/h). Range 469 miles (755km). **Photo:** Gazelle HT Mk 3.

Aérospatiale AS350 Ecureuil France

The six-seat Ecureuil (Squirrel) was developed by Aérospatiale to serve as a successor to the Alouette, and a prototype made its first flight on 27 June 1974, with a Lycoming LTS101 turboshaft. The second prototype, flown on 14 February 1974, introduced a Turboméca Arriel and production versions with these engines were designated AS350C and AS350B respectively, the former being known as the Astar in North America. The AS350D, with uprated (616shp) Lycoming LTS101-600A2 engine, has replaced the AS350C in production, and a twin-engined version, the AS355E Ecureuil 2 or Twin Star, has also been developed, making its first flight on 27 September 1979. The first military customer for helicopters of this family is the Brazilian Navy, which has acquired six AS350Bs from the Helibras assembly line in Brazil — with the local name of Esquilo — to serve aboard oceanographic survey ships in place of Fairchild FH-1100s. **Data** (AS350B): Rotor diameter 35ft 0.75in (10.69m). Length 42ft 8in (13.00m). Gross weight 4,300lb (1,950kg). Max cruising speed 144mph (232km/h). Range 440 miles (710km). **Photo:** AS350 Esquilo.

Aérospatiale SA365N Dauphin (HH-65A Dolphin) France

The Dauphin was originally developed to fill a gap in the Aérospatiale range between the Alouette III and the Puma, and was first produced as the single-engined SA360, flown in prototype form on 2 June 1972. A military version, with 1,400shp Turboméca Astazou XXB turboshaft, is identified as the SA361H, and a prototype of this version has been demonstrated as the HCL (*Hélicoptère Combat Leger*) with eight HOT missile launchers and a nose-mounted forward-looking infra-red system. The SA365C, first flown on 24 January 1975, is a twin-engined derivative, mostly for civil use, followed in turn by the SA365N on 31 March 1979 with a completely new, more streamlined fuselage and a retractable undercarriage. This same fuselage is used by the SA365F, which is armed with four AS15TT ASMs and carries Agrion search radar for anti-shipping duty. The Saudi

Arabian Navy has ordered 20 SA365Fs and four SA365Ns. A version with Lycoming LTS101-750 engines in place of the Turboméca Arriels, the SA366G, won a US Coast Guard competition for a Short Range Recovery helicopter in 1979 and 90 have been ordered with the designation HH-65A Dolphin. The first HH-65A flew on 23 July 1980. **Data** (SA365N): Rotor diameter 38ft 4in (11.68m). Length 43ft 7.25in (13.29m). Gross weight 7,936lb (3,600kg). Cruising speed 172mph (277km/h). Range 540 miles (870km). **Photo:** SA365/AS15TT mock-up.

Aérospatiale TB30 Epsilon   France

Interest in the development of a new primary trainer began within the Aérospatiale organisation early in 1977, at first as a small jet-powered aircraft. This was soon superseded by the TB30, a side-by-side trainer derived from the SOCATA TB10, but a tandem layout was adopted later in 1977 and the project lost virtually all commonality with the TB10. Alternatives with 260hp (TB30A), 300hp (TB30B) and 400hp (TB30C) engines were studied in 1978 and in response to an Armée de l'Air request for proposals in June 1978, the TB30B was chosen for submission in November, this being accepted in February 1979. Two prototypes were ordered in

June 1979 and these flew, respectively, on 22 December 1979 and 12 July 1980. The prototypes were flown with the 300hp AEIO-540-L1B5D engine but to overcome a handling problem caused by an unusual pitch-yaw coupling, major changes had to be made and the modified first prototype resumed testing on 31 October 1980. Changes include rounded and slightly upturned wingtips and a totally redesigned tail unit with a larger tailplane mounted on the fuselage and a ventral fin fitted. **Data:** Span 25ft 11.5in (7.92m). Length 24ft 10.5in (7.59m). Gross weight 2,590lb (1,175kg). Max speed 230mph (370km/h).

Aérospatiale/Potez CM170 Magister, Super Magister and CM175 Zephyr

France

The first of three prototypes of the Magister tandem two-seat jet trainer flew on 23 July 1952. Eleven months later, the French Air Force placed a pre-production order for 10 (first flown 7 July 1954) followed by production orders for a total of 387 (first flown 29 February 1956). The original design and manufacturing company, Fouga, became part of the Potez group, which continued production until the Magister was taken over by Sud-Aviation (now Aérospatiale) in 1967. Magisters built by these companies continue to serve in Algeria, France, Belgium, Cameroun, Bangladesh, Guatemala, Eire, Morocco, Lebanon, Libya, Rwanda, El Salvador, and Togo. Others, built under licence by Valmet of Finland and Israel Aircraft Industries, serve in Finland

and Israel and eight of the latter have been supplied to Uganda. The standard CM170 Magister has two 880lb (400kg) st Turboméca Marboré IIA turbojets and can carry two machine guns, plus underwing racks for two 50kg bombs, four 25kg rockets, up to 36 smaller rockets or two AS11 guided missiles. The last 130 aircraft for the French Air Force were Super Magisters with 1,058lb (480kg) st Marboré VI engines. 32 CM175 Zephyrs for the French Navy (first flown 30 May 1959) were equipped for deck landing training. **Data** (Magister): Span 39ft 10in (12.14m). Length 33ft (10.06m). Gross weight 7,055lb (3,200kg). Max speed 444mph (714km/h). Range 735 miles (1,200km). **Photo:** Magister, Irish Army Air Corps

Aerotec T-23 Uirapuru and T-18 Tangára

Brazil

The prototype of this side-by-side two-seat all-metal light aircraft flew on 2 June 1965, powered by a 108hp Lycoming O-235-C1 engine. A second Uirapuru followed, this time with a 150hp Lycoming O-320-A engine, and was offered to the Brazilian Air Force as a replacement for its locally-built Fokker S11 and S12 Instructor basic trainers. Seventy Uirapurus were ordered for this purpose in 1968-69, under the military designation T-23, with a further batch of 30 ordered later. Eight Uirapurus were acquired by the Paraguayan Air Force and 18 by the Bolivian Air Force. All have a 160hp Lycoming O-320-B2B and differ from the civilian model in

having fully-adjustable seats, stick-type controls and a modified cockpit canopy. As the A-132 Uirapuru II, an improved version was evolved during 1980, with improved cockpit canopy and updated equipment. Renamed the T-17 Tangará, a prototype first flew on 26 February 1981. **Data** (Uirapuru): Span 27ft 10.75in (8.50m). Length 21ft 8in (6.60m). Gross weight 1,825lb (840kg). Max speed 140mph (225km/h). Range 495 miles (800km). **Photo:** T-17 Tangará.

Agusta A109A

Italy

The first of three prototypes of the basic A109 helicopter, with seats for one or two pilots and six passengers, flew on 4 August 1971. Deliveries initially to customers in the USA, began in 1976, powered by two 420shp Allison 250-C20B turboshaft engines. In early 1977, the Italian Army began evaluating two A109s as transport/liaison helicopters and three others in the anti-tank role, armed with four TOW missiles; as a result, development was launched. of the specialised Agusta A129 Mangusta anti-tank helicopter, using A109 dynamic components. This helicopter with a new narrow-profile fuselage and two seats in tandem, was to enter flight test in 1981. Meanwhile, standard general-purpose A109s have been ordered by a number of foreign armed services, including those of the Argentine and Portugal. A special naval version is also in development for anti-submarine, anti-surface vessel, electronic warfare, search and rescue, and utility duties with several navies. Powered by R-R Gem turboshafts, the A129 prototypes are to fly in 1982. **Data:** Rotor diameter 36ft 1in (11.00m). Fuselage length 35ft 1.75in (10.71m). Gross weight 5,400lb (2,450kg). Max cruising speed 165mph (266km/h). Range 351 miles (565km). **Photo:** Anti-tank version.

AIDC T-CH-1

Taiwan

The T-CH-1 is a product of the Aero Industry Development Center of the Chinese Air Force on Taiwan (Nationalist China), and is a tandem two-seat trainer similar in overall concept and size to the North American T-28, but with a turboprop engine. Construction of two prototypes began early in 1972 and the first of these, as the XT-CH-1A, made its first flight on 23 November 1973. The second prototype, flown on 27 November 1974, incorporated modifications to permit its use as a weapons trainer and for counter-insurgency missions; this prototype is designated XT-CH-1B. A batch of 50 T-CH-1s was put into production at the AIDC in 1976. **Data:** One 1,450ehp Lycoming T53-L-701 turboprop. Span 40ft 0in (12.19m). Length 33ft 8in (10.26m). Gross weight 11,150lb (5,057kg). Max speed 368mph (592km/h). Range 1,250 miles (2,010km).

AIDC XC-2

Taiwan

As its second major design project, the Chinese Air Force's Aero Industry Development Center in Taiwan undertook the development of a light twin-turboprop transport, on which work began in early 1973. Powered by two 1,451ehp Lycoming T-53-L-701A turboprops, this XC-2 is able to seat 38 passengers in the cabin, which has quick-change provisions and a rear ramp to allow the rapid loading of supplies and the dropping of paratroops. The XC-2 has a high wing and a retractable tricycle undercarriage, the main units of which retract into fuselage-side fairings. A prototype was completed at the end of 1978 and began its flight tests in May 1979. **Data:**

Span 81ft 8.5in (24.90m). Length 64ft 9in (19.74m). Gross weight 25,000lb (11,340kg). Max speed 265mph (426km/h). Range 1,324 miles (2,131km) with max fuel and 357 miles (574km) with max payload.

Antonov An-2 (NATO code-name 'Colt')

USSR

First flown in 1947, the An-2 was designed as a rugged and versatile replacement for aircraft like the little Po-2, particularly for agricultural work in 'outback' areas. Its ability to operate from short strips, thanks to its large wing area, and to carry a payload of around 1.25ton, made it an ideal utility transport for the Soviet Air Force, and more than 13,000 have been built in the Soviet Union and Poland. Examples were supplied for military use in nearly 20 other countries, including Afghanistan, Bulgaria, Cuba, Czechoslovakia, East Germany, Hungary, Iraq, North Korea, Romania, Somalia and

Tanzania. The An-2 was built under licence also in China; production in Poland continued into 1980, by which time that country alone had built over 8,200 mostly for export to the USSR, with many for civil use. Powered by a 1,000hp Shvetsov ASh-61IR engine, the An-2 carries 14 troops, six stretchers or freight, and can operate on wheels, skis or floats. **Data:** Span 59ft 8.5in (18.18m). Length 40ft 8.25in (12.40m). Gross weight 12,125lb (5,500kg). Max speed 157mph (253km/h). Range 562 miles (900km) at 124mph (200km/h). **Photo:** An-2 Poland

Antonov An-14 (NATO code-name 'Clod') USSR

First flown on 15 March 1958, the An-14 underwent a lengthy period of flight development, during which major changes were made to the wing and tail design and more powerful engines were introduced. Production aircraft have 300hp Ivchenko AI-14RF engines and normally seat six passengers in the cabin. Since 1967, examples of the An-14 have been in service with the Soviet Air Force and some Communist bloc countries, including Bulgaria and East Germany. A turboprop derivative, the 15/19-passenger An-28 (NATO code-name *Cash*), appeared in 1972 and has entered production for Aeroflot. A version of the An-28 can be expected to appear in military guise in due course. **Data** (An-14): Span 72ft 2in (21.99m). Length 37ft 6.5in (11.44m). Gross weight 7,935lb (3,600kg). Max cruising speed 118mph (190km/h). Range 404 miles (650km) with 1,590lb (720kg) payload. **Photo:** An-14, Bulgaria.

Armstrong Whitworth Sea Hawk UK

Of 555 Sea Hawks produced by Armstrong Whitworth and Hawker, only about six remained in front line service in 1981. These equip the fighter squadron which serves, together with Breguet Alizés, aboard the Indian Navy's aircraft carrier *Vikrant*. India purchased 24 Sea Hawk FGA Mk 6s, to the same production standard as the final version for the Royal Navy, which acquired a total of 434 in six marks. Other export orders were from Germany (64 Mk 100 and Mk 101) and the Netherlands (36 Mk 50). India later acquired 12 more Sea Hawks ex-Royal Navy and 28 from Germany and will soon retire the last few in favour of the Sea Harrier. All versions were powered by a Rolls-Royce Nene turbojet, with the 5,400lb (2,450kg) st Nene 103 in the Sea Hawk FGA Mk 6. **Data:** Span 39ft 0in (11.89m). Length 39ft 8in (12.09m). Gross weight 16,200lb (7,348kg). Max cruising speed 590mph (950km/h) at sea level.

Atlas C4M Kudu   South Africa

The C4 Kudu was evolved by the Atlas Aircraft Corporation, in the Transvaal, out of its experience in assembling the Aeritalia/Aermacchi AM3C Bosbok for the SAAF. The wings, tail assembly, undercarriage and 340hp Piaggio-built Lycoming GSO-480-B1B3 power plant are all virtually identical with those of the Bosbok, while the fuselage is derived from the original design of the Lockheed AL60, a utility transport for which Aermacchi was responsible in Europe. A six/eight-seat light transport, the C4M can be converted quickly to operate in the freighting role and can be flown into and out of semi-prepared strips. A civil prototype Kudu first flew on 16 February 1974 and was used to obtain certification, granted on 16 June 1975, two days before the first flight of the military prototype C4M, which was subsequently evaluated by the SAAF. Production was begun to re-equip No 43 Squadron, one of the South African Active Citizen Force squadrons and about 20 were in service in 1980. **Data:** Span 42ft 10.75in (13.08m). Length 30ft 6.25in (9.31m). Gross weight 4,497lb (2,040kg). Max speed 161mph (259km/h). Range 806 miles (1,297km).

Beechcraft Bonanza   USA

The prototype Bonanza flew for the first time on 22 December 1945, and the type has now been in continuous production, in progressively improved versions, for more than 30 years. The 10,000th example of the basic V-tailed Model 35 Bonanza was flown in early 1977. Since 1959, variants have included a conventional-tail family of lightplanes, known originally as Debonairs, but currently designated F33 series Bonanzas. The first military order for Bonanzas, placed by the Imperial Iranian Air Force in 1972, was for F33As for training and liaison duties. Contracts for F33Cs, approved for aerobatic flying, have followed, and by 1978, the IIAF had a total of 49 of these two variants in service. All are basically four/five-seaters, with a 285hp Continental IO-520 engine. Other operators are the Mexican Air Force and Naval Aviation, with 23 Bonanza F33Cs, and the Spanish Air Force, with 25 F33Cs and 29 F33Es. **Data** (F33C): Span 33ft 6in (10.21m). Length 26ft 8in (8.13m). Gross weight 3,400lb (1,542kg). Max speed 209mph (338km/h). Range 1,023 miles (1,648km). **Photo:** F33C (E.24A), Spain.

Beechcraft C-12 Huron and RU-21J　　　USA

Both the USAF and the US Army adopted the Beech Super King Air 200 during 1974, to meet a requirement for a liaison and staff transport. The commercial prototype had first flown on 27 October 1972. By the beginning of 1978, the USAF had taken delivery of 30 C-12As, for use by US attaches overseas and by military missions. The US Army ordered 80 C-12A Hurons for utility transport and liaison duties and these, like the USAF C-12As, have 750shp PT6A-38 turboprops. However, in 1979, the Army adopted the 850shp PT6A-41 for the later production examples and some conversions of these in service, under the designation C-12C; five C-12Ds featured enlarged cargo doors. The US Navy acquired 66 UC-12Bs as passenger/cargo transports,

with PT6A-41s and large cargo doors. The Irish Army Air Corps has acquired three Super King Airs. In 1974, the US Army also took delivery of three RU-21Js. These are Super King Airs fitted with standard 850shp PT6A-41 engines and extensive aerial arrays for electronic reconnaissance. Beech also has developed a maritime patrol version of the Super King Air and the Japanese Maritime Safety Agency has acquired 13, with tip tanks, radar in a ventral radome and other special equipment. The Uruguayan Navy has also acquired one of this variant. **Data** (C-12A): Span 54ft 6in (16.60m). Length 43ft 9in (13.16m). Gross weight 12,500lb (5,670kg). Max cruising speed 262mph (421km/h). Range 1,824 miles (2,935km). **Photo:** UC-12B.

Beechcraft Musketeer　　　USA

The Musketeer and its successors have been in production since 1962 and by the end of 1980 over 5,000 had been sold for service throughout the world. The majority were delivered for private or club use, in two-, four- or six-seat variants. During January 1970, the Fuerza Aérea Mexicana took delivery of 20 two-seat Musketeer Sport models to be used as instrument trainers, each with a 150hp Lycoming O-320-E2C engine and fixed tricycle undercarriage. During 1971, the Canadian Armed Forces took delivery of 25 Musketeers (CAF

designation CT-134) to replace Chipmunk primary trainers; the Royal Hong Kong Auxiliary Air Force has two and the Algerian national pilot training school has three. **Data:** Span 32ft 9in (9.98m). Length 25ft 0in (7.62m). Gros weight 2,250lb (1,020kg). Max speed 140mph (225km/h). Range 880 miles (1,420km). **Photo:** CT-134, CAF.

Beechcraft T-34 Mentor

USA

Derived from the civil Bonanza lightplane, as a private venture, the Mentor first flew on 2 December 1948. Three YT-34s were ordered by the USAF for evaluation in 1950. Subsequently, 350 T-34As were built for the USAF, and the US Navy took delivery of 423 similar T-34Bs before production ended in October 1957. The Mentor was also built by Canadian Car and Foundry for the USAF (100) and RCAF (25); by Fuji Industries in Japan (140 for JASDF, now out of service, and 36 for Philippine Air Force) and at Cordoba in the Argentine (75). Mentors were supplied to several other nations through MAP, and continue to fly with at least a dozen air forces. **Data:** One 225hp Continental O-470-13 engine. Span 32ft 10in (10.0m). Length 25ft 11.25in (7.90m). Gross weight 2,950lb (1,338kg). Max speed 189mph (304km/h). Range 735 miles (1,183km). **Photo:** T-34A, Spain (E.17).

Beechcraft T-34C Turbo Mentor

USA

In 1973 Beech received a US Navy contract to modify two T-34B Mentor trainers to YT-34C Turbo Mentor standard. This involved installing the 715shp (derated to 400shp) Pratt & Whitney PT6A-25 turboprop engine and the latest electronics. The first YT-34C flew on 21 September 1973. By March 1975 the two prototypes had completed 700 flying hours, including 300 hours of Navy evaluation, as a result of which the type was ordered into production as a replacement for the piston-engined T-34B and T-28. Total procurement of 184 for the US Navy was completed by 1980, the T-34C having entered service with the NATC in November 1977. In addition, orders have been placed by Morocco (12), Argentina (16), Ecuador (20), Indonesia (16), Peru (6) and Algeria (6) some of these being for the armed version known as the T-34C-1. **Data:** Span 33ft 3.875in (10.15m). Length 28ft 8.5in (8.75m). Gross weight 4,274lb (1,939kg). Max cruising speed 247mph (397km/h). Max range 749 miles (1,205km). **Photo:** T-34C.

Beechcraft T-42A Cochise   USA

In February 1965, the USAF chose the Beech B55 Baron to meet its requirement for a twin-engined instrument trainer, following a design competition limited to 'off-the-shelf' types. Subsequently, Beech received contracts for 65 aircraft, to be designated T-42A. In 1971, five more T-42As were sold, to Turkey, and in 1972 the Spanish Air Force ordered seven B55 Barons (since supplemented by a further 12). The B55 is a four/six-seat light transport, powered by two 260hp Continental IO-470-L engines. **Data:** Span 37ft 10in (11.53m). Length 27ft 0in (8.23m). Gross weight 5,100lb (2,313kg). Max speed 236mph (380km/h). Range 1,225 miles (1,971km). **Photo:** B55, Spain (E20).

Beechcraft U-8 Seminole and Queen Air   USA

Final version of the U-8 Seminole series supplied to the US Army was a variant of the commercial Queen Air designated U-8F, with a fuselage seating up to six passengers, and 340hp Lycoming IGSO-480 engines. Three pre-production and 68 production U-8Fs were delivered. The standard Queen Air is used by the Japan Maritime Self-Defence Force as a transport and navigation trainer, and others are used by the air forces of Israel, Peru, Venezuela and Uruguay. Earlier Seminoles in US Army service had included the U-8D, with 340hp GSO-480 engines, and the U-8E, with 295hp GO-480 engines, similar to the commercial Model F50 and D50 Twin Bonanzas respectively; some of these earlier models have been modified to U-8Gs. **Data** (U-8F): Span 45ft 10.5in (13.98m). Length 35ft 6in (10.82m). Gross weight 7,700lb (3,493kg). Max speed 239mph (384km/h). Range 1,220 miles (1,963km). **Photo:** Queen Air JGSDF.

Beechcraft U-21 Ute, T-44A and King Air   USA

During 1963, Beech converted a Queen Air airframe to have Pratt & Whitney PT6A-6 turboprops, and this aircraft was evaluated by the US Army as the NU-8F. In production guise, with the designation U-21A, the same basic airframe has a double freight-loading door, extensive avionics and an interior layout for 10 troops, 6-8 command personnel or three stretchers. Delivery of the U-21As began in May 1967 and subsequent contracts brought the total to 184. These include U-21A, RU-21A and RU-21D variants with 550hp PT6A-20 engines and RU-21B, RU-21C and RU-21E variants with 620hp PT6A-20s and 10,900lb (4,994kg) gross weight. Many of these aircraft have extensive aerial arrays for electronic reconnaissance duties and several were supplied to Israel in 1980 to monitor troop movements in the Sinai desert. Five U-21Fs acquired by the US Army in 1971 are similar to the commercial, pressurised King Air A100 and 17 U-21Gs are updated USAF versions of the U-21A. The single VC-6B is a VIP transport similar to the King Air 90, and about ten foreign air forces have bought King Airs. In 1976, the US Navy also ordered a version of the King Air 90 as a new multi-engined pilot trainer, designated T-44A. Deliveries of 61 began in August 1977, to replace piston-engined Grumman TS-2As and Bs. **Data** (U-21F): Span 45ft 10.5in (13.98m). Length 39ft 11.25in (12.17m). Gross weight 11,500lb (5,216kg). Max cruising speed 285mph (459km/h). Range 1,395 miles (2,245km). **Photo:** U-21A.

Bell AH-1 HueyCobra   USA

Bell developed the HueyCobra from the UH-1 Iroquois (also known as the Huey), initially as a private venture, against US Army requirements for an armed helicopter. The prototype Bell 209 HueyCobra flew on 7 September 1965, and two pre-production aircraft and an initial production batch of 110 were ordered in April 1966, with the designation AH-1G, powered by the 1,100shp Lycoming T53-L-13B. Operational service in Vietnam began in autumn 1967. Early Army AH-1Gs had a TAT-102A nose turret with a six-barrel 7.62mm Minigun. Later aircraft have the XM-28 armament system with two Miniguns or two XM-129 40mm grenade launchers, or one of each; production totalled 1,078, plus 20 for the Spanish Navy (designated Z16); six have been supplied to Israel and the US Marine Corps received 38 from the Army. Some AH-1Gs were fitted with dual controls as TH-1Gs. In 1973, the Army began a programme to convert AH-1Gs to AH-1Q standard, with provision to carry eight Hughes TOW (Tube-launched Optically-tracked Wire-guided) missile containers and associated equipment, including a helmet sight sub-system. All but 11 of 93 AH-1Qs are being further modified to AH-1S when fitted with the 1,800hp T53-L-703 and upgraded gearbox and transmission. The Army also ordered 297 new-build AH-1S helicopters, some with a 20mm turret cannon, plus conversion of 208 AH-1Gs to the same standard; other AH-1Gs became AH-1Rs with the new engines but without TOW provision. Orders for AH-1S TOW-equipped helicopters have also been placed by Morocco, Greece and Spain. Japan acquired two in 1979 and is expected to produce 54 under licence. **Data** (AH-1S): Rotor diameter 44ft 0in (13.41m). Gross weight 10,000lb (4,535kg). Max speed 141mph (227km/h). Max range 315 miles (507km). **Photo:** AH-1G.

Bell AH-1J/1T SeaCobra

USA

The SeaCobra was originally ordered by the US Marine Corps in May 1968 as an improved version of the AH-1G HueyCobra, the principal difference being the use of a Pratt & Whitney T400-CP-400 coupled free-turbine turboshaft, flat rated to give a continuous output of 1,100shp or 1,250shp for take-off. Armament comprised an electrically-driven turret system in the nose with a 20mm General Electric SM-197 three-barrel cannon, plus four external weapon points under stub-wings carrying rockets, Minigun pods, etc. Delivery of 69 AH-1Js to the USMC began in mid-1970, but the last two were converted before delivery to AH-1T standard with

1,970shp T400-WV-402 engine, larger main rotor, lengthened fuselage and other new features. 57 of these AH-1Ts had been ordered by the Marine Corps by early 1978 and deliveries of TOW-equipped AH-1Ts to the USMC Squadron HMA-269 began on 19 November 1979. Through the US government, the Imperial Iranian Army Aviation service acquired 202 Bell 209s similar to the AH-1Js. **Data** (AH-1J): Rotor diameter 44ft 0in (13.41m). Fuselage length 44ft 7in (13.59m). Gross weight 10,000lb (4,535kg). Max speed 207mph (333km/h). Max range 359 miles (577km). **Photo:** AH-1J.

Bell OH-58A Kiowa and TH-57A Sea Ranger

USA

Bell flew the first of five OH-4A (Model 206) prototypes for the Army Light Observation Helicopter competition on 10 December 1962 and subsequently built 2,200 Model 206As for the US Army as OH-58A Kiowa observation helicopters. The US Navy acquired 40 similar TH-57A SeaRangers for training duties. Among many other users of the type in its unarmed version are the Canadian Armed Forces (75 CH-136 and 14 Model 206Bs), Australian Army (56, built by CAC as CA-36), Brazilian Navy (18), Austria, Brunei, Spain, Turkey, Iran, Italy and Saudi Arabia. In 1980, Bell developed the TexasRanger as an armed version of Model 206L LongRanger, with Allison 250-C30 engine and lengthened fuselage. In Italy, Agusta added the five-seat Bell Model 206 to its range of

licence-built helicopters in 1967, since which time more than 500 examples have been built in Italy for commercial and military use. Of the latter, those for the Swedish Navy (HKP 6) are equipped for anti-submarine and anti-shipping patrol and attack, carrying assorted weapons beneath the fuselage, and feature the high-skid landing gear (originally developed by Bell for use in rough terrain) to permit clearance for these weapons. Some military models have a larger rotor and carry the Agusta designation AB-206A-1. **Data** (206B): Rotor diameter 33ft 4in (10.16m). Fuselage length 31ft 2in (9.50m). Gross weight 3,200lb (1,451kg). Max speed 140mph (226km/h). Max range 418 miles (673km). **Photo:** CH-136, CAF.

Bell UH-1 Iroquois
(and Agusta-Bell 204B/205)

USA/Italy

Deliveries of the HU-1A (Model 204) Iroquois, with T53-L-1A engine, began on 30 June 1959, for utility transport and casualty evacuation, with six seats or two stretchers. First flown in 1960, the HU-1B (now UH-1B) had a larger cabin for eight passengers or three stretchers, and 960shp T53-L-5 engine. Large numbers were built for the US Army, and for the Australian, Austrian, Italian, Netherlands, Norwegian, Saudi Arabian, Spanish, Swedish and Turkish Services, and by Fuji in Japan. The UH-1C was similar with 1,100shp T53-L-11 engine and wide-chord rotor. The UH-1D (Model 205) has a larger cabin, for 12-14 troops or six stretchers, and a T53-L-11 driving a larger-diameter rotor. In addition to large US Army orders, this model serves in numerous foreign air arms and was built by Dornier for the German Service. For the US Army and New Zealand, the UH-1H superseded the D, with 1,400shp T53-L-13 engine, and 118 of this model were produced in Taiwan for the Chinese Nationalist Army. A similar version used by the Canadian Forces is known as the CH-118, and the USAF bought 30 HH-1Hs for local base rescue duties. A version of the UH-1B won a US Marines design contest for an assault support helicopter in 1962 and is in service as the UH-1E; in 1963 the USAF adopted the UH-1F, with 1,100shp T58-GE-3 engine, for support duties. The HH-1K is a Navy air-sea rescue version of the UH-1E; the TH-1L and UH-1L are Navy training and utility versions. In Italy, Agusta has built equivalent models in large numbers as AB-204 and AB-205, and for the Italian and Spanish Air Arms a special version was developed for anti-submarine duties. Special features of this variant, known as the AB-204AS, include automatic approach-to-hover system and all-weather instrumentation, sonar equipment, optional AN/APN-195 search radar and provision to carry two Mk 44 homing torpedoes. The power plant is a 1,290shp General Electric T58-GE-3 turboshaft, and the gross weight is 9,500lb (4,310kg). **Data** (UH-1H): Rotor diameter 48ft 0in (14.63m). Fuselage length 41ft 10.75in (12.77m). Gross weight 9,500lb (4,309kg). Max speed 127mph (204km/h). Range 318 miles (511km) at 127mph (204km/h). **Photo:** UH-1H.

Below: TH-1L Iroquois

Bell UH-1N and Model 212 (and Agusta-Bell 212ASW)

USA/Italy

The Bell Model 212 was developed from the basic Model 205 Huey during 1968 to take advantage of the Pratt & Whitney (Canada) PT6T coupled turboshaft engine, offering improved performance and twin-engined safety. Initial orders were placed simultaneously by the US government and the Canadian government. The US version was designated UH-1N and a total of 300 has been built for service with the USAF, USN and Marine Corps, including some VH-1N command transports. The Canadian variant was designated CUH-1N when ordered but now serves with the Canadian Forces as the CH-135. Deliveries of the UH-1N, with 1,800shp Pratt & Whitney T400-CP-400 engine, began in 1970, followed by the first CUH-1N in May 1971. During 1973, 14 Bell 212s were ordered for use by

the Peruvian Air Force; the Argentine Air Force has ordered eight, and several other air forces have acquired Model 212s for general duties. The Bell 212 is also built in Italy by Agusta, and this company has developed an extensively-modified version for anti-submarine search and attack as the AB212ASW. Carrying search radar, sonar and homing torpedoes, the AB212ASW has been ordered by the Italian Navy, Spanish Navy, Peru and Turkey, and the general-purpose AB212 has been ordered by the Austrian Army. **Data** (AB212ASW): Rotor diameter 48ft 0in (14.63m). Fuselage length 46ft 0in (14.02m). Gross weight 11,196lb (5,079kg). Max speed 122mph (196km/h). Range 414 miles (667km). **Photo:** Agusta-Bell AB212ASW.

Bell Model 214 (Isfahan)

USA

During 1970, Bell flew the prototype of an improved version of the UH-1H, known as the model 214 Huey Plus. Powered by a 1,900shp Lycoming T53-L-702 turboshaft, it had an enlarged main rotor, strengthened airframe and increased gross weight of 11,000lb (4,995kg). From this prototype was developed the Model 214A with a T55-L-7C engine and after demonstrations in Iran, the Iranian government placed an order for 287 examples of the Model 214A, powered in the production model by the 2,930shp Lycoming LTC4B-8D engine, derated

to 2,050shp. Known in Iran as the Isfahan, the first production Model 214A flew on 13 March 1974; deliveries began in April 1975 and were completed in 1978. The Imperial Iranian Army subsequently ordered 39 Model 214Cs, which are similar but are equipped for search and rescue duties. **Data** (Model 214A): Rotor diameter 50ft 0in (15.24m). Gross weight with external load 15,000lb (6,803kg). Cruising speed 161mph (259km/h). Range 283 miles (455km). **Photo:** Model 214A Isfahan, Iran.

Boeing E-4   USA

The well-known Boeing 747 'jumbo-jet' entered USAF service in 1974 to serve as the National Emergency Airborne Command Post and HQ Strategic Air Command airborne command post, able to control the entire US deterrent force of manned bombers and missiles in time of war or crisis. The first three NEACP aircraft were delivered to E-4A interim standard, with electronic systems transferred from EC-135 command posts, and were to be updated eventually to E-4B standard, with new avionics having greater capabilities. Three new-build E-4Bs are also being procured by the USAF for NEACP and SAC ABNCP missions, and the first of these, less the complete avionics, flew on 8 June 1978. The E-4s are each powered by four 52,500lb (23,815kg) st General Electric F103-GE-100 turbofans, which replaced the Pratt & Whitney F105-PW-100s fitted temporarily to the first two.

Data: Span 195ft 8in (59.64m). Length 231ft 4in (70.51m). Gross weight (E-4A) 778,000lb (352,895kg). Unrefuelled endurance 12 hours. **Photo:** E-4B.

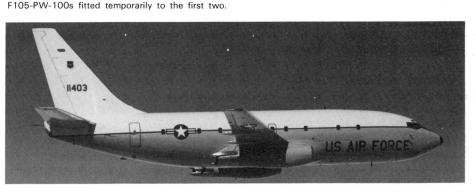

Boeing T-43A and Model 737   USA

Choice of the Boeing 737 as a navigation trainer to replace the Convair T-29 was announced by the USAF in May 1971. This type, powered by two Pratt & Whitney JT8D turbofans, had been produced previously only in commercial versions. The USAF order for T-43As was for 19; the first flew on 10 April 1974 and deliveries to Mather AFB were completed in mid-1974. In 1980, 13 remained in service there, the other six being assigned to the ANG. Each has positions in the cabin for 12 students, four advanced students and three instructors. Among air forces operating 737s as standard or VIP transports are those of Brazil and Venezuela. **Data** (T-43A): Span 93ft 0in (28.35m). Length 100ft 0in (30.48m). Gross weight 115,500lb (52,390kg). Max speed 586mph (943km/h). Range over 2,000 miles (3,200km). **Photo:** USAF T-43A.

Boeing 727 USA

Although it is the world's most successful commercial jet transport, with sales of more than 1,800 announced by the end of 1980, the Boeing 727 has seen virtually no military application. From time to time, Boeing has projected special-purpose military variants but the first military user is the Belgian Air Force, which acquired two 727QC (quick-change) versions with side-loading freight doors, from Sabena. These are operated by No 21 Squadron, which has responsibility for VIP and communications flying and is based at Melsbroek. Two Boeing 727s acquired by JAT are similarly assigned for VIP duty in Yugoslavia, and the Mexican Air Force has one. **Data:** Span 108ft 0in (32.92m). Length 133ft 2in (40.59m). Gross weight 169,000lb (76,655kg). Max speed 632mph (1,017km/h). Range 2,025 miles (3,260km).

Boeing Vertol CH-46 Sea Knight USA/Japan

The Sea Knight is a derivative of the Boeing Vertol 107-II tandem-rotor helicopter, which itself originated as a Piasecki design. Three Model 107s underwent US Army evaluation and the type was then adopted by the US Marine Corps as the CH-46A Sea Knight with 1,250shp General Electric T58-GE-8B engines; the first example flew on 16 October 1962. After 160 CH-46A, production switched to the CH-46D, with 1,400shp T58-GE-10 engines; 266 'Ds' were built, and a change was then made to the CH-46F with added avionics and instrument panel changes, 174 being built by the time production ended in 1970. During 1975, the Marine Corps began a programme to convert 273 Sea Knights to CH-46E standard, with 1,870shp T58-GE-16 engines and other improvements. For use in supplying stores to combatant vessels at sea, the US Navy bought 14 UH-46As and 10 UH-46Ds, similar to the Marine Corps models. Variants of the Model 107 were supplied by Boeing to Canada for use by the RCAF as CH-113 Labradors and by the Army as CH-113A Voyageurs; and to Sweden (with Bristol Siddeley Gnome engines) for use by the Air Force and Navy as HKP-7s. **Data** (CH-46D): Rotor diameter 51ft 0in (15.55m) each. Fuselage length 44ft 10in (13.66m). Gross weight 23,000lb (10,442kg). Max speed 166mph (267km/h) at sea level. Range 230 miles (370km). **Photo:** CH-113A Voyageur.

Boeing Vertol CH-47 Chinook   USA

The Vertol Model 114 tandem-rotor helicopter was selected in March 1959 as the winner of a US Army design competition for a 'battlefield mobility' helicopter, capable of carrying a two-ton load internally or eight tons on an external sling. Five prototypes were ordered with the designation YHC-1B, and the first of these flew on 21 September 1961, by which time the Vertol company had become a Division of Boeing. Delivery to the Army began in December 1962, the first production version being the CH-47A, with 2,200hp T55-L-5 or, later, 2,650shp T55-L-7 engines. In early October 1966, the CH-47B made its first flight, with 2,850shp T55-L-7C engines, and production of this version began in 1967. On October 1967, Boeing Vertol flew the first CH-47C, with 3,750shp T55-L-11 engines, and the first production type reached Vietnam in 1968. Production totals of these three models for the US Army were 354, 108 and 270 respectively; about 70 of these were transferred to the Vietnam Air Force. Exports by Boeing Vertol include Thailand, four CH-47A; RAAF, 12 Model 165; Spain, 10 Model 176 and three Model 414 (HT17); Argentina, three Model 308; Canada, nine Model 173 (CH-147). The Chinook is also built in Italy by Agusta, which has sold 26 to the Italian Army, 95 to Iran, six to Morocco, two to Tanzania, 20 to Libya and 15 to Egypt. During 1977, Boeing-Vertol began converting one each of the CH-46A, B and C models to YCH-47D prototypes, with 3,700shp T55-L-712 engines, composite rotor blades and improved instrumentation; the first of these flew on 11 May 1979 and the Army plans eventually to convert 436 of its Chinooks to this standard. The RAF has bought 33 Model 352s as Chinook HC Mk 1s, and the first of these flew on 23 March 1980. **Data** (CH-47C): Rotor diameter (each) 60ft 0in (18.29m). Length 51ft 0in (15.54m). Gross weight 46,000lb (20,865kg). Max speed 190mph (306km/h) at sea level. Mission radius 115 miles (185km) at 160mph (257km/h) with 13,450lb (6,080kg) payload. **Photo:** Chinook HC Mk 1.

British Aerospace (BAC) One-Eleven   UK

First military Service to purchase BAC One-Elevens was the Royal Australian Air Force, which took delivery of two for VIP transport duties. They are used by No 34 (VIP) Squadron, which operates from Fairbairn, Canberra, on transport and liaison work for the Australian government. Basically Series 200 aircraft, they are each powered by two 10,410lb (4,722kg) st Rolls-Royce Spey-2 Mk506 engines. Two others fly in British military markings at the RAE Bedford. Three Srs 475s were ordered in 1974 by the Sultan of Oman's Air Force, and these were subsequently modified to have a large freight door on the port side of the fuselage. **Data:** Span 88ft 6in (26.97m). Length 93ft 6in (28.50m). Gross weight 78,500lb (35,610kg). Max speed 541mph (871km/h). Typical range 1,155 miles (1,860km). **Photo:** Srs 475, Oman.

British Aerospace HS125 Dominie T Mk 1 (and Mercurius)

UK

The Hawker Siddeley 125 Srs 2 was ordered for the RAF in September 1962, as a navigational trainer, under the name Dominie T Mk 1. The first of 20 production models flew on 30 December 1964, and deliveries to No 1 Air Navigation School at Stradishall, Suffolk, began in the autumn of 1965. They are now used by No 6FTS at Finningley. The Dominie T1 is similar to the commercial twin-jet executive versions of the HS125, with 3,000lb (1,360kg) st Rolls-Royce Viper 520 turbojets, but is equipped to carry a pilot, pilot assister, two students and an instructor. The RAF also has five HS125

CC Mk 1s and two lengthened CC Mk 2s (Srs 600) for communication duties, serving with No 32 Squadron. Other air forces using the HS125 include those of Malaysia (2), Brazil (8, as VC-93), South Africa (4, named Mercurius) and the Irish Air Corps, which has a Srs 600 and a Srs 700. **Data** (Srs 600): Span 47ft 0in (14.32m). Length 50ft 5.75in (15.37m). Gross weight 25,000lb (11,340kg). Max speed 359mph (578km/h). Range 1,876 miles (3,020km). **Photo:** Irish Air Corps HS125.

British Aerospace (HS) Sea Vixen

UK

Retired from service with the Fleet Air Arm in 1972, the Sea Vixen was a carrier-borne two-seat all-weather fighter that entered service in July 1959. Production totalled 119 F(AW) Mk 1s and 29 F(AW) Mk 2s, with 67 of the former also converted to the latter standard. During 1977, Flight Refuelling Ltd in conjunction with the RAE developed the D Mk 3 pilotless drone conversion for service at the RAE Llandbedr range in succession to Meteor and Canberra drones and about 25 stored Sea Vixens were made available for conversion to this standard. **Data:** Powered by two 11,250lb (5,100kg) st Rolls-Royce Avon 208 turbojets. Span 51ft 0in (15.54m).

Length 55ft 7in (16.94m). Gross weight 41,575lb (18,875kg). Max speed 690mph (1,110km/h). **Photo:** Sea Vixen D Mk 3.

British Aerospace (Scottish Aviation) Bulldog UK

This two-seat primary trainer was developed originally by Beagle Aircraft as the B125 Series 1. Its all-metal airframe was basically similar to that of the civil Pup, with structural and equipment changes to suit it for military use. In particular, the Bulldog has a large rearward-sliding jettisonable canopy over its side-by-side seats and is powered by a 200hp Lycoming IO-360-A1B6 engine. The Beagle prototype flew for the first time on 19 May 1969 and the Scottish Aviation prototype Bulldog 100 Series on 14 February 1971. Deliveries began in July 1971, to meet orders from Sweden (58 Model 101 for Swedish Air Force and 20 for Swedish Army; designation SK 61), Malaysia (15 Model 102) and

Kenya (5 Model 103). First flown on 30 January 1973, the Series 120 has a strengthened centre-section and increased aerobatic gross weight. The RAF bought 130 as Bulldog T Mk 1 (Model 121), the Ghana Air Force 13 (Model 122/122A), the Nigerian Air Force 32 (Model 123), the Jordanian Royal Academy of Aeronautics 18 (Model 125), the Lebanese Air Force 6 (Model 126), the Kenya Air Force 9 (Model 127), the Royal Hong Kong Auxiliary Air Force 2 (Model 128) and the Botswana Defence Force, 6. **Data** (Series 120): Span 33ft (10.06m). Length 23ft 3in (7.09m). Gross weight 2,350lb (1,065kg). Max speed 150mph (240km/h). Range 621 miles (1,000km). **Photo:** T Mk 1.

British Aerospace (Scottish Aviation) Jetstream UK

After a chequered history, the Jetstream was given a new surge of life by its choice as the type to replace RAF Varsity multi-engined pilot training aircraft. The order was for 26 Jetstream T Mk 1s, for delivery in 1973-5. Power plant comprises two 940shp Turboméca Astazou XVI turboprops, permitting higher operating weights and performance than the Astazou XIIs and XIVs fitted in the prototype (first flown 18 August 1967) and early Mk 1 aircraft built by Handley Page before the company ceased operations. In 1972 full responsibility for the programme was taken over by Scottish Aviation (now British Aerospace), and the 26 aircraft had all

been delivered by spring 1976. After a period in store, 12 were delivered to the RAF for multi-engine training and serve with 6 FTS at RAF Finningley. Fourteen have been converted to T Mk 2 standard, to replace the Royal Navy's Sea Princes in an observer training role, with weather/mapping radar in a nose 'thimble'. The T Mk 2 first flew on 7 April 1977 and these aircraft serve with No 750 Squadron at Culdrose. **Data** (T Mk 1): Span 52ft 0in (15.85m). Length 47ft 1.5in (14.37m). Gross weight 12,566lb (5,700kg). Max speed 282mph (454km/h). Max range 1,380 miles (2,224km). **Photo:** Jetstream T Mk 2.

CAARP/Mudry CAP10 and CAP20   France

Developed from the well-known Piel Emeraude, the side-by-side two-seat CAP10 is intended for training, touring or aerobatic use. Construction is of wood, except for fabric covering on the rear fuselage and some plastics components, such as the engine cowlings. Standard power plant is a 180hp Lycoming IO-360-B2F. Thirty of the first 50 CAP10s built were delivered to the French Air Force, for service with the Equipe de Voltige Aérienne at Salon-de-Provence, and at the basic flying training school at Clermont-Ferrand-Aulnat; 20 more were delivered in 1980 for the primary training school at Cognac. A

small number also serve with Aéronavale. The Equipe de Voltige also acquired six CAP20s, which are single-seat derivatives of the CAP10 with a 200hp Lycoming AIO-360-B1B engine. **Data** (CAP10): Span 26ft 5.25in (8.06m). Length 23ft 11.5in (7.30m). Gross weight 1,829lb (830kg). Max speed 168mph (270km/h). Range 745 miles (1,200km). **Photo:** CAP10 (Aéronavale).

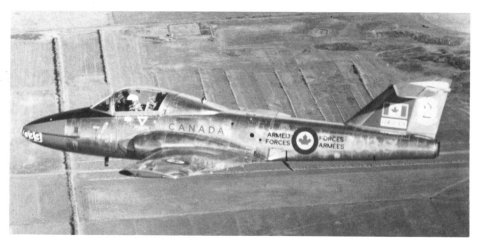

Canadair CL-41 (CT-114) Tutor   Canada

The first of two prototypes of the Canadair CL-41 two-seat basic trainer flew on 13 January 1960, powered by a 2,400lb (1,090kg) st Pratt & Whitney JT12A-5 turbojet. It was developed to meet the anticipated needs of the RCAF for a basic jet trainer and, after evaluation of the prototypes, the RCAF ordered 190 CL-41A production models, powered by the locally-built 2,633lb (1,194kg) st General Electric J85-Can-40, under the designation CT-114 Tutor. The first of these was delivered on 29 October 1963, and all were in service by 1966. They

continue in service as the standard basic trainer of the Canadian Armed Forces. Twenty CL-41Gs were supplied to the Royal Malaysian Air Force in 1967/68 and currently equip two squadrons. The CL-41G, which has the RMAF name of Tebuan (Wasp), has underwing and fuselage strong points for light weapons. **Data:** Span 36ft 6in (11.13m). Length 32ft 0in (9.75m). Gross weight 11,288lb (5,131kg). Max speed 480mph (774km/h) at 28,500ft (8,700m). Max range 1,340 miles (2,155km) with six underwing tanks.

Canadair CL-215

Canada

The CL-215 amphibian was evolved as a specialised water-bomber, following several years' close study by Canadair of the requirements for this type of operation. The prototype flew for the first time on 23 October 1967; first customers were the Province of Quebec and the Securité Civile of France, each of which acquired 15. Being designed for simplicity of operation and maintenance, and capable of operating from short airstrips, small lakes and bays, the CL-215 is equally suited to a variety of other duties. Thus, the Spanish Air Force has 10 (designated UD13) which are intended primarily for search and rescue, carrying up to 18 passengers or nine stretchers, but are available for other tasks, including fire-fighting. The Hellenic Air Force flies eight CL-215s for general transport and fire-fighting duties; the Royal Thai Navy has two for search and rescue. **Data:** Two 2,100hp Pratt & Whitney R-2800-83AM2AH engines. Span 93ft 10in (28.60m). Length 65ft 0.5in (19.82m). Gross weight 43,500lb (19,731kg). Max cruising speed 181mph (291km/h). Range 1,405 miles (2,260km). **Photo:** CL-215, Spain (UD13).

Caproni C-22J

Italy

First flown on 21 July 1980, the C-22J is an attempt to produce an ultralight and low-cost jet training aeroplane primarily to permit the screening of students prior to their being committed to expensive military flying training programmes that they might not have the aptitude to complete. As the appearance suggests, the C-22J is based on the Caproni company's lengthy experience of high performance sailplane design, and is in fact an extrapolation of the A-21SJ jet-powered sailplane. Considerable use is made of plastics in the construction of the C-22J, the basic structure of which is metal. The prototype is powered by a pair of 247lb (112kg) st KHD T 317 turbojets but the Microturbo TRS 18 is available as an alternative. **Data:** Span 32ft 9.75in (10.00m). Length 20ft 3.5in (6.19m). Gross weight 2,425lb (1,100kg). Max speed 329mph (530km/h). Max range 658 miles (1,060km).

CASA C207 Azor

Spain

The Azor flew for the first time on 28 September 1955 and was produced subsequently for the Spanish Air Force in two versions, under the designation T7. The first series of 10 aircraft are CASA C207-As (T7As), equipped to carry a crew of four and 30-40 passengers in an air-conditioned cabin. The second series of 10, known as CASA C207-Cs (T7Bs) are freighters with a large cargo-door. Powered by 2,040hp Bristol Hercules 730 engines, five C207-Cs and two C207-As remain in service in 1980 with Escuadron 405, primarily for target-towing. **Data:** Span 91ft 2.5in (27.80m). Length 68ft 5in (20.85m). Gross weight 36,375lb (16.500kg). Max speed 284mph (455km/h). Range 1,620 miles (2,610km)

CASA C101 Aviojet

Spain

The Spanish Ministerio del Aire signed a contract with CASA in September 1975 for the construction of four prototypes (plus two static test specimens) of a new advanced jet trainer for use by the Ejercito del Aire. The C101 was designed along conventional lines, with a straight wing and a single 3,500lb (1,590kg) st Garrett-AiResearch TFE 731-2 engine. Construction is on modular lines, with space for additional equipment that may be required to meet future training needs. The design also provides for the addition of weapons on six wing pylons and a fuselage centreline hardpoint, up to a total external load of 4,410lb (2,000kg). The first prototype of the C101 flew at Getafe on 27 June 1977, and the first production model flew on 8 November 1979. Deliveries of 60 C101s to the Ejercito del Aire began in March 1980 when the first four entered service with Escuadron 793, with the designation E25. **Data:** Span 34ft 9.5in (10.60m). Length 40ft 2.25in (12.25m). Gross weight (trainer) 10,360lb (4,700kg). Max speed 479mph (771km/h) at 27,000ft (8,230m).

CASA C212 Aviocar   Spain

Design of the C212 was undertaken to provide a locally-produced replacement for the CASA C352L (Ju52/3m) and Douglas C-47 transport aircraft serving with the Spanish Air Force. The Spanish Air Ministry ordered two prototypes in September 1968 and these flew, respectively, on 26 March and 23 October 1971, powered by 755hp AiResearch TPE 331 turboprops. Orders totalled over 200 for seven countries by 1980, including 68 for the Spanish Air Force, 25 for the Portuguese Air Force, five for Ecuador, four for the Royal Jordanian Air Force, 10 for Chile and at least 45 for the armed forces of Indonesia, where an Aviocar assembly line has been opened by Nurtanio. The Spanish Air Force orders include the C212A (T12B) utility transport, C212B (TR12A) photo-survey version, C212AV (T12C) VIP transport and C212E (TE12B) navigation trainer. The 138th production Aviocar, first flown on 30 April 1978, is the prototype C212-10, with an increased gross weight of 16,500lb (7,485kg) and 865hp TPE 331-10-501C engines. **Data** (C212C): Span 62ft 4in (19.00m). Length 49ft 10.5in (15.20m). Gross weight 14,330lb (6,500kg). Max speed 223mph (359km/h). Range 300-1,100 miles (480-1,750km). **Photo:** C212A, Jordan.

Cessna O-1 Bird Dog   USA

One of the first light liaison and reconnaissance aircraft developed for the US Army Field Forces after the end of World War 2, the O-1 (formerly L-19) Bird Dog won a design competition in April 1950. By March 1964, a total of 3,431 had been delivered to the Army under the designations O-1A and O-1E and to the Marine Corps as O-1B (60 built). The Marines also received 25 O-1Cs, a similar but more powerful type with square-cut fin. TO-1A, TO-1D and TO-1E versions were used by the Army as trainers. The USAF used the modified O-1F and O-1G for forward air control duties in Vietnam. The O-1 was also supplied to France (90), Canada, Cambodia, Austria, Brazil, Chile, Indonesia, Italy, Kenya, South Korea, Laos, Lebanon, Norway, Pakistan, the Philippines, Spain (designated U12), Thailand, Turkey and South Vietnam, and was built in Japan by Fuji; it remains in service in several of these countries. **Data** (O-1E): One 213hp Continental O-470-11. Span 36ft 0in (10.9m). Length 25ft 10in (7.89m). Gross weight 2,430lb (1,103kg). Max speed 115mph (184km/h). Range 530 miles (848km). **Photo:** L-19A, JGSDF.

Cessna O-2 (and Summit O2-337) USA

The USAF adopted this version of the 'push and pull' Cessna 337 Super Skymaster late in 1966, to replace the Cessna O-1 in FAC (forward air controller) missions, for which purpose a number of modifications were introduced including four underwing pylons for gun pods, rockets, flares etc. Powered by two 210hp Continental IO-360-C/D engines, the O-2 has dual controls for the pilot and observer, and can carry one passenger. The USAF acquired 346, and 12 were purchased by the Iranian Imperial AF. In addition, the USAF acquired more than 100 O-2Bs, equipped for psychological warfare duties with high-power air-to-ground broadcast systems; these are no longer in service. The

Ecuadorean Air Force and Venezuelan Navy are among military users of the basic Skymaster. In France, Reims Aviation produced the similar F-337 in several military versions, some with STOL modifications and early in 1980 became solely responsible for all Model 337 Skymaster/O-2/FH-337 production. In the USA, the Summit company produces the military Sentry O2-337 conversion of the basic civil Skymaster; examples have been sold to Haiti, Honduras, Nicaragua, Senegal and the Royal Thai Navy. **Data:** Span 38ft 2in (11.63m). Length 29ft 9in (9.07m). Gross weight 5,400lb (2,450kg). Max speed 199mph (320km/h). **Photo:** O-2B.

Cessna U-17 USA

The Cessna 185 Skywagon has been adopted for military duties by several nations and has also been built in quantity under USAF contract for delivery to foreign nations, with the designation U-17. Since 1963 a total of 169 U-17As and 136 U-17Bs, plus some U-17Cs with O-470-L engines, have been delivered. Among the nations which received U-17s under this programme were Bolivia, Costa Rica, South Vietnam and Laos. Skywagons, powered by the 300hp Continental IO-520-D engine, have also been purchased direct from Cessna by the South African Air Force and Peru. The larger Model 207 Turbo-Skywagon has been purchased by the

Indonesian Air Force. **Data:** Span 35ft 10in (10.92m). Length 25ft 9in (7.85m). Gross weight 3,300lb (1,500kg). Max speed 178mph (286km/h). Range 1,075 miles (1,730km). **Photo:** U-17 Greece.

Cessna U-3, Model 310, 402 and 411　　　USA

The U-3A (originally known as the L-27A) is the commercial Cessna 310A (first flown on 3 January 1953) as modified for a USAF design competition for a light twin-engined administrative liaison and cargo aircraft. It won this competition, and an initial contract for 80 was subsequently doubled. The U-3A seats five in a roomy cabin, and can be identified by its unswept fin. It was followed by 36 'all-weather' U-3Bs, based on the commercial 310E with swept fin. At least nine other air forces operate standard Cessna 310s. The French Air Force acquired 12 somewhat similar but larger six/eight-seat Cessna 411s, with 340hp GTSIO-520 turbo-supercharged engines, and 12 Cessna 310s which serve in the

communications role at the CEV bases at Bretigny and Istres. Twelve Cessna 402s were bought by the Royal Malaysian Air Force and the RNZAF has acquired three Model 421s. **Data** (U-3A): Two 240hp Continental O-470M piston-engines. Span 36ft (10.97m). Length 27ft 1in (8.25m). Gross weight 4,600lb (2,086kg). Max speed 232mph (373km/h). Range 850 miles (1,368km). **Photo:** Model 310, France.

Cessna T-41 Mescalero　　　USA

In 1964 the USAF ordered 170 standard Cessna 172 light aircraft as basic trainers, under the designation T-41A; a further 34 followed in 1967, and about half these remain in service for preliminary flight screening of pilot candidates. Eight T-41As were delivered to Ecuador, 20 to Greece, five to Honduras and 20 to Peru. The US Army bought 255 similar T-41Bs, with a 210hp Continental IO-360-D engine. Also similar are the T-41C, of which Cessna delivered 52 to the USAF Academy, and the T-41D, 226 of which were built for MAP supply to various nations including Bolivia, Colombia, Dominican Republic, Ecuador, Indonesia, Laos, The Philippines,

Thailand and Turkey. Other military users of the Cessna 172 include the Malagasy Air Force, the Royal Saudi Air Force and the Irish Army Air Corps, which has eight Reims-built FR172Hs. Other countries use various Cessna lightplanes including the Model 180, with tailwheel undercarriage and 230hp Continental O-470-R engine, and the Model 182 with O-470-R and nose-wheel undercarriage. **Data** (T-41A): One 145hp Continental O-300-C engine. Span 35ft 10in (10.92m). Length 26ft 11in (8.20m). Gross weight 2,300lb (1,043kg). Max speed 138mph (222km/h). Range 720 miles (1,160km). **Photo:** T-41A, Greece.

Convair C-131 (and Canadair CC-109) USA

The USAF procured substantial numbers of the basically-civil Convair Model 240/340/440 series in two groups — as T-29 special purpose trainers and as C-131 transports. None remain in service, but during 1977, the US Coast Guard acquired 22 C-131As ex-USAF, from long term storage, for conversion to HC-131A search-and-rescue aircraft. 17 of these have now entered the USCG inventory, with the original R-2800 piston engines to fill the gap until delivery of HU-25A Guardians. One USN Reserve squadron still flies turboprop-engined C-131Hs. A few Convair-liners still operate with other air forces, while the Canadian Armed Forces has in service seven CC-109 Cosmopolitans, these being Canadair-built versions of the C-440 with Allison T56 engines. **Data** (VC-131H): Span 105ft 4in (32.10m). Length 79ft 2in (24.13m). Gross weight 54,600lb (24,788kg). Cruising speed 342mph (550km/h). Range 1,605 miles (2,582km). **Photo:** C-131H, USNR VR-48.

Convair F-102 Delta Dagger USA

Convair initiated design of the Delta Dagger in 1950, basically by scaling up in size its earlier XF-92A, the world's first jet-powered delta. The first YF-102 flew on 24 October 1953 but when initial trials revealed deficiencies in performance, a YF-102A was built with the first-ever area-ruled ('waisted') fuselage. For service with Air Defense Command, 875 similar F-102As were built, each powered by a 17,200lb (7,808kg) st Pratt & Whitney J57-P-23 or -25 afterburning turbojet and armed with up to four Falcon missiles. They were supplemented by 63 two-seat (side-by-side) F-102A combat trainers. About 60 F-102As and TF-102As were passed on to the Turkish and Hellenic Air Forces; but only a few Delta Daggers remained operational in 1980, in Turkey. In the US 'Pave Deuce' programme, Sperry Flight Systems and Fairchild Aircraft Service Division have produced 63 PQM-102A and 66 PQM-102B unmanned drone conversions of F-102As; first flight was made on 13 August 1974 and first operational use on 25 June 1975. Five QF-102A drones have provision for manned operations. **Data:** (PQM-102B): Span 38ft 1.5in (11.62m). Length 68ft 4.5in (20.81m). Gross weight approx 32,000lb (14,515kg). Max speed Mach 1.2 (792mph; 1,274km/h). Mission endurance, 40-55min. **Photo:** PQM-102A.

Dassault MD-452 Mystère IVA and Super Mystère B-2

France

Altogether, 421 Mystère IVAs were built, all but the first 50 with a 7,716lb (3,500kg) st Hispano-Suiza Verdon 350 turbojet. None remain in first-line service, but a few still fly in Israel. The supersonic Super Mystère B-2, evolved from the Mystère IV series, retired from French service in 1977. Israel, which purchased 24, still had one squadron operational in a fighter-bomber role at the time of the October 1973 war. By that time, the original Atar 101G turbojet fitted to these aircraft had been replaced by a 9,300lb (4,218kg) st Pratt & Whitney J52-P-8A, with lengthened jet pipe, as installed in early Israeli Skyhawks. 12 of these J52-engined Super Mystères were sold to Honduras in 1976/77. **Data** (Super Mystère B-2): Span 34ft 6in (10.51m). Length 46ft 1in (14.04m). Gross weight 22,046lb (10,000kg). Max speed 646mph (1,040km/h) at sea level. Range 600 miles (965km). **Photo:** Super Mystère B-2.

Dassault-Breguet Falcon 10 MER

France

The Falcon 10 was developed by Dassault-Breguet in the late 1960s as a 'baby brother' for the successful Mystère/Falcon 20 business jet. Basically a scaled-down version of that design, it has smaller overall dimensions and less powerful engines; but a more advanced wing bestows on the Falcon 10 a somewhat higher cruising speed. The cabin normally seats four, with a crew of two. The first Falcon 10 flew on 1 December 1970, with General Electric CJ610 engines, followed by a second prototype on 15 October 1971, with 3,230lb (1,466kg) st Garrett-AiResearch TFE 731-2 engines which have been adopted as the production standard. Three Falcon 10s are in service with the French Aéronavale, as systems trainers for the Super Etendard programme and for fleet support and instrument training duties in general; these are known as Falcon 10 MER (*Marine Entratainement Radar*) and are operated by the Section Reacteur de Landivisiau. **Data:** Span 42ft 11in (13.08m). Length 45ft 5in (13.85m). Gross weight 18,740lb (8,500kg). Max speed 568mph (915km/h).

Dassault-Breguet Falcon 20 (Mystère 20) and Guardian

France

Powered in the Falcon 20D and F version by a pair of 4,500lb (2,041kg) st General Electric CF700 turbofans, this biz-jet normally carries a crew of two and eight passengers but several special-duty arrangements of the cabin are possible. As a VIP transport, Falcons of this type are used by several air forces including those of Australia, Belgium, Norway, Egypt, Pakistan and Spain (designated T11). The Canadian Armed Forces bought seven (CC-117s) for communications but three have been converted for the electronic warfare training. French use includes seven VIP transports with the GLAM (a communications unit), one target tug and two (Mystère 20ST) fitted with Mirage IIIE-type nose radar. Libya uses one in the latter configuration and the Spanish Air Force has one for radio calibration (as TM.11) The

French Aèronavale ordered five examples of the Mystère 20H for overwater surveillance duty replacing P-2 Neptunes; this version is powered by 5,538lb (2,512kg) st Garrett ATF 3-6-2C turbofans and carries extra fuel in the rear fuselage. The same engines power the Mystère 20G Guardian, which first flew in prototype form on 28 November 1977. In 1977, the US Coast Guard ordered 41 specially-equipped versions of the Mystere 20G; the first production model flew on 4 August 1978 after assembly in the USA and these were entering service in 1981 as HU-25A Guardians. **Data** (HU-25A): Span 53ft 6in (16.30m). Length 56ft 3in (17.15m). Gross weight 32,000lb (14,515kg). Max cruising speed, 531mph (855km/h). Range 2,590 miles (4,170km). **Photo:** Mystère 20ST.

Dassault-Breguet Falcon 50 (Mystère 50)

France

Development of the Mystère/Falcon 50 began in 1974 to provide a biz-jet of similar size to the Mystère/Falcon 20 but of greater range and improved cruising performance. This was achieved by introducing a new wing and extending the fuselage to incorporate extra fuel tankage and a third engine (required to match the higher operating weights). The first of two prototypes flew on 7 November 1976, and the first full production aircraft (No 4) with 3,700lb (1,678kg) st Garrett AiResearch

TFE731-3 turbofans, flew on 2 March 1979. Next aircraft off the line, the Mystère 50 No 5, was delivered later in 1979 to the Groupes de Liaisons Aériennes Militaires of the French Air Force and was assigned for priority use by the President of the Republic. It bears the individual name *Rambouillet*. **Data:** Span 61ft 10.5in (18.86m). Length 60ft 0.5in (18.30m). Gross weight 37,478lb (17,000kg). Max cruising speed 540mph (870km/h). Range, over 4,000 miles (6,500km).

Dassault-Breguet Super Mirage 4000   France

The Super Mirage 4000 was developed (at first as the Super Mirage Delta) as a company-funded private venture after the Armée de l'Air abandoned its Avion de Combat Futur (ACF) programme for a twin-engined aircraft and adopted the Mirage 2000 instead. The Super Mirage 4000 is a relatively large aircraft with a typical Dassault delta wing layout, featuring canard surfaces on the intakes, and is powered by two 18,704lb (8,500kg) st SNECMA M53-2 turbofans. The sole prototype flew on 9 March 1979 and further development depended upon the financial backing of one or more customers.

Data: Span 39ft 4.5in (12.0m). Length 61ft 4.25in (18.70m). Gross weight about 50,000lb (23,000kg). Max speed at least Mach 2.2.

De Havilland DHC-1 Chipmunk   Canada/UK

First original design by de Havilland Canada, the Chipmunk was built in quantity on both sides of the Atlantic, DHC producing a total of 218 and 1,014 being built by de Havilland in the UK. Most of those operated by the RAF (as Chipmunk T Mk 10) have been replaced by Bulldogs but some remain in use in Air Experience Flights, for the benefit of the ATC, and have undergone a programme to give them a further 10-year life. Chipmunks were supplied to about a dozen overseas air forces and are still used in the training role by a few of them, including those of Burma, Sri Lanka and Thailand, and the Irish Air Corps. **Data** (T Mk 10): One 145hp Gipsy Major 8 piston-engine. Span 34ft 4in (10.46m). Length 25ft 5in (7.48m). Gross weight 2,014lb (915kg). Max speed 138mph (222km/h). Range 280 miles (450km). **Photo:** T Mk 10, RAF.

De Havilland DHC-3 Otter and UH-1   Canada

First flown on 12 December 1951, the 11-seat Otter is 'big brother' to the Beaver. A total of 460 were built for military and commercial use and about 11 air forces have flown the type. The 69 Canadian Armed Forces Otters (CSR-123) were supplied primarily for Arctic search and rescue, paratroop dropping and photographic duties and continue in service with units of the Air Reserve Group. The US Army purchased a trial batch of six YU-1s in 1955 and followed this order with another for 84 U-1As which were used as supply aircraft in forward areas; they are no longer in service. U-1Bs were US Navy purchases for use in the Antarctic. All Otters can operate on wheels, floats or skis. **Data:** One 600hp R-1340 piston-engine. Span 58ft (17.69m). Length 41ft 10in (12.80m). Gross weight 8,000lb (3,629kg). Max speed 160mph (257km/h). Range 945 miles (1,520km). **Photo:** CSR-123.

De Havilland DHC-6 Twin Otter and UV-18   Canada

The original 19-passenger DHC-6 made its first flight on 20 May 1965. Both the Series 100 and Series 200 have 579eshp Pratt & Whitney PT6A-20 turbo-props, while the Series 300 has 652eshp PT6A-27 engines, increased gross weight and higher performance. Over 700 Twin Otters have been delivered to date, mostly for service with airlines and as business aircraft. Military orders have come from the Argentine Air Force (5) and Army (3); Canadian Forces (9, designated CC-138); Chilean Air Force (11); Ecuadorean Air Force (3); Jamaica Defence Force (1); Peruvian Air Force (12, including eight floatplanes); Royal Norwegian Air Force (5); Uganda Police Air Wing (1); Paraguayan Air Force (1) and Panamanian Air Force (1). The US Army has acquired four as UV-18As for service in Alaska, and the USAF bought two UV-18Bs in 1977 to be used at the Air Academy. **Data:** Span 65ft 0in (19.81m). Length 51ft 9in (15.77m). Gross weight 12,500lb (5,670kg). Max speed 210mph (338km/h). Range 794 miles (1,277km). **Photo:** Twin Otter, Norway

De Havilland Canada Dash-7 (and Ranger)   Canada

Two examples of the Dash-7 STOL airliner were purchased by the Canadian Armed Forces in 1979, for service in support of the Canadian forces based in Federal Germany. Powered by four 1,120shp Pratt & Whitney PT6A-50 turboprops each, the Dash-7s are designated CC-132 by the CAF and were delivered in mid-1979 to No 412 Squadron. Replacing CC-109 Cosmopolitans, they have large freight-loading doors and rapid-change interiors for conversion between all-passenger and all-cargo configuration. The Canadian Coast Guard has ordered two of the DHC-7R Ranger variants, which have extra fuel capacity, special nose-mounted radar and other search and observation facilities. **Data:** Span 93ft 0in (28.35m). Length 80ft 7.75in (24.58m). Gross weight 44,000lb (19,958kg). Max cruising speed 261mph (420km/h). Range 840 miles (1,352km).

De Havilland (Hawker Siddeley)   UK
DH104 Dove, Devon
and Sea Devon, and Sea Heron C Mk 1

The Dove was adopted for service with the RAF in 1948, as the Devon C Mk 1. A change of designation to C Mk 2 indicated replacement of the original 380hp Gipsy Queen 70-4 or -71 engines with Gipsy Queen 175s; introduction of an enlarged Heron-type canopy was indicated by the designation C Mk 2/2. The Devon's primary role was that of staff transport, most of the 44 examples acquired having been allocated for the personal use of officers commanding Groups and Commands. 14 remained in RAF service in 1980 with No 207 Communications Squadron. Thirteen similar aircraft were acquired by the Royal Navy for communications duties, as Sea Devon C Mk 20s. Eight remained in use until early 1981, together with four Sea Heron C Mk 1s, with four Gipsy Queen engines and seats for 14-17 passengers. A few other air forces still use Doves in the communications and training rôle. **Data:** Span 57ft (17.40m). Length 39ft 3in (11.96m). Gross weight 8,950lb (4,060kg). Max speed 230mph (370km/h). Range 880 miles (1,415km). **Photo:** Devon C Mk 2.

De Havilland Vampire
UK

Having flown for the first time on 20 September 1943, the Vampire is one of the oldest jet fighters still in service. The Dominican Republic has a fighter-bomber squadron of F Mk 1s and FB Mk 50s, acquired from Sweden. Zimbabwe has one squadron of FB Mk 9s. Switzerland uses some FB Mk 6s as weapons trainers and in 1980 these were receiving modified noses containing UHF radio, removed from Venoms as they were retired from Swiss service. Also in service is the two-seat training variant of the Vampire, first flown in private-venture prototype form on 15 November 1950. The prototype was followed by two examples for evaluation by the Royal Navy, and then by production deliveries for the RAF, under the designation T Mk 11. Trainers were exported to about 20 countries and are still used by several, including Burma, Chile, Venezuela and Switzerland. **Data** (T Mk 11): Span 38ft 0in (11.58m). Length 34ft 6.5in (10.51m). Gross weight 11,150lb (5,060kg). Max speed 549mph (885km/h). Range 853 miles (1,370km). **Photo:** FB Mk 6, Switzerland.

De Havilland Venom
UK

The DH112 Venom prototype first flew on 2 September 1949 as a direct modification of the Vampire with thinner, slightly sweptback wings and tip-tanks. Production deliveries of the Venom FB Mk 1 to the RAF began in 1951 and the type was used to equip squadrons of the 2nd TAF in Germany and others in the Middle and Far East. Re-equipment of these squadrons with the Venom FB Mk 4, with powered ailerons, redesigned tail unit and other changes, began in the mid-1950s. The last air force to use the Venom operationally is that of Switzerland, where 150 Mk 1 and 100 Mk 4 Venoms were produced locally. By 1980, most had been retired; those that remain have additional UHF equipment in modified noses. **Data** (FB Mk 4): Powered by one 4,850lb (2,200kg) st de Havilland Ghost 103 turbojet. Span 41ft 8in (12.70m). Length 31ft 10in (9.70m). Gross weight 15,400lb (6,985kg). Max speed 640mph (1,030km/h). Range over 1,000 miles (1,610km) with external fuel. **Photo:** FB Mk 4, Switzerland.

Dornier Do27

Germany

Until aircraft manufacture was again permitted in Germany, many German designers worked abroad. Thus, the prototype of this design, designated Do25 and powered by a 150hp ENMA Tigre G-IVB engine, was built in Spain to meet a Spanish Air Force requirement. It flew on 25 June 1954, and was followed by the prototype Do27 with 275hp Lycoming GO-480 engine on 27 June 1955. Production of the latter was transferred to Germany, where the first of 428 Do27As ordered for the German Air Force and Army flew on 17 October

1956. Others were acquired by about ten air forces and are still used by a few, including that of Spain, where 50 were built as CASA 127s for the Spanish Air Force (with the designation U9). The basic Do27A is a five-seater, convertible for freighting or casualty evacuation. **Data** (Do27A): Span 39ft 4.5in (12.0m). Length 31ft 6in (9.6m). Gross weight 4,070lb (1,850kg). Max speed 141mph (227km/h). Range 685 miles (1,100km). **Photo:** Do27B, Germany.

Dornier Do28D Skyservant

Germany

The 14/15-seat Skyservant is a successor to the STOL Do28, of which 120 were built. A few Do28As serve in military guise for communications duties (in Spain, designated U14). The Do28D represented a completely new design, with much increased capacity, and the prototype flew on 23 February 1966. After seven Do28Ds had been built, production switched to the Do28D-1/2 with a small increase in wing span and higher gross weight. The largest single order for the Do28D-2 was from the German Armed Forces, comprising 20 for the Navy and 101 for the Luftwaffe. Two were bought by the Turkish Army for its Flying Training School and other

military users include the Zambian, Israeli, Malawi, Ethiopian, Nigerian, and Kenyan Air Forces. The Skyservant is powered by two 380hp Lycoming IGSO-540 engines but during 1980 those in service with the Luftwaffe were being converted to Do28D-7 standard with turbosupercharged TIGO-540 engines. A maritime surveillance version with search radar under the forward fuselage has also been developed. **Data:** Span 51ft 0.25in (15.55m). Length 37ft 5.25in (11.41m). Gross weight 8,470lb (3,842kg). Max cruising speed 170mph (273km/h). Range 1,255 miles (2,020km). **Photo:** Do28D-2, Malawi.

159

Douglas C-47 and C-117 Skytrain and Dakota   USA

C-47 variants remain in service with several air forces throughout the world, sometimes under the British name Dakota, although numbers inevitably are dwindling with the passage of time. The C-47 Skytrain was the basic production model for the USAF, supplemented by the externally-similar C-117A, B and C staff transports. The C-117D was an improved model for the US Navy with new wings and tail and 1,535hp Wright R-1820 engines. Heavily-armed gunship versions of the type, designated AC-47D 'Spooky', operated in Vietnam with great effectiveness; some AC-47s were later transferred to Cambodia. The few C-47s remaining in Canada are now used by the Air Reserve Group and carry the designation CC-129. The largest single user in 1980 was believed to be the South African Air Force, with 28. **Data** (C-47): Two 1,200hp Pratt & Whitney R-1830-90C piston engines. Span 95ft (28.95m). Length 64ft 5.5in (19.64m). Gross weight 26,000lb (11,793kg). Max speed 229mph (369km/h). Range 1,500 miles (2,414km). **Photo:** CC-129.

Douglas A-3 Skywarrior   USA

The Skywarrior was the largest aircraft that had been produced for carrier operations when the prototype first flew on 28 October 1952, designated XA3D-1. All Skywarriors were built with A3D designations, changed to A-3 in 1962. The first production three-seat A-3A flew on 16 September 1953, and deliveries to the Navy began in March 1956. The A-3B which began to reach the fleet in 1957, had more powerful engines and provision for flight refuelling; 164 were built. The EA-3B for electronic countermeasures had a crew compartment in the bomb-bay, seating four, and first flew on 10 December 1958; 24 were built. The US Navy was sole user of the Skywarrior and by 1980 only a few remained in service in the EKA-3B tanker aircraft/ countermeasures or strike (TACOS) version, 30 examples of which were converted from A-3Bs. **Data** (A-3B): Two 10,500lb (4,763kg) st Pratt & Whitney J57-P-10 turbojets. Span 72ft 6in (22.07m). Length 76ft 4in (23.27m). Gross weight 73,000lb (33,112kg). Max speed 610mph (982km/h) at 10,000ft (3,050m). Range over 2,900 miles (4,667km). **Photo:** EA-3B.

Douglas C-118 Liftmaster and DC-4/DC-6/DC-7 variants   USA

The USAF acquired a total of 101 DC-6Cs for service with MATS, under the designation C-118A, following development under military contracts of the prototype DC-6. Designated XC-112A, this prototype first flew on 15 February 1946, and was a development of the C-54. A further 65 similar aircraft were purchased by the US Navy and contributed to MATS operations — 61 as R6D-1s and four as R6D-1Zs with executive interiors. These were subsequently redesignated C-118B and VC-118B respectively, and were assigned to Reserve units (to replace C-54s), with which a few were still being flown in 1978. Commercial DC-6/DC-7 variants passed into military service elsewhere, such as six DC-6A/BFs used for long range logistic support by the Portuguese Air Force, and five in service with the Paraguayan Air Force. A handful of the earlier and smaller C-54 (DC-4) transports also remain in service, particularly with the South African Air Force, which has five. **Data** (C-118): Span 117ft 6in (35.81m). Length 105ft 7in (32.18m). Gross weight 102,000lb (46,266kg). Max speed 360mph (579km/h). Range 3,860 miles (6,212km). **Photo:** C-118B, US Navy.

EKW C-3605   Switzerland

This is the final variant in a family of general-purpose monoplanes originated by the Swiss factory of Eidgenössiches Konstruktionswerkstätte (EKW), in 1939, when the C-3601 was flown for the first time. The Swiss Air Force took delivery, between 1942 and 1945, of 150 C-3603s and ten C-3604s as reconnaissance bombers. After they had been replaced by newer types, 35 C-3603s remained in service as target tugs and two as trainers, powered by the Hispano HS12Y-51 engine. On 19 August 1968, EKW flew the C-3605, a converted C-3603 with a 1,150shp Avco Lycoming T5307A turboprop engine. The Swiss Air Force ordered conversion of 23 of the surviving C-3603s to this standard for continued use as target tugs and these began to enter service in 1972. **Data:** Span 45ft 1in (13.74m). Length 39ft 5.75in (12.03m). Gross weight 8,185lb (3,710kg). Max speed 268mph (432km/h). Range 610 miles (970km).

EMBRAER EMB-121 Xingu

Brazil

Development of the Xingu was started by EMBRAER in 1974 as one of several projected derivatives of the EMB-110 Bandeirante, and a prototype flew on 10 October 1976. The original idea was to 'shrink' the Bandeirante to produce a business transport with a smaller fuselage, but as finally produced little of the Bandeirante remained except the basic wing structure (of reduced span) and the installation of the 680shp PT6A-28 turboprops. The fuselage is pressurised, and in the Xingu 2, for introduction in 1981, is stretched by 33in (84cm) to improve the cabin space. The Xingu 2 also features uprated PT6A-42 engines. The first production Xingu flew on 20 May 1977 and in 1978 five of the early production aircraft were delivered to the Grupo de Transporte Especial of the Brazilian Air Force, with the designation VU-9. In 1980, France placed contracts with EMBRAER for 25 Xingu to replace the Flamants used as trainers by the Armée de l'Air and 16 to replace DC-3s used by Aéronavale. **Data:** Span 47ft 5in (14.45m). Length 40ft 2.25in (12.25m). Gross weight 12,500lb (5,670kg). Max cruising speed 280mph (450km/h). Range 1,035 miles (1,666km).

EMBRAER EMB-312 (T-27)

Brazil

First flown on 16 August 1980, the EMB-312 was developed by EMBRAER to meet Brazilian Air Force needs for a fully aerobatic basic trainer to replace ageing Cessna T-37s in service at the Air Force Academy. Powered by a 750shp Pratt & Whitney PT6A-25C turboprop, the EMB-312 has been designated T-27 by the Brazilian Air Force, the two prototypes being YT-27s. Production of an initial batch was expected to allow the T-27 to enter service at the Academy in 1982/83 and subsequently the type was likely to remain in production also to succeed the Neiva T-25 Universal. Four wing strong points allow the T-27 to be used for weapons training and light attack duties, carrying up to 1,235lb (560kg) of practice bombs, rocket pods or flush-fitting underwing gun pods each containing a 7.62mm machine gun and 350 rounds. **Data:** 36ft 6.5in (11.14m). Length 32ft 4.5in (9.86m). Gross weight 180lb (2,350kg). Max speed 247kts (457km/h) at 13,100ft (3,993m). Range, up to 1,140nm (2,112km).

Fairchild C-119 Flying Boxcar　　　　USA

A total of 1,051 Flying Boxcars was built for the USAF and for countries associated with the Mutual Aid Programme. By 1980 the principal remaining users of the Flying Boxcar were the Chinese Nationalist Air Force, with about 40, the Ethiopian Air Force, with about 10 C-119Ks, the Italian Air Force, with about 20 C-119G/Js and the Indian Air Force with about 40 C-119Gs in three squadrons (Nos 12, 19 and 48). During 1963-64, 26 of the Indian Air Force machines were modified to Steward-Davis Jet Packet standard, by having a Westinghouse J34-WE-36 auxiliary turbojet mounted above the fuselage. More powerful Orpheus turbojets have since replaced the J34s. **Data** (C-119K): Two 3,700hp Wright R-3350-99 TC18EA2 piston engines, plus two 2,850lb (1,293kg) st General Electric J85-GE-17 turbojets. Span 109ft 3in (33.30m). Length 86ft 6in (26.36m). Gross weight 77,000lb (34,925kg). Max speed 243mph (391km/h) at 10,000ft (3,050m). Range 990 miles (1,595km) with max payload. **Photo:** C-119, China.

Fairchild C-123 Provider　　　　USA

This tactical assault transport was derived from a cargo glider designed in 1949 by Chase Aircraft. Five pre-production C-123Bs were built for Chase at Willow Run by the Kaiser-Frazer Corporation in 1953, after which the production contract was transferred to Fairchild. As the C-123B Provider, Fairchild flew the first of 300 on 1 September 1954. First flown on 30 July 1962, the YC-123H added CJ610 podded turbojets under each wing and was tested in South Vietnam in the counter-insurgency role. A modification programme was put in hand for the conversion of 183 aircraft to similar standard with J85 engines in the pods; the first of these, designated C-123K, flew on 27 May 1966. Many of the USAF Providers used in Vietnam were transferred to the VNAF, but were withdrawn in the closing stages of the war, leaving only a few to be captured by the Vietnamese People's Air Force. Other users of the type included the Cambodian Air Force, but these aircraft also were flown out to Thailand, which had about 40 in service in 1980. The Chinese Nationalist Air Force has about 10 and four US Air Force Reserve squadrons still fly C-123Ks in 1981. **Data:** Two 2,300hp Pratt & Whitney R-2800-99W piston-engines and two 2,850lb (1,293kg) st General Electric J85-GE-17 turbojets. Span 110ft 0in (33.53m). Length 76ft 3in (23.92m). Gross weight 60,000lb (27,215kg). Max speed 228mph (367km/h) at 10,000ft (3,050m). Normal range 1,035 miles (1,666km) with 15,000lb (6,800kg) payload. **Photo:** C-123B, Thailand.

FFA AS202 Bravo

Switzerland

This side-by-side lightplane and primary trainer was developed for joint production in Switzerland and Italy, by Flug-Fahrzeugwerke and Siai-Marchetti, but all production has been handled by FFA in Switzerland, with that company's subsidiary Repair AG responsible for marketing. The prototype AS202/15 flew on 7 March 1969, with a 150hp Lycoming O-320-E2A; the later AS202/18A has a 180hp Lycoming AEIO-360-B1F. More than 150 had been built by mid-1980, almost all for export. The principal users include the air forces of Iraq, Indonesia and Morocco, and government training schools in Uganda and Oman. **Data** (AS202/18A): Span 31ft 11.75in (9.75m). Length 24ft 7.25in (7.50m). Gross weight 2,315lb (1,050kg). Max cruising speed 141mph (227km/h). Range 600 miles (965km). **Photo:** AS202/18A, Oman.

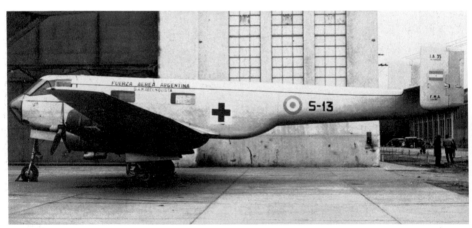

FMA IA35 Huanquero

Argentina

The IA35 Huanquero (first flown 21 September 1953) was built in four versions for the Argentine Air Force. The first production machine flew on 29 March 1957; of the total of 47 delivered about 35 remain in service. The IA35 Type 1A is an advanced instrument flying and navigation trainer, carrying two pilots, radio operator, instructor and four pupils. Type III is an ambulance version with accommodation for a crew of three, four patients and attendant. Type IV is a photographic version serving with the 1 Escuadron Fotografico. Each of these three models is powered by two 620hp IA19R El Indio engines. Fourth version, being replaced by the IA58 Pucara, is the Type IB used by the II Escuadron de Exploration y Ataque, powered by 750hp IA19R engines and armed with two 0.50in machine guns, plus underwing racks for 440lb of bombs or rockets. **Data:** (Type IA): Span 64ft 3in (19.60m). Length 45ft 10in (13.98m). Gross weight 12,540lb (5,700kg). Max speed 225mph (362km/h). Range 975 miles (1,570km).

FMA IA50 GII
Argentina

In its original Guarani Mk I form, this design utilised many components of the Huanquero, including the twin-fin tail unit. The IA50 GII introduced many changes, including a single swept fin and rudder, de-icing equipment, a shorter rear fuselage and more powerful (930hp) Turboméca Bastan VI-A turboprops. The first of two prototypes flew on 23 April 1963, followed by one pre-production model and two series of 18 and 15 production aircraft. The first batch comprised 14 troop transports, a VIP transport and two survey aircraft for service with the Argentine Air Force and one Navy staff transport. One example was fitted with skis and another furnished as a Presidential transport. **Data:** Span 64ft 3.25in (19.59m). Length 50ft 2.5in (15.30m). Gross weight 16,200lb (7,350kg). Max speed 310mph (500km/h). Max range 1,600 miles (2,575km).

Fokker-VFW F28
Netherlands

First military order for an F28 of the basic Mk 1000 series, announced in 1970, came from the Argentine Air Force, for use as a Presidential aircraft. Another was acquired by the Dutch Royal Flight; one was delivered for the President of Colombia, another for VIP use by the Government of Nigeria and similar aircraft to the Congo Republic, Peru and Togo. The Malaysian government bought two and the Argentine Air Force acquired five Mk 1000C freighters for operation by LADE. Another Mk 1000C and a Mk 1000 went to Ivory Coast. The F28 prototype made its first flight on 9 May 1967 and deliveries for commercial use began on 24 February 1969. Most aircraft sold for military or government VIP use have been to Mk 1000/1000C standard, with 9,850lb (4,468kg) st Rolls-Royce RB183-2 Spey Mk 555-15 engines. Current commercial aircraft are the Mk 3000 and Mk 4000, with improved engines and greater wing span. **Data** (Mk 1000): Span 77ft 4.25in (23.58m). Length 89ft 10.75in (27.40m). Gross weight 65,000lb (29,485kg). Max cruising speed 528mph (849km/h) at 21,000ft (6,400m). Range 956 miles (1,538km). **Photo:** Mk 1000, Nigeria.

Fuji LM-1/LM-2 Nikko and KM-2 (T-3)   Japan

The four-seat LM-1 Nikko liaison aircraft was developed from the Beech T-34 Mentor by Fuji, who built the latter under licence in Japan. The first Nikko, with 225hp Continental O-470-13A engine, flew on 6 June 1955, and 27 were delivered subsequently to the Japan Ground Self-Defence Force. Some were converted to LM-2 standard, with more powerful engine and optional fifth seat. Generally similar in appearance are KM-2 two/four-seat primary trainers of the Maritime Self-Defence Force; but these have a 340hp Lycoming IGSO-480-A1C6 engine. The KM-2B trainer is similar, but with only two seats in tandem like the original Mentor; the prototype flew on 26 September 1974 and in 1975 the KM-2B was selected by the JASDF as a replacement for the Mentor in the primary training role, designated T-3. The first of six pre-production models flew on 17 January 1978 and the first production model on 7 March 1978; 50 have been ordered. **Data** (KM-2): Span 32ft 10in (10.0m). Length 26ft 0.75in (7.94m). Gross weight 3,860lb (1,750kg). Max speed 230mph (370km/h). Range 570 miles (915km). **Photo:** KM-2.

Fuji T1   Japan

Designed to replace the T-6 piston-engined trainers of the JASDF, the prototype of this tandem two-seat intermediate jet trainer was ordered in 1956 and flew on 19 January 1958. The first 40 production machines each had a 4,000lb (1,814kg) st Bristol Siddeley Orpheus 805 turbojet and bear the company designation T1F2 (JASDF designation T1A). They were followed by 20 T1F1s (T1B) with 2,645lb (1,200kg) st Ishikawajima-Harima J3-IHI-3, the prototype of this version making its first flight on 17 May 1960. Both versions have provision for one 0.50in machine gun and 1,500lb (680kg) of underwing bombs, rockets or missiles instead of drop tanks. **Data** (T1A): Span 34ft 5in (10.50m). Length 39ft 9in (12.12m). Gross weight 11,000lb (5,000kg). Max speed 575mph (925km/h). Range 1,210 miles (1,950km). **Photo:** T1B.

Gates Learjet   USA

The world's most successful biz-jet, with over 1,000 sold by mid-1980, the Learjet also serves in small numbers in military or quasi military rôles. A few examples operate as VIP and Presidential transports, differing little from the commercial versions other than in their external livery and markings, as for example the Learjet 24D illustrated in service with the Mexican Navy. More extensively modified are two Model 25Bs used by the Peruvian Air Force for aerial surveys, with cameras in a special housing under the forward fuselage; the Bolivian Air Force has a similar Model 25B. Swedair, in Sweden, has two (civil-registered) Model 24s used as high-speed target tugs; in 1980 Gates Learjet was marketing an alternative Model 35 target tug, three examples of which were ordered by Finland, and also the Sea Patrol version of the Learjet 35A, with Litton radar in a ventral radome and wing strong points to carry flares, smoke markers, sonobuoys etc. **Data** (Model 24D): Span 35ft 7in (10.84m). Length 43ft 3in (13.18m). Gross weight 13,500lb (6,124kg). Max speed 545mph (877km/h). Range 1,848 miles (2,974km). **Photo:** Learjet 24D, Mexico.

Grumman Ag-cat   USA

Perhaps the most improbable type of aircraft operating in military service in 1980 was the Ag-cat agricultural biplane, about six examples of which are operated by the Greek Air Force in fulfilment of its social responsibilities (together with a number of helicopters). Originally developed by the Grumman company and first flown on 27 May 1957, the Ag-Cat was built by Schweizer and later marketed by Grumman American — from which company the Greek examples were procured — before the latter company was acquired by Gulfstream American. The basic Ag-Cat is powered by a 450hp Pratt & Whitney R-985 radial engine; alternatives are the 525hp Continental R-975 and the 600hp P & W R-1340. **Data:** Span 42ft 3in (12.88m). Length 25ft 11in (7.90m). Gross weight 6,075lb (2,755kg). Max cruising speed 117mph (188km/h). Range 249 miles (401km).

Grumman C-2A Greyhound

USA

Grumman developed the C-2A under US Navy contract as a carrier on-board delivery (COD) aircraft, taking the E-2A Hawkeye as the basis for the design. The wing, main landing gear, flight deck and tail unit are basically the same as the equivalent components of the E-2A, the fuselage being the obvious new feature. This was designed to seat up to 39 passengers in a high-density layout, and can also accommodate a wide variety of stores and supplies used on an aircraft carrier including spare jet engines, small vehicles and standard US freight pallets. Loading doors and a ramp are incorporated in the rear fuselage. The initial US Navy order was for three C-2A airframes, including one for static testing. The first prototype flew on 18 November 1964, and the Navy began accepting production C-2As in 1966. Manufacture of the production batch of 17 ended in 1968. **Data:** Two 4,050shp Allison T56-A-8A or 8B turboprops. Span 80ft 7in (24.56m). Length 56ft 8in (17.27m). Gross weight 54,830lb (24,870kg). Max speed 352mph (567km/h). Range 1,650 miles (2,660km) at 297mph (478km/h) at 27,300ft (8,320m).

Grumman HU-16 Albatross

USA

The XJR2F-1 Albatross prototype, built for the US Navy as a utility transport amphibian, first flew on 24 October 1947. The USAF ordered a total of 305, as SA-16As, for search and rescue. Most of these were converted to SA-16Bs with increased span and higher weights. Designations were changed to HU-16A and HU-16B respectively in 1962. The US Navy purchased aircraft similar to the SA-16As as UF-1s, and put in hand a similar conversion programme, to produce UF-2s; these became HU-16C and HU-16D respectively, while the Coast Guard version became HU-16E. Nations still using the type in 1980 include Argentina, Brazil, Chile, Indonesia, Mexico, Nationalist China, Peru, the Philippines, Spain and Venezuela. A special model for anti-submarine duties was produced in 1961, with a large nose radome, retractable MAD in the rear fuselage, an ECM radome on the wing, an underwing searchlight and provision for carrying depth charges. In 1980, Spain was operating nine of these ASW aircraft and Greece had eight, acquired in 1969 from Norway. The Albatross has two 1,425hp Wright R-1820-76A engines. **Data:** Span 96ft 8in (29.46m). Length 62ft 10in (19.18m). Gross weight 37,500lb (17,010kg). Max speed 236mph (379km/h) at sea level. **Photo:** HU-16A, Philippines.

Grumman TC-4C Academe (and Gulfstream I) USA

A single example of the Grumman Gulfstream executive transport was purchased for use by the US Coast Guard in 1963 with the designation VC-4A; it serves as a VIP transport. Plans to buy a training variant for use by the USN as TC-4B were shelved; but in December 1966 the Navy ordered nine TC-4Cs as flying classrooms for training bombardier/navigators for service in the A-6 Intruder. For this purpose a large radome was incorporated in the nose and the cabin was modified to house a complete A-6 avionics system. Powered by two 2,185ehp Rolls-Royce Dart 529-8X turboprops, the TC-4C made its first flight on 14 June 1967 and these aircraft have been progressively updated to incorporate TRAM sensors. A single Gulfstream I is used by the Greek Air Force as a VIP transport. **Data:** Span 78ft 6in (23.92m). Length 67ft 11in (20.70m). Gross weight 36,000lb (16,330kg). Max cruising speed 348mph (560km/h). **Photo:** Gulfstream I, Greece.

Grumman Gulfstream II and III (VC-11A) USA

Developed as a jet-powered derivative of the Gulfstream I, with a similar fuselage but a new wing and tail unit, the Gulfstream II first flew on 2 October 1966, as a product of Grumman Aircraft. It serves almost exclusively in the civil role but a single example was acquired by the US Coast Guard as the VC-11A, for use as a VIP transport. Gulfstream IIs are also used as VIP and governmental transports in Gabon, Ivory Coast and Morocco. After Gulfstream American Corp acquired production rights in the Gulfstream II, a switch was made to Gulfstream III, featuring a slightly lengthened fuselage, increased fuel capacity and winglets at the wing tips. The prototype Gulfstream III, powered by 11,400lb (5,170kg) st Rolls-Royce Spey 511-8 turbofans, first flew on 2 December 1979 and early production deliveries in 1981 were to include three for the Royal Danish Air Force, equipped for fishery protection, search and rescue and staff transport duties. **Data:** (G-III): Span 77ft 10in (23.72m). Length 82ft 11in (25.27m). Gross weight 68,200lb (30.935kg). Cruising speed 518mph (824km/h). Range 4,330 miles (6,968km). **Photo:** VC-IIA.

HAL HAOP-27 Krishak Mk 2   India

This two/three-seat air observation post aircraft was developed by Hindustan from its two-seat Pushpak light aircraft and utilises the same basic fabric-covered metal wing. The first of two prototypes flew in November 1959, with a 190hp Continental engine. Production Krishaks, of which 68 were supplied to the Indian Army, have 225hp Continental O-470-J engines. Dual controls are standard and the cabin can be adapted to carry a stretcher for air ambulance duties. **Data:** Span 37ft 6in (11.43m).

Length 27ft 7in (8.41m). Gross weight 2,800lb (1,270kg). Max speed 130mph (209km/h). Max range 500 miles (805km).

HAL HJT-16 Kiran   India

This side-by-side two-seat jet basic trainer was designed to replace the Indian Air Force's Vampires. Detailed design work began in 1961, under the leadership of Dr V. M. Ghatage, but the need to give priority to the HF-24 fighter delayed the first flight of the prototype Kiran until 4 September 1964. A second prototype followed and deliveries of the initial series of 24 pre-production aircraft began in March 1968. From the 119th aircraft, deliveries were of the Kiran Mk 1A variant, with two underwing hardpoints for weapons or drop-tanks. Standard power plant of the Kiran Mk 1/1A is the 2,500lb (1,135kg) st Rolls-Royce Viper 11 turbojet. On 30 July 1976, Hindustan flew the prototype of the Kiran II with a derated Orpheus 701 engine, built-in gun armament, updated avionics and four hardpoints on the wings. Production of the Kiran was ending in 1981 with nearly 200 built. **Data:** (Kiran Mk I): Span 35ft 1.25in (10.70m). Length 34ft 9in (10.60m). Gross weight 9.039lb (4,100kg). Max speed 432mph (695km/h). Endurance 1hr 45min on internal fuel. **Photo:** Kiran Mk1

HAL HPT-32

India

Design of a new fully-aerobatic basic trainer for use by the Indian Air Force as a replacement for the HT-2 was launched by Hindustan Aeronautics in 1975 and a conventional low-wing piston-engined monoplane was evolved. The first of two prototypes of the HPT-32 flew on 6 January 1977, at Bangalore and upon conclusion of flight trials, production was authorised with deliveries to the Indian Air Force expected to begin in 1981/82. With side-by-side seating for pupil and instructor, the HPT-32 has provision for a third seat in the rear of the cockpit and is designed to be used for a wide range of ab initio training, including instrument, navigation, night flying and formation flying, and also for armed patrol, observation, weapon training, glider towing and target towing. It is powered by a 260hp Lycoming AEIO-540-D4B5 flat-six engine. **Data:** Span 31ft 2in (9.50m). Length 25ft 4in (7.72m). Gross weight 3,490lb (1,583kg). Max speed 145mph (233km/h). Range 745 miles (1,199km).

HAL HT-2

India

India's first domestically-designed aeroplane, the HT-2 was a product of the Hindustan Aeronautics factory at Bangalore. The first HT-2, a conventional tandem-seat basic trainer, flew on 13 August 1951, with a de Havilland Gipsy Major 10 engine. The second prototype, flown on 19 February 1952, had a 155hp Blackburn Cirrus Major III engine and production HT-2s for the Indian Air Force and Navy were to this standard. About 70 were in service in 1980, for replacement by HPT-32s by the mid-1980s. **Data:** 35ft 2in (10.72m). Length 24ft 8.5in (7.53m). Gross weight 2,240lb (1,016kg). Max speed 130mph (209km/h). Range 350 miles (563km)

Hawker Siddeley (BAe) Trident UK

Although the three-engined Trident was conceived solely for airline use and all 117 examples built between 1962 and 1978 were sold to civil operators, about half of the 39 acquired by the Chinese airline CAAC are believed to have been transferred to the Chinese Air Force to serve as personnel and VIP transports. CAAC originally acquired from British production 33 Trident 2Es and a pair of larger Super 3Bs; in addition, four Trident 1Es were acquired from Pakistan International Airlines. Those used in Chinese Air Force markings are believed to be only Srs 2Es. The Trident is powered by three 11,900lb (5,425kg) st Rolls-Royce Spey 512 turbofans. **Data:** Span 98ft 0in (29.87m). Length 114ft 9in (34.97m). Gross weight 144,000lb (65,315kg). Cruising speed 596mph (959km/h) at 30,000ft (9,150m). Range with max fuel 2,500 miles (4,025km).

Hispano HA-200 Saeta and HA-220 Super Saeta Spain

The HA-200 serves with the Spanish Air Force as the E-14 two-seat advanced flying and AE10A armament trainer. The first prototype flew on 12 August 1955, followed by five pre-production models and 30 HA-200s (first flight 11 October 1962) with 880lb (400kg) st Turboméca Marboré IIA turbojets and armament of two 7.7mm machine guns and underwing rockets. Also in service, but allocated to a counter-insurgency squadron, are HA-200Ds (AE10Bs), with modernised systems; of 55 built, 40 have the heavier armament specified for the HA-200E which was to be powered by 1,058lb (480kg) st Marboré VI turbojets, but did not enter production. From it was developed the single-seat HA-220 ground-attack aircraft (A-10C), of which 25 were built for the Spanish Air Force and continue to equip a light strike squadron. Egypt bought 10 and built 90 HA-200Bs with the local name of Al-Kahira; a few may still survive. **Data:** (HA-220): Span 34ft 2in (10.42m). Length 29ft 5in (8.97m). Gross weight 8,157lb (3,700kg). Max speed 413mph (665km/h). Range 1,055 miles (1,700km). **Photo:** AE-10A

Hughes AH-64
USA

YAH-64 prototypes of the Hughes Model 77 attack helicopter first flew on 30 September and 22 November 1975 respectively and in November 1976 the US Army selected this aircraft over the Bell YAH-63 after a competitive fly-off. The prototypes flew about 750hr up to May 1978 and were then modified to production configuration, flight testing being resumed on 28 November 1978. Three more prototypes were then built, the first of these flying on 31 October 1979 and introducing a low-mounted stabilator in place of the original fixed T-tailplane. A definitive, smaller stabilator and a larger tail rotor were introduced on the fifth prototype, flown on

16 March 1980. The AH-64 features a Martin Marietta target acquisition and designation system and pilot's night vision system (TADS/PNVS) in the nose and an armament of a 30mm Hughes XM-320 chain gun in an underfuselage turret plus up to 16 Hellfire anti-tank missiles or 76 rockets on stub wings. Power is provided by two 1,536shp General Electric T700-GE-700 turboshaft engines. The US Army plans acquisition of up to 536 AH-64s by 1989. **Data:** Rotor diameter 48ft 0in (14.63m). Length 49ft 5in (15.06m). Gross weight 17,650lb (8,006kg). Max speed 192mph (309km/h). Range (external fuel) 380 miles (611km).

Hughes OH-6A Cayuse and Model 500M-D Defender
USA

The OH-6A was chosen by the US Army for production in May 1965. Deliveries began in 1966 against contracts which eventually totalled 1,434; of these, about 400 remained in service in 1980, mostly with the National Guard. The OH-6A is powered by a 252.5shp Allison T63-A-5A turboshaft, driving a four-blade main rotor, and carries a crew of two, plus two passengers or four soldiers sitting on the floor, or equivalent freight. The similar Hughes 500M has been delivered to numerous foreign armed forces including those of Colombia, Argentina, Denmark, Mexico, the Philippines and the Spanish Navy (in a special version for anti-submarine use) and is built by Kawasaki in Japan (as OH-6J for JGSDF) and BredaNardi in Italy (for Italian Army). Latest military

variant is the Model 500M-D Defender, with 420shp Allison 250-C20B turboshaft, five-blade main rotor, a small T-tail, self-sealing tanks, armour and provision for a variety of weapons, including 14 rockets and a Minigun, a 30mm chain gun, ASW weapons or four TOW air-to-surface missiles. The Defender has been ordered by Colombia (10), Mauritania (4), Israel (30), Morocco (12) South Korea (34, plus local manufacture), Kenya (32) and Taiwan (12). In 1980 Hughes introduced the Defender II with rotor mast weapon site and increased weapons capability. **Data** (500M-D): Rotor diameter 26ft 5in (8.05m). Length 23ft 0in (7.01m). Gross weight 3,000lb (1,360kg). Max speed 160mph (258km/h). Range 335 miles (540km). **Photo:** Defender.

Hughes TH-55A Osage

USA

Hughes entered the light helicopter field in 1955, when it began design and development of the two-seat Model 269. The prototype flew in October 1956. The design was then simplified for production and the US Army purchased five of the resulting Model 269A for evaluation, under the designation YHQ-2HU; commercial sales began in 1961. The version now in production, as Model 300C, has three seats and a 190hp Lycoming HIO-360 engine. In mid-1964, the US Army ordered 20 Model 269A-1s, under the designation TH-55A and follow-up orders brought the total of TH-55As to 792, to meet the Army's needs for a standard light helicopter primary trainer; 246 remained in the inventory in 1980. Small numbers were bought for military use by other countries, including Algeria, Brazil, Colombia, Guyana, India and Nicaragua. Kawasaki built 38 TH-55Js for the JGSDF in Japan. **Data** (TH-55A): Rotor diameter 25ft 3.5in (7.71m). Length 21ft 11.75in (6.80m). Gross weight 1,670lb (757kg). Max speed 86mph (138km/h). Range 204 miles (328km). **Photo:** 269A-1, Spain (HE20).

Hunting Pembroke

UK

First to order military versions of the Prince feeder-liner was the Royal Navy; but the last of its Sea Prince T Mk 1s, equipping the Air Observer School at Culdrose, was retired in 1978 with the introduction of the Jetstream. The RAF acquired 44 Pembroke C Mk 1 staff transports, each powered by two 540/560hp Alvis Leonides 127 piston-engines and furnished to carry a crew of two and eight passengers. To prolong their life into the 1980s, a modernisation programme was begun during 1969, under which 14 of the Pembrokes were re-sparred. Of these, eight remain in service with No 60 Squadron at Wildenrath, Germany, one with No 207 Squadron at Northolt and two are in storage. **Data:** Span 64ft 6in (19.66m). Length 46ft 0in (14.02m). Gross weight 13,500lb (6,125kg). Max speed 224mph (360km/h). Range 1,150 miles (1,850km).

Israel Aircraft Industries IAI-201 Arava

Israel

Israel Aircraft Industries began development of this twin-turboprop STOL light transport in 1966 and first flew the IAI-101 civil prototype on 27 November 1969, followed by a second on 8 May 1971. A prototype of the military IAI-201 was flown on 7 March 1972. This was powered by two 750shp Pratt & Whitney PT6A-34 engines and had accommodation for 24 fully-equipped troops, 17 paratroops and a despatcher, twelve stretchers and two seated casualties or medical attendants, or 2.5 tons of freight. The first production Arava 201 flew on 4 February 1973. Deliveries to the Mexican Air Force (which now has more than 10) began later in 1973 and known customers among the purchasers of nearly 100 sold by 1980 include the Israeli Air Force (14), Bolivian Air Force (6), Ecuadorian Army (6), Ecuadorian Navy (3), Guatemalan Air Force (10), Honduran Air Force (3), Nicaraguan Air Force (2) and Salvadorean Air Force (5). **Data:** Span 68ft 9in (20.96m). Length 42ft 9in (13.03m). Gross weight 15,000lb (6,803kg). Max speed 203mph (326km/h). Max range 812 miles (1,306km).

Israel Aircraft Industries Sea Scan (Westwind 1124N)

Israel

Sea Scan is the name given to the version of the IAI Westwind biz-jet equipped for coastguard duties and for naval tactical support. For this purpose it carries Litton search radar in an extended nose and has strongpoints on the fuselage sides to carry flare dispensers, rescue packs or offensive weapons. Three Sea Scans are in service with the Israeli Navy. They were acquired in 1977 from the Westwind Model 1123 production but have since been converted to 1124N standard by exchanging their original General Electric CJ610-5 engines for Garrett AiResearch TFE 731-3-1G turbofans. In 1980, Rhein Flugzeugbau ordered four Westwind Is (which lack the Sea Scan's nose radar) for use as high-speed target tugs. **Data** (Westwind I): Span 44ft 9.5in (13.65m). Length 52ft 3in (15.93m). Gross weight 22,850lb (10,365kg). Max cruising speed, 504mph (811km/h). Range 2,800 miles (4,510km).

Ilyushin Il-12 and Il-14 USSR
(NATO code-names 'Coach' and 'Crate')

The Il-12 (NATO 'Coach') first flew in 1944 as a general-purpose military transport to succeed the Li-2, the Russian-built Dakota. It could carry only 27 passengers because of its high structure weight, but was put into service by the Soviet Air Force with 1,775hp Shvetsov ASh-82FNV two-row radials. The Il-14 (NATO 'Crate') appeared in 1953, with reduced structure weight and 1,900hp ASh-82T engines. In the Il-14P, gross weight was reduced to 36,380lb (16,500kg), leading to improved take-off and climb performance while carrying 18-26 passengers. In the Il-14M, which appeared in 1956, the fuselage was stretched by 3.3ft (1.0m) and the gross weight restored to 38,000lb (17,235kg) with 32 passengers. Air forces of the Warsaw Pact nations, and their allies, continue to fly the Il-14 in small numbers, including versions specially equipped for ECM duties. **Data** (Il-14M): Span 103ft 11in (31.67m). Length 73ft 3.5in (22.34m). Gross weight 38,000lb (17,235kg). Max speed 258mph (415km/h). Range 937 miles (1,508km). **Photo:** Il-12 (ECM).

Kaman SH-2 Seasprite USA

The Seasprite was developed and produced originally as a single-engined utility helicopter powered by a 1,250shp T58-GE-8B turboshaft. The prototype flew for the first time on 2 July 1959. Subsequently, the US Navy took delivery of 88 UH-2As, equipped for all-weather operation and 102 UH-2Bs, with instruments for VFR operation only. Conversion of the entire inventory to twin-engined configuration was undertaken under the basic designation of UH-2C, deliveries beginning in August 1967. In 1971, two Seasprites were modified for evaluation in an anti-ship missile defence (ASMD) role under the US Navy's LAMPS (Light Airborne Multi-Purpose System) programme. As a result of these tests, 20 Seasprites were converted to SH-2D LAMPS configuration, with Canadian Marconi LN66 high-power surface search radar in a chin housing, towed magnetic anomaly detector in the starboard side of the fuselage, sonobuoys, smoke markers, flares, homing torpedoes and other equipment. The first SH-2D flew on 16 March 1971, and this version has been followed by conversion of 87 more Seasprites to improved SH-2F standard, with new rotor, LN 66HP radar, a repositioned tailwheel midway along the rear fuselage, 1,350shp T58-GE-8F engines and other changes. The SH-2Ds have been uprated to 'F' standard. **Data** (SH-2F): Rotor diameter 44ft 0in (13.41m). Length, nose and blades folded, 38ft 4in (11.68m). Gross weight 12,800lb (5,805kg). Max speed 165mph (265km/h). Range 422 miles (679km). **Photo:** SH-2F.

Kamov Ka-25 (NATO code-name 'Hormone')　　USSR

The Ka-25 (NATO code-name 'Hormone-A') was first seen in prototype form in the Soviet Aviation Day display over Moscow on 9 July 1961. It then carried two dummy air-to-surface missiles, on outriggers on each side of its cabin. No such installation has been seen on production Ka-25s, which serve on board ships of the Soviet Navy, including the aircraft carrier *Kiev* and the helicopter cruisers *Moskva* and *Leningrad*; but there is a weapons bay below the cabin floor of most aircraft, able to house ASW torpedoes and nuclear depth charges. Equipment includes an undernose search radar, optional equipment pod at the base of the central tail-fin and cylindrical housing above the tail-boom, and, usually,

inflatable pontoons on each wheel of the undercarriage. A version with special electronics to acquire targets for ship-launched missiles has the NATO reporting name of 'Hormone-B' and can be identified by its more spherical nose radome. The Ka-25 has a commercial counterpart in the Ka-25K which was exhibited at the 1967 Paris Aero Show, and is itself used also for transport and general-purpose duties. The engines are 900shp Glushenkov GTD-3 turboshafts. **Data** (based on Ka-25K): Rotor diameter 51ft 8in (15.74m). Length 32ft 0in (9.75m). Gross weight 16,100lb (7,300kg). Max speed 137mph (220km/h). Max range 405 miles (650km). **Photo:** 'Hormone-A'.

Kawasaki KV-107　　Japan

During 1962, Kawasaki flew the first example of the Boeing Vertol 107 tandem-rotor helicopter built in Japan under licence, and since 1965 the company has held world-wide sales rights in the KV-107 from Boeing. In addition to a series of KV-107/II variants offered by Kawasaki, the company has developed the improved KV-107/IIA, with 1,400shp General Electric CT58-140-1 engines (which can be of Japanese origin, built by Ishikawajima). Production is continuing to meet the requirements of the Japanese armed forces, which have bought nine KV-107/II-3 or IIA-3 mine-countermeasures variants (JMSDF), 59 KV-107/II-4 or IIA-4 transports (JGSDF) and 30 KV-107/II-5 or IIA-5 search and rescue versions (JASDF). The Swedish Navy also bought eight KV-107/II-5s which were fitted in Sweden with

Gnome engines to standardise with the KKP-7s previously acquired from the USA. Saudi Arabia bought four KV-107/IIA-SM-1s equipped for fire fighting and two KV-107/IIA-SM-2s equipped for rescue and aeromedical duty. **Data** (KV-107/IIA): Rotor diameter 50ft 0in (15.24m) each. Fuselage length 44ft 7in (13.59m). Gross weight 21,400lb (9,706kg). Max speed 158mph (254km/h). Range 682 miles (1,097km). **Photo:** KV-107, JASDF.

Lockheed C-140 JetStar USA

Five JetStars, designated C-140A, are used by USAF's Air Force Communications Service which is responsible for checking world-wide military navigation aids. Six others, designated VC-140B, are 11/16-seat transports operated by the 89th Military Airlift Group, Special Missions, Military Airlift Command. Three JetStars were acquired by the Federal German Air Force for VIP transport duties; other are operated by the air forces of Indonesia (1), Libya (1), Mexico (1) and Saudi Arabia (2). The prototype JetStar flew on 4 September 1957, powered by two Bristol Siddeley Orpheus turbojets. Production models have four 3,000lb (1,360kg) st Pratt & Whitney JT12A-6A or 3,300lb (1,497kg) st JT12A-8 engines, mounted in pairs on each side of the rear fuselage. **Data:** Span 54ft 5in (16.60m). Length 60ft 5in (18.42m). Gross weight 42,000lb (19,051kg). Max speed 566mph (911km/h). Range 2,235 miles (3,595km). **Photo:** VC-140B.

Lockheed T-33A and RT-33A USA

The final single-seat fighter version of America's first operational jet-fighter, the Shooting Star, was the F-80C, with a 5,400lb (2,450kg) st Allison J33-A-35 turbojet and armament of six 0.50in machine guns and two 1,000lb (454kg) bombs or 10 rockets. The T-33A advanced trainer is similar, except for having two seats in tandem, and is still used by more than 20 air forces throughout the world, in some cases in AT-33 armed trainer/attack form. A total of 5,691 T-33As, and similar T-33Bs for the US Navy, were built by Lockheed, and USAF still uses up to 300 for combat support duties, and for proficiency and radar target evaluation training. A further 210 were produced under licence by Kawasaki in Japan. Canadair built 656 as CL-30 Silver Stars with the 5,100lb (2,313kg) st Rolls-Royce Nene 10. Also in service in Pakistan, Thailand and Yugoslavia is the RT-33A photographic reconnaissance aircraft with camera-carrying nose. **Data** (T-33A): Span 38ft 10.5in (11.85m). Length 37ft 9in (11.51m). Gross weight 14,440lb (6,550kg). Max speed 600mph (965km/h). Range 1,345 miles (2,165km). **Photo:** T-33A.

MBB 223 Flamingo

Spain

First flown on 1 March 1967, this all-metal light aircraft was developed in Germany by the former SIAT company, now part of MBB, after winning a 1962 design competition organised by the German Ministry of Economics. Only 50 were built in Germany, including a batch of 15 MBB 223A1 two-seat utility/trainers for the Turkish Air Force. Production was then transferred to CASA in Spain, where a further series of 50 was built, including 32 for the Syrian Air Force. Most of the CASA aircraft are 223K1s which are fully aerobatic when flown as single-seaters. The jigs and tools were next transferred to Pilatus in Switzerland, which then built a further 16 of these trainers for the Syrian Air Force. Iraq was reported to have acquired a batch of about 15-20. Power plant is a 200hp Lycoming AIO-360. **Data** (223K1): Span 27ft 2in (8.28m). Length 24ft 4.5in (7.43m). Gross weight 1,810lb (821kg). Max speed 155mph (249km/h).

MBB BO105

Germany

This twin-turbine utility helicopter has been adopted for large-scale service with the German Army in two special versions. The first, designated BO105M (VBH: *Verbindungs-und Beobachtungshubschrauber*) is a five-seat liaison and observation helicopter of which 90 were ordered in 1976 to replace Alouette IIs from 1979. The BO105P (PAH-1: *Panzerabwehr-Hubschrauber*) is an anti-tank version, carrying six HOT missiles on outriggers and fitted with a stabilised sight above the cabin. Following trials with four prototypes, 212 production PAH-1s are being manufactured for the German Army, with deliveries starting in late 1979. The standard BO105CB utility version has been ordered for military use by several nations, including Spain (60, assembled by CASA), Nigeria (20), the Netherlands (30), Philippines (built by PADC), Indonesia (built by Nurtanio) and Malaysia (12 from Indonesia). The standard version is powered by two 420hp Allison 250-C20B turboshafts. **Data:** Rotor diameter 32ft 3.5in (9.84m). Fuselage length 28ft 1in (8.56m). Gross weight 5,070lb (2,300kg). Max speed 167mph (270km/h). Range 408 miles (656km). **Photo:** PAH-1.

MBB HFB 320 Hansa

Germany

The unique sweptforward wings of the Hansa were adopted to permit the wing centre-section structure to pass through the fuselage without impairing the space available in the main cabin, and to give passengers an exceptional downward view. Standard versions carry seven or twelve passengers. The prototype flew for the first time on 21 April 1964, and deliveries began in September 1967, later aircraft having 3,100lb (1,406kg) st General Electric CJ610-9 turbojets in rear-mounted pods. A total of 47 was built and of these eight were delivered to the Luftwaffe for VIP transport and military flight test duties. Eight others have been equipped for ECM missions, and for flight checks and avionics calibration, the last of these being delivered in 1980. **Data:** Span 47ft 6in (14.49m). Length 54ft 6in (16.61m). Gross weight 20,280lb (9,200kg). Max speed 513mph (825km/h). Range 1,472 miles (2,370km) at 420mph (675km/h). **Photo:** ECM version.

McDonnell Douglas C-9 Nightingale/Skytrain II

USA

The USAF selected the C-9A Nightingale version of the commercial DC-9 Series 30 during 1967 to meet a requirement for a new aeromedical transport. The initial order was for eight; 13 more were ordered subsequently. The C-9A can carry up to 40 patients on stretchers or more than 40 in standard seats and contains a special-care compartment. Powered by 14,500lb (6,575kg) st Pratt & Whitney JT8D-9 turbofans, the first C-9A was delivered to Scott AFB on 10 August 1968. Three VC-9Cs ordered by the USAF in 1974 are for use as VIP transports. Also based on the DC-9 Series 30, the US Navy's C-9B Skytrain II is a fleet logistic support transport of which 15 have been acquired. The Italian and Kuwait Air Forces each fly two DC-9 Srs 30s as VIP transports. **Data** (C-9A): Span 93ft 5in (28.47m). Length 119ft 3.5in (36.37m). Gross weight 108,000lb (48,988kg). Max cruising speed 565mph (909km/h) at 25,000ft (7,620m). Range more than 2,000 miles (3,220km). **Photo:** C-9A Nightingale.

McDonnell Douglas DC-8   USA

France's air transport command — the *Commandement du transport aerien militaire* or Cotam — has among its responsibilities the maintenance of a regular link between France and the French territories in the Pacific. This link is performed by Escadron 3/60 'Esterel' using three DC-8 Srs 55s and a Srs 62CF with cargo loading door for mixed traffic operations. A fifth DC-8 (Srs 33) is equipped for electronic surveillance duties. The commercial DC-8 is powered by Pratt &

Whitney JT3D turbofans but the Armée de l'Air plans to acquire another Srs 62 and to fit both with CFM-56 turbofans. The Spanish Air Force operates a single Srs 52, which it designates T15. **Data** (Srs 55): Span 142ft 5in (43.41m). Length 150ft 6in (45.87m). Gross weight 325,000lb (147,415kg). Cruising speed 580mph (933km/h). Range over 5,000 miles (8,050km).

Mikoyan/Gurevich MiG-15   USSR
(NATO code-names 'Fagot' and 'Midget')

The MiG-15 first flew on 30 December 1947, and was produced in very large numbers, in Czechoslovakia and Poland as well as in Russia. The basic version (S-102 in Czechoslovakia, LiM-1 in Poland) had an RD-45 turbojet, which was a copy of the Rolls-Royce Nene with a rating of around 5,450lb (2,470kg) st. This engine was replaced by a developed 5,950lb (2,700kg) st Klimov VK-1 turbojet in the MiG-15*bis* (S-103 in Czechoslovakia, LiM-2 in Poland). Armament comprised one 37mm N-37 and two 23mm NR-23 cannon. The basic single-seat fighter (NATO 'Fagot') was supplied in

large numbers to countries in the Soviet sphere of influence and a few examples survive. The tandem two-seat MiG-15UTI operational trainer (NATO code-name 'Midget') was also built in quantity, with an RD-45 turbojet (this version being known as the CS-102 in Czechoslovakia). The MiG-15UTI remains in use as an advanced trainer in many countries. **Data** (MiG-15UTI): Span 33ft 1in (10.08m). Length 32ft 11.25in (10.04m). Gross weight 11,905lb (5,400kg). Max speed 630mph (1,015km/h). Range 885 miles (1,424m) at 32,800ft (10,000m) with underwing tanks. **Photo:** MiG-15UTI, East Germany.

Mil (WSK-PZL-Swidnik) Mi-2   Poland
(NATO code-name 'Hoplite')

By utilising two small and lightweight turboshaft engines, mounted above the cabin, Mil produced a helicopter that can carry 2.5 times the payload of the piston-engined Mi-1 without any significant change in overall dimensions. Known in Russia as the V-2, the Mi-2 was announced in the autumn of 1961 and has since been in large-scale production, exclusively at the WSK-Swidnik in Poland, for both military and civil use. Nearly 3,000 had been built by 1980. The basic version carries a pilot and up to eight passengers and is powered by 400 or 450shp Isotov GTD-350P turboshaft engines. The ambulance version carries four stretchers and an attendant; cargo can be carried internally or slung underneath from a hook. Air forces that operate the Mi-2 include those of Czechoslovakia, Hungary, Poland, Romania and the Soviet Union. **Data:** Rotor diameter 47ft 6.75in (14.50m). Length 39ft 2in (11.94m). Normal gross weight 7,862lb (3,550kg). Max speed 130mph (210km/h). Max range 360 miles (580km) at 118mph (190km/h).

Mil Mi-4 (NATO code-name 'Hound')   USSR

Soviet counterpart of the American Sikorsky S-55, the Mi-4 has been in service with the Soviet Air Force since 1953. Powered by a 1,700hp Shvetsov ASh-82V piston engine, the basic transport version ('Hound-A') carries a crew of two and 14 troops, or 3,525lb (1,600kg) of freight or vehicles, which are loaded via clamshell rear doors beneath the tailboom. The fairing under the front fuselage can house a navigator or observer, and carries a machine gun. This can be supplemented with air-to-surface rockets for army support duties. Although largely superseded by turbine-powered types in the Soviet Services, Mi-4s continue to operate with about 25 foreign air forces. Most are transports, but anti-submarine variants ('Hound-B') can also be seen, with undernose search radar, an MAD towed 'bird' stowed against the rear of the fuselage pod and racks for flares, markers or sonobuoys on each side of the cabin. First identified in 1977 was a communications jamming Mi-4 ('Hound-C') with multiple antennae projecting from the front and rear of the cabin on each side. Several hundred Mi-4s have been built at the Harbin complex in China, where the type is known as the H-5; in 1979, a prototype installation of a Pratt & Whitney PT6T-6 turboshaft engine was made in an H-5. **Data:** Rotor diameter 68ft 11in (21.00m). Length 55ft 1in (16.80m). Gross weight 17,200lb (7,800kg). Max speed 130mph (210km/h). Range 250 miles (400km) with eight passengers. **Photo:** Mi-4, India.

Mil Mi-6 and Mi-26   USSR
(NATO code names 'Hook' and 'Halo')

Several hundred examples of the Mi-6 have been built since this large helicopter first appeared in 1957, at which time it was the world's largest rotorcraft. This distinction has now passed to the Mi-26, which made its first appearance in 1981, although it had probably first flown several years earlier. The Mi-26 is of similar configuration to the Mi-6, and of about the same overall dimensions, but is has some twice the installed power, with a pair of 11,000shp D-136 turboshafts compared with the two 5,500shp Soloviev D-25Vs in the Mi-6. The Mi-26 is unique in having an eight-bladed main rotor, whereas the Mi-6 has a conventional four-bladed rotor, and with a max gross weight of 110,230lb (50,000kg), it can lift a 44,100lb (20,000kg) slung load. The Mi-6 itself is in large-scale service as a troop and cargo transport with the Soviet armed forces and has been exported in small numbers to Indonesia (no longer in service), Bulgaria, Egypt, Iraq, Syria, North Vietnam and Peru. Some examples have a nose gun armament. **Data** (Mi-6): Rotor diameter 114ft 10in (35.00m). Length 108ft 10.5in (33.18m). Gross weight 93,700lb (42,500kg). Max speed 186mph (300km/h). Range 620 miles (1,000km) with 9,920lb (4,500kg) payload. **Photo:** Mi-6, Peru.

Mil Mi-8 (NATO code-name 'Hip')   USSR

Similar in overall size to the Mi-4, and able to use Mi-4 rotor blades and secondary gearboxes in an emergency, the Mi-8 made its first appearance in 1961 powered by a single 2,700shp Soloviev turboshaft engine. A version with two 1,500shp Isotov TV2-117A turboshafts flew for the first time on 17 September 1962, and became the prototype for some 6,000 production Mi-8s that have since entered service, mainly with the Soviet Air Force but also with at least 25 other air forces throughout the world. The standard assault transport ('Hip-C') carries a crew of two or three and up to 32 passengers or 8,820lb (4,000kg) of internal freight. Three tons can be carried externally, and twelve stretcher patients and a medical attendant can be carried on return flights from combat areas. The heavily-armed 'Hip-E' version has a flexibly mounted 12.7mm machine gun in the nose and a triple rack on an outrigger each side of the cabin to carry anti-tank missiles, bombs or rocket pods. **Data:** Rotor diameter 69ft 10.25in (21.29m). Length 60ft 0.75in (18.31m). Gross weight 26,455lb (12,000kg). Max speed 161mph (260km/h). Range 264 miles (425km) with 28 passengers. **Photo:** 'Hip-C', Czech.

Mil Mi-10 (NATO code-name 'Harke')   USSR

This very large flying crane was put back into production in 1976, to meet a Soviet military requirement, and more than 60 are thought to be in service, a few others also having been reported to have been delivered to Iraq. The Mi-10 was first displayed at Tushino on Aviation Day 1961. Subsequent photographs showed it to be almost identical with the Mi-6 above the line of the cabin windows, but the depth of the cabin is reduced considerably and the tailboom deepened to give a continuous flat undersurface. The stalky four-leg undercarriage enables loads as big as prefabricated buildings or a motor coach to be carried on an open cargo platform between the legs, plus 28 passengers or freight in the cabin. With two 5,500shp Soloviev D-25V turboshafts, max payload is 33,070lb (15,000kg). **Data:** Rotor diameter 114ft 10in (35.00m). Fuselage length 107ft 9.75in (32.86m). Gross weight 96,340lb (43,700kg). Max speed 124mph (200km/h). Range 155 miles (250km) with 26,455lb (12,000kg) payload.

Mil Mi-14 (NATO code-name 'Haze')   USSR

A float-equipped version of the Mi-8 was reported to be under development in the Soviet Union in early 1974, with the designation V-14 (Mi-14). This is now believed to be the shore-based anti-submarine helicopter (known to NATO as 'Haze') which, with the Ka-25, has largely replaced Mi-4s in the Soviet Navy's force of around 500 helicopters. Although the power plant is similar to that of the Mi-8, the addition of a boat-hull, with a sponson on each side, should give the aircraft a degree of amphibious capability and the ability to sit on the water in order to use its submarine detection sensors. Other features that can be identified in the few pictures released to date include a large undernose radome, a towed magnetic anomaly detection (MAD) 'bird' stowed against the rear of the fuselage pod, and fully-retractable undercarriage. **Data** (Estimated): Rotor diameter 69ft 10.25in (21.29m). Length 59ft 7in (18.15m). Gross weight 26,455lb (12,000kg). Max cruising speed 130mph (210km/h). Range 280 miles (450km).

Mil Mi-24 (NATO code-name 'Hind') USSR

The introduction of up to 1,000 Mi-24 assault helicopters into service with the Soviet Union armed forces by the end of 1980 has given a completely new dimension to the mobility and hitting power of the Warsaw Pact ground forces confronting NATO in Europe. The initial multi-role version, which appeared in service in 1974 and is known to NATO as 'Hind-A', has been followed by the complementary 'Hind-C' and 'D'. The first of these is an armed assault transport, carrying a crew of four on a large flight deck and a squad of eight heavily-armed combat troops in its armoured cabin. Four pylons under its stub-wings enable it to carry up to 128 rockets or other weapons to keep down the heads of any

opposition in the drop zone. In addition, the assault craft are intended to be escorted by 'Hind-D' gunships, with weapon operator and pilot in tandem cockpits in a completely redesigned front fuselage. Additional wingtip pylons carry anti-tank (NATO 'Swatter') missiles, and there is a four-barrel Gatling-type gun under the nose. A special sensor pack is believed to house infra-red and low-light-level TV for operations by night or in bad weather. 'Hind-E' was reported to be in service in 1979 and has an armament of four laser-homing (NATO 'Spiral') anti-tank missiles. 'Hinds' are in service with all Warsaw Pact countries and have been exported to Afghanistan, Algeria, Iraq, Libya and South Yemen.

Mitsubishi MU-2 Japan

The first prototype of this 6/14-seat STOL utility transport flew on 14 September 1963, powered by two 562shp Turboméca Astazou turboprop engines. The early production versions had 605shp AiResearch TPE 331-25A turboprops and a 3ft 3.5in (1.0m) greater wing span than the prototypes. Initial military versions were the MU-2C, of which four were delivered to the Japanese Ground Self-Defence Force, with reconnaissance cameras and provision for two nose machine guns, bombs, rockets, etc; and the MU-2E search and rescue model, of which 16 were produced for the Japanese Air Self-Defence

Force, with nose radome, extra fuel, bulged observation windows and sliding door for lifeboat dropping. Military designations are LR-1 and MU-2S respectively. They have been followed by four more LR-1s and seven MU-2A search and rescue aircraft, all with 724ehp TPE 331-6-251M engines, corresponding to commercial MU-2K. **Data** (MU-2K): Span 39ft 2in (11.95m). Length 33ft 3in (10.13m). Gross weight 9,920lb (4,500kg). Max cruising speed 365mph (590km/h). Range 1,680 miles (2,700km). **Photo:** MU-2S.

NAMC YS-11

Japan

First flown in prototype form on 30 August 1962, the basic YS-11-100 is a 52/60-passenger short-range transport powered by two 3,060ehp Rolls-Royce Dart Mk 542-10K turboprop engines. It entered commercial service in the spring of 1965. Military versions include the YS-11-103/105 32/48-seat VIP transport (4 for JASDF), YS-11-112 cargo transport (1 for JMSDF), YS-11A-218 transport (1 for JASDF), YS-11A-206 anti-submarine trainer (4 for JMSDF), YS-11A-305 passenger/cargo transport (1 for JASDF), and YS-11A-402 cargo transport (7 for JASDF). **Data** (YS-11-200 series): Span 104ft 11.75in (32.00m). Length 86ft 3.5in (26.30m). Gross weight 54,010lb (24,500kg). Max cruising speed 291mph (469km/h). Max range 2,000 miles (3,215km).

NDN Firecracker

UK

The NDN-1 Firecracker was developed under the guidance of Desmond Norman to provide a lightweight and relatively cheap training aircraft capable of simulating the handling characteristics of more advanced jet trainers to which military pilots would progress. Powered by a 260hp Lycoming AEIO-540-B4D5 engine, the NDM-1 prototype made its first flight on 26 May 1977; an alternative version with 300hp Lycoming AEIO-540-L is designated NDN-1A, and a second prototype, under construction in 1981, is powered by a Pratt & Whitney PT6A-25 turboprop and is designated NDN-5. NDN Aircraft plans to license other companies to produce the Firecracker, with technical and manufacturing support from the parent company. **Data** (NDN-1): Span 26ft 0in (7.92m). Length 25ft 3in (7.70m). Gross weight 2,840lb (1,288kg). Max speed 205mph (326km/h). Range 1,285 miles (2,068km). **Photo:** NDN-1 prototype.

Neiva C-42 and L-42 Regente Brazil

The Regente is of all-metal construction. It flew for the first time on 7 September 1961 and was ordered for the Brazilian Air Force in two versions. These comprised 80 C-42 four-seat utility models and 40 air observation post L-42s, with stepped-down rear fuselage for improved all-round visibility. The prototype Regente had a 145hp Continental O-300 engine, but the production models, which continue in service in 1980, are powered by a 210hp Continental IO-360-D. **Data:** Span 29ft 11.5in (9.13m). Length 23ft 8in (7.21m). Gross weight 2,293lb (1,040kg). Max speed 153mph (246km/h). Range 590 miles (950km). **Photo:** L-42.

Neiva N621 Universal (T-25) Brazil

This two/three-seat basic trainer was designed to meet a Brazilian Air Force requirement for a replacement for its Fokker S-11/S-12 Instructors and T-6 Texans. The prototype flew for the first time on 29 April 1966, and was followed on 7 April 1971 by the first of 150 production Universals delivered in 1971-78 to the Air Forces of Brazil (140) and Chile (10). The power plant is a 300hp Lycoming IO-540-K1D5 piston-engine and construction is all-metal. The pilot and instructor sit side-by-side, with space for a third person to the rear. The Brazilian Air Force designation is T-25. A prototype of the N622 Universal II (YT-25B), with a 400hp Lycoming IO-720 engine and six underwing attachments for light bombs and rocket pods was flown on 22 October 1978 but development was discontinued when Neiva was acquired by EMBRAER in 1980. **Data:** Span 36ft 1in (11.00m). Length 28ft 2.5in (8.60m). Gross weight 3,748lb (1,700kg). Max speed 195mph (315km/h). Max range 975 miles (1,570km).

Nord 2501/2504 Noratlas

France

The original prototype Nord 2500 (first flown 10 September 1949) had 1,600hp Gnome-Rhone 14R engines. The second prototype, designated Nord 2501 and first flown on 28 November 1950, switched to 2,040hp SNECMA-built Bristol Hercules 738 engines and 200 aircraft of this type were built for the French Air Force; 30 were acquired by Israel and more than 20 by the Portuguese Air Force, including some bought second-hand. 25 were built for Federal Germany, where a further 161 were produced under licence by Flugzeugbau Nord. A few Noratlas remain in service for special duties in Germany; France continues to use them as transports as does Greece, which acquired 40 from Germany and 20 from Israel; Niger has three from Germany and Djibouti has two from France. **Data:** Span 106ft 7in (32.50m). Length 72ft 0in (21.96m). Gross weight 45,415lb (20,600kg). Max speed 273mph (440km/h). Range 1,550 miles (2,500km) with a 4.5ton payload. **Photo:** Nord 2501, Greece.

North American (and Cavalier) F-51D Mustang (and Enforcer)

USA

A few North American F-51D Mustang fighters of World War 2 vintage remain in service, with small air forces such as that of Dominica, but most of those that were long in service in South America had gone by 1980. They had included examples acquired from Cavalier Aircraft Corporation, which received a USAF contract in 1967 to build (from existing components) a small batch of Mustangs for duties with air forces which received MAP assistance. The basic Cavalier F-51D was a tandem two-seat fighter assembled from component parts, some manufactured as new. The height of the fin was increased, and armament and avionics updated to 1968 standards. Cavalier also developed a prototype conversion of the Mustang with a Rolls-Royce Dart replacing the Merlin piston engine and this Turbo Mustang III was further developed into the Enforcer in 1971 with a 2,445ehp Lycoming T55-L-9 turboprop. Rights in the Enforcer were acquired by Piper Aircraft and in 1980 the USAF was preparing to undertake a further evaluation of this prototype for potential use as a light strike aircraft. **Data** (Cavalier F-51D): Span 37ft 0.5in (11.29m). Length 32ft 2.5in (9.81m). Gross weight 12,500lb (5,670kg). Max speed 457mph (735km/h). Max range 1,980 miles (3,185km) at 290mph (466km/h). **Photo:** Enforcer.

North American T-6 Texan   USA

Remembered in Britain as the Harvard, this veteran two-seat basic trainer remained in production in the United States and, later Canada, from 1938 until 1954 and more than 10,000 were built. In 1949-50, a total of 2,068 early models were modernised as T-6G Texans, and considerable numbers of these are still in service with more than 20 air forces throughout the world. The Spanish Air Force designates its T-6Ds as AE-6s for light strike duties, and its T-6Gs as E16s for training. The Texan has a 550hp Pratt & Whitney R-1340-AN-1 engine and can carry underwing rockets and light bombs for weapon training and close support duties. **Data:** Span 42ft (12.80m). Length 29ft 6in (8.99m). Gross weight 5,617lb (2,548kg). Max speed 212mph (341km/h). Range 870 miles (1,400km). **Photo:** T-6G.

North American T-28 Trojan   USA/France

At the time of its introduction into service, the T-28 was the most powerful aircraft ever used for primary training and was adopted by both the USAF and the US Navy. Production trainers for the USAF, with an 800hp Wright R-1300 engine, were designated T-28A; the prototype flew on 26 September 1949. With a 1,425hp R-1820-56S engine, the US Navy's T-28B was similar; the T-28C had deck landing arrester gear for training purposes. Trainer versions continue in service with some foreign air forces. In addition, several hundred surplus T-28s were adapted for ground attack duties. Carrying bombs, rockets and gun packs under the wings, the T-28D was evolved as a US version for operation in South Vietnam and the Congo, and still serves with several air forces, such as Dominica, Ethiopia, Kampuchea, Laos, South Korea, the Philippines, Thailand and Honduras. A version of the T-28 with a turboprop engine, developed in Taiwan for the Nationalist Chinese Air Force, is described separately. **Data:** Span 40ft 7.5in (12.38m). Length 32ft 10in (10.00m). Gross weight 8,495lb (3,853kg). Max speed 380mph (611km/h). Range over 500 miles (805km) with full weapon load. **Photo:** T-28B.

Northrop T-38A Talon   USA

Structurally, the T-38A two-seat supersonic basic trainer is almost identical with the F-5A/B tactical fighter (described separately). It lacks the fighter's wing leading-edge flaps and is powered by two 3,850lb (1,746kg) st General Electric J85-GE-5A afterburning turbojets. The first prototype ordered by the USAF flew on 10 April 1959, powered by YJ85-GE-1 engines without afterburners. The second aircraft was similar and was followed by four YT-38 trials aircraft with 3,600lb (1,633kg) st YJ85-GE-5 afterburning engines. The first production T-38As became operational in March 1961 and a total of 1,187 were eventually built. 46 were purchased by the Luftwaffe for training German pilots in the USA; the Nationalist Chinese Air Force received 30; the US Navy has five; and the Portuguese Air Force has six. **Data:** Span 25ft 3in (7.70m). Length 46ft 4.5in (14.12m). Gross weight 11,820lb (5,360kg). Max speed Mach 1.3 (860mph; 1,385km/h). Range 1,140 miles (1,835km).

Pazmany/CAF PL-1B Chienshou   Taiwan

In 1968 the Chinese Nationalist Air Force was looking for a small primary trainer which could be built in Taiwan as the first stage in creating an aircraft industry. The type selected was the PL-1, of which construction plans are marketed by the designer, Ladislao Pazmany of San Diego, California. The slightly modified prototype, designated PL-1A and powered by a 125hp Lycoming O-290-D engine, was built in 100 days at the Aeronautical Research Laboratory, Taichung, and flew for the first time on 26 October 1968. It was followed by two more PL-1A prototypes, and then by the first of 55 production PL-1Bs (10 for the Chinese Army) with wider cockpit, larger rudder and more powerful (150hp) Lycoming O-320-E2A engine. The PL-1B is a side-by-side two-seater, of all-metal construction. **Data:** Span 28ft (8.53m). Length 19ft 8in (5.99m). Gross weight 1,440lb (653kg). Max speed 150mph (241km/h). Max range 405 miles (650km). **Photo:** PL-1B Chienshou.

Piaggio P149D

Italy

The P149 started out as a four-seat touring development of the P148 two/three-seat primary trainer, with a tricycle undercarriage and more powerful engine. It was flown in prototype form (with 260hp Lycoming GO-435) on 19 June 1953, but did not enter large-scale production until West Germany chose it as the standard basic trainer/liaison aircraft for the Luftwaffe. The first of 72 Piaggio-built P149Ds (with 270hp GO-480) was delivered to Germany in May 1957, and was followed six months later by the first of 190 which were licence-built by Focke-Wulf. About 40 of these continue in service and plans for their early replacement were postponed in 1980. P149Ds are used also by the air forces of Nigeria and Uganda. Up to five persons can be carried in the liaison role. **Data:** Span 36ft 6in (11.12m). Length 28ft 9.5in (8.78m). Gross weight 3,704lb (1,680kg). Max speed 192mph (310km/h). Range 680 miles (1,095km). **Photo:** P149D, Nigeria.

Piaggio P166M (and Albatross)

Italy

Piaggio developed the P166 light transport from its P136 twin-engined amphibian, with a normal fuselage instead of a flying-boat hull, but with similar basic outline. More than 100 were built, including 51 P166Ms for training, ambulance and communications duties with the Italian Air Force. Powered by two 340hp Lycoming GSO-480-B1C6 engines, driving pusher propellers, the P166M can carry up to ten people or items of freight as large as an Orpheus turbojet. Final production version was the P166S, of which the South African Air Force purchased 20 (in two batches) for coastal patrol, with the local name Albatross. No military orders had been reported for the latest P166-DL2 with 380hp Lycoming IGSO-540 engines, or the turboprop P166-DL3, up to 1980. **Data** (P166M): Span 46ft 9in (14.25m). Length 38ft 1in (11.60m). Gross weight 8,115lb (3,680kg). Max speed 222mph (357km/h). Range 1,200 miles (1,930km). **Photo:** P166M.

Piaggio PD-808

Italy

The El Segundo Division of Douglas Aircraft Company was responsible for the basic design of this 6/10-seat twin-jet utility transport; detail design and manufacture were entrusted to Piaggio. The Italian Government paid for two prototypes, and the first of these flew on 29 August 1964. Of the 13 PD-808s that went into service subsequently with the Italian Air Force, four are six-seat VIP transports, six are PD-808TA communications aircraft and three are ECM aircraft with a crew of five. Power is provided by two 3,360lb (1,524kg) st Rolls-Royce Bristol Viper 526 turbojets, mounted on the sides of the rear fuselage. **Data:** Span 43ft 3.5in (13.20m). Length 42ft 2in (12.85m). Gross weight 18,000lb (8,165kg). Max speed 529mph (852km/h). Range 1,322 miles (2,128km).

Pilatus P-2

Switzerland

This tandem two-seat basic trainer, like all aircraft designed for the Swiss armed forces, is capable of operating from high-altitude alpine airfields and has a sturdy structure. It is powered by a 465hp Argus As410A-2 engine and carries comprehensive night flying instrumentation, oxygen and radio equipment. The prototype flew for the first time on 27 April 1945, and was followed by 53 production models for the Swiss Air Force. The first 27, designated P-2/05s, were intended only for flying training. The remainder, designated P-2/06s, each have a 7.9mm machine gun in the fuselage and underwing racks for practice bombs and rockets for weapon training, plus provision for cameras in the rear cockpit for observer training. **Data:** Span 36ft 1in (11.00m). Length 29ft 9in (9.07m). Gross weight 4,335lb (1,966kg). Max speed 211mph (340km/h). Range 535 miles (860km).

Pilatus P-3

Switzerland

The tandem two-seat Pilatus P-3 is used by the Swiss Air Force as a basic trainer, before the pupil graduates on to the Vampire jet advanced trainer. The first of two prototypes flew on 3 September 1953 and a total of 72 was acquired by the Swiss Air Force to replace its T-6 Texans, a few also serving in the liaison role. Power plant is a 260hp Lycoming GO-435-C2A piston-engine, and one 7.9mm machine gun and racks for two rockets or four small bombs can be fitted for weapon training. **Data:** Span 34ft 1.5in (10.40m). Length 28ft 8in (8.75m). Gross weight 3,300lb (1,500kg). Max speed 193mph (310km/h). Range 465 miles (750km).

Pilatus PC-6 Porter and Turbo-Porter (and Fairchild AU-23A Peacemaker)

Switzerland/USA

This family of aircraft stemmed from the basic Swiss Pilatus PC-6 Porter 8/10-seat STOL utility transport, with a Lycoming piston-engine. Turbo-Porters, similar except for having a Turboméca Astazou (PC-6/A series), Pratt & Whitney PT6A (PC-6/B series) or AiResearch TPE 331 (PC-6/C series) turboprop, were manufactured also by Fairchild in the USA. From them was evolved the AU-23A Peacemaker, of which 15 were acquired by the USAF for evaluation, 14 later being assigned to the Royal Thai Air Force. Powered by a 650shp TPE 331-1-101F, the AU-23A carries a side-firing 20mm cannon and has five racks under its fuselage and wings for gun or rocket pods, bombs, broadcasting equipment, or camera and flare packs. Five more AU-23As were bought by the Thai Police, and another batch of 20 was delivered to the Thai Air Force in 1975/76. The numerous customers for Porters and Turbo-Porters include the Australian Army, Austria, Angola, Bolivia, Colombia, Ecuador, Israel, Peru and Sudan and the US Army which in 1979 bought two Turbo Porters for service in Berlin, with the designation UV-20A and the name Chiricahua. **Data** (PC-6/B2): Span 49ft 8in (15.13m). Length 36ft 1in (11.00m). Gross weight 4,850lb (2,200kg). Max cruising speed 161mph (259km/h). Max range 1,006 miles (1,620km). **Photo:** Turbo-Porter, Switzerland.

Pilatus PC-7 Turbo-Trainer

Switzerland

In the mid-1960s, Pilatus decided to update the P-3 intermediate trainer by developing a turboprop version. An early P-3 was retrofitted with a 550shp Pratt & Whitney PT6A-20, and flew for the first time in its new form on 12 April 1966. Known originally as the P-3B, it was subsequently redesignated PC-7 Turbo-Trainer. The project was revived in the spring of 1975, by which time the design had undergone considerable refinement. The original framed canopy was replaced by a one-piece type. Provision for underwing tanks superseded the former wingtip tanks. The engine is now a 550shp PT6A-25A. The result is a thoroughly modern, fully-aerobatic tandem two-seater, orders for which totalled 160 for eight air forces by 1980. Customers included Burma (16), Bolivia (12), Chilean Navy (10), Guatemala (12), Iraq (52), Mexico (38), Argentine Navy and Philippines. **Data:** Span 34ft 1.5in (10.40m). Length 32ft 0in (9.75m). Gross weight 5,952lb (2,700kg). Max cruising speed 252mph (405km/h). Max range 807 miles (1,300km). **Photo:** PC-7, Burma.

Pilatus Britten-Norman BN-2A Islander and Defender

UK

Among the first military customers for the basic Islander was the Abu Dhabi Defence Force, which has four for communications duties. Numerous others are now in use with various overseas Services, including the Ghana Air Force (8) and Jamaica Defence Force (2). Intended for more specific military roles, including search and rescue, border patrol and reconnaissance, the Defender appeared in 1971. It has nose-mounted Bendix or RCA radar, the gun or rocket pods on four pylons under the wings. The Maritime Defender differs in having larger search radar. First orders for the Defender came from the Sultan of Oman's Air Force, for eight, and from the Malagasy Air Force; among more recent customers are the Belgian Army (12), Mauritanian Islamic Air Force (9), Guyana Defence Force (8), Indian Navy (5), Philippine Navy (at least 10) Botswana Defence Force (6) and several others with one or two examples each. The basic BN-2A is powered by 260hp Lycoming O-540-E4C5 engines and was first flown on 13 June 1965. The Defender has 300hp IO-540s. **Data** (Defender): Span 49ft 0in (14.94m) or 53ft 0in (16.15m). Length 35ft 8in (10.86m). Gross weight 6,600lb (2,993kg). Cruising speed 165mph (265km/h) at 10,000ft (3,050m). Range up to 1,723 miles (2,772km) with optional tanks in wingtips. **Photo:** BN2A-21, Belgium.

Piper PA-24 Comanche and PA-28-120 Cherokee 140   USA

First country to adopt this two/four-seat sporting and training aircraft for military use was Tanzania, which took delivery of five in the first half of 1972. They are being used as ab initio trainers for the Tanzanian People's Defence-Force Air Wing. The Cherokee 140 is powered by a 150hp Lycoming O-320 engine. Two of the 'stretched' six/seven-seat Cherokee Six version of the same basic design are operated by the Chilean Army and one by the Tanzanian Air Wing. Five Cherokee Arrows, with retractable undercarriage, were loaned to the Finnish Air Force by private owners and these were replaced in 1980 by four Arrow IVs purchased by the Air Force. A two-seat military training version of the Cherokee Arrow, with a 260hp Lycoming AEIO-540 engine, has also been developed in Argentina by the Chincul company. The older and slightly larger PA-24 Comanche, with 260hp or 400hp Lycoming engine, is also in limited military use for communications and training duties. **Data** (Cherokee 140): Span 36ft 2in (11.02m). Length 23ft 3.5in (7.10m). Gross weight 2,150lb (975kg). Max speed 142mph (229km/h). Max range 839 miles (1,350km). **Photo:** Chincul Arrow.

Piper PA-31 Turbo Navajo   USA

The prototype of the basic Navajo six/nine-seat light transport was flown on 30 September 1964, as the first of a new Piper family of larger aircraft for business and commuter airline service. It was followed by the turbocharged Turbo Navajo and then, in 1970, by the PA-31P Pressurised Navajo. The French Navy has 12 Navajos and the Argentine Navy has four. The Chilean Army has one Turbo Navajo. The Spanish Air Force has one Pressurised Navajo; the Nigerian Air Force has two Pressurised Navajo and one Navajo Chieftain, the Syrian Air Force has two for air survey duties, and Kenya Air Force has two Chieftains. **Data** (Turbo Navajo): Powered by two 310hp Lycoming TIO-540-A engines. Span 40ft 8in (12.40m). Length 32ft 7.5in (9.94m). Gross weight 6,500lb (2,948kg). Max speed 261mph (420km/h). Max range 1,730 miles (2,780km). **Photo:** Navajo, Kenya.

Piper PA-34 Seneca (and EMB-810C)   USA/Brazil

The Seneca light twin has been part of the Piper range of commercial aircraft since its introduction in 1971. The current production model is the Seneca II, introduced in 1975; this version is also being built in Poland by PZL Mielec as the M-20 Mewa (Gull) with PZL-Franklin engines in place of the usual 200hp Continental TSIO-360-E flat fours. It is also built in Brazil by EMBRAER, with the designation EMB-810C, and among nearly 300 sold in Brazil by the end of 1980 are 32 acquired by the Brazilian Air Force for communications duties, with the designation U-7. One of these aircraft is illustrated. **Data:** Span 38ft 10.75in (11.85m). Length 28ft 6in (8.69m). Gross weight 4,570lb (2,073kg). Cruising speed 191mph (308km/h). Range 674 miles (1,084km). **Photo:** U-7.

Piper U-11A Aztec   USA

The PA-23-250 Aztec was introduced by Piper in 1959 as a five-seat development of their Apache four-seat light twin, with more powerful engines and swept fin. The US Navy ordered 20 of this original version, with 250hp Lycoming O-540-A1A engines, 'off the shelf' for utility transport duties and some of these remain in service under the designation U-11A (originally UO-1). The later six-seat Turbo Aztec E, with 250hp TIO-540-C1A engines and longer nose, serves with the Spanish Air Force, which acquired six in 1972 (as E19). The French Air Force also bought two Aztecs. The Malagasy Air Force has one, Nigeria one, the Peruvian Navy one, Senegal one and Uganda two. **Data** (Turbo Aztec E): Span 37ft 2.5in (11.34m). Length 31ft 2.75in (9.52m). Gross weight 5,200lb (2,360kg). Max speed 253mph (407km/h). Range 1,310 miles (2,108km). **Photo:** U-11A.

PZL-104 Wilga/Gelatik 32   Poland/Indonesia

The original Wilga 1 prototype flew for the first time on 24 April 1962, powered by a 180hp Narkiewicz WN-6B engine. The fuselage and tail unit were then redesigned completely, giving the aircraft its present unique spindly outline. The resulting Wilga 2 flew on 1 August 1963, with a 195hp WN-6RB engine. Other prototypes followed, equipped for both four-seat liaison and agricultural duties, including one with a Continental O-470 engine. Thirty-nine of this version were built under licence in Indonesia, with the name Gelatik (Rice-bird) and are serving with the Indonesian Air Force. Early aircraft have a 225hp O-470-13A; Gelatik 32s have a 230hp O-470-L. The Polish Air Force has received standard Polish-built Wilgas, and a few are in service with the Egyptian Air Force, with 260hp AI-14R radial engines, to replace its Yak-12s. **Data** (Gelatik): Span 36ft 5in (11.10m). Length 26ft 6.75in (8.10m). Gross weight 2,711lb (1,230kg). Max speed 127mph (205km/h). Range 435 miles (700km). **Photo:** Wilga 35, Poland.

PZL-Mielec TS-11 Iskra   Poland

The TS-11 Iskra (Spark) flew for the first time on 5 February 1960. It came second to the Czech L-29 Delfin in the competition to find a new jet trainer for the Warsaw Pact nations; but Poland decided to continue development and production of the Iskra to meet its own requirements and the first formal delivery to the Air Force was made in March 1963. Quantity deliveries began in the following year and several hundred had been built by 1980, the only other user being the Indian Air Force, which acquired 50 in 1976. Design is conventional, with two seats in tandem and a 2,205lb (1,000kg) st nationally-designed SO-3 turbojet (1,760lb; 800kg st HO-10 in early aircraft). The basic two-seat trainer, with two wing hard points, is the Iskra-Bis A, and the Iskra-Bis B (also known as Iskra 100) has four hard points; the Iskra-Bis D (Iskra 200) is similar with improved weapon load versatility. The Iskra-Bis C (also known as Iskra 200) is a single-seat reconnaissance version with increased fuel capacity and the Iskra-Bis DF is similar with the same increased armament capability as the Iskra-Bis D. **Data:** Span 33ft 0in (10.07m). Length 36ft 5in (11.17m). Gross weight 8,465lb (3,840kg). Max speed 447mph (720km/h). Range 907 miles (1,460km). **Photo:** Iskra-Bis D, India.

Republic F-84F Thunderstreak   USA

The Republic company, now a part of Fairchild Industries, built a total of 718 RF-84F Thunderflash reconnaissance aircraft, in addition to 2,711 of the F-84F Thunderstreaks, the former having a camera carrying nose and wing-root intakes whereas the latter featured a nose intake and an armament of six 0.50in (12.7mm) machine guns, plus underwing pylons for 6,000lb (2,720kg) of stores. Both types saw wide service with the USAF and many NATO air forces, but had been withdrawn by the mid-1970s from almost all of these. In 1980, RF-84Fs still equipped one front-line unit of the Greek Air Force, and the same service was using F-84Fs for advanced and proficiency training. **Data** (F-84F): Span, 33ft 7.25in (10.24m). Length 43ft 4.75in (13.23m). Gross weight 28,000lb (12,700kg). Max speed 695mph (1,118km/h) at sea level. Max range over 2,000 miles (3,220km). **Photo:** RF-84F (Greek).

RFB Fantrainer 400   Germany

First military prototypes to emerge from Rhein-Flugzeugbau's experiments with ducted fan propulsion systems were two Fantrainers, the first of which flew on 27 October 1977. Of extremely neat layout, the Fantrainer has the now customary sloping tandem cabin, giving the instructor a clear view forward over the head of his pupil. The first prototype, designated AWI-2, was originally powered by two 150hp Audi NSU/RFB Wankel EA871-L rotating-piston engines, mounted one above the other in the centre-fuselage and driving a Dowty Rotol seven-blade variable-pitch ducted fan built into the cruciform rear fuselage. The second prototype, designated ATI-2, flew on 31 May 1978 with a single 420shp Allison 250-C20B turboshaft and this same engine was subsequently fitted in the first prototype, in which a 650shp 250-C30 was substituted during 1980. The prototypes were funded by the Federal German Defence Ministry, but a hoped-for Luftwaffe order for the Fantrainer to replace Piaggio P149Ds did not materialise. In conjunction with Vought, a twin-engined version of the Fantrainer was offered in 1980 in the USAF Next Generation Trainer (NGT) competition as the Vought V-538 Eaglet, to which the following data refer. **Data** (V-538, PT6B-34 or 250-C30 engines): Span 40ft 11in (12.47m). Length 32ft 3in (9.83m). Gross weight 5,197lb (2,357kg). Cruising speed 374mph (602km/h). **Photo:** ATI-2

Rockwell B-1 USA

Although the B-1 supersonic bomber, developed to meet the USAF requirement for an Advanced Manned Strategic Aircraft (AMSA), was cancelled on 30 June 1977, prototype testing has continued and in 1981 further development programmes for the B-1 were being considered by the USAF. The B-1 design, by what was then the Los Angeles Division of North American Rockwell, had been selected by the USAF in June 1970 and the first prototype flew on 23 December 1974. Further prototypes flew on 1 April (the avionics test bed) and 14 June 1976, followed by the fourth and last on 14 February 1979, featuring the full offensive and defensive weapons system. Two of the B-1s have been retired but Nos 3 and 4 are still in use, and No 3 was to be used in 1981/82 to evaluate the suitability of the B-1 as a Strategic ALCM Launcher carrying AGB-86B air-launched cruise missiles internally and externally. Powered by four General Electric F101-GE-100 turbofans, the B-1 has variable-sweep wings and carries a crew of four. **Data:** Span (spread) 136ft 8.5in (41.66m). Span (fully swept) 78ft 2.5in (23.84m). Length 150ft 2.5in (45.78m). Gross weight 395,000lb (179,172kg). Max speed Mach 2.1 (1,450mph; 2,335km/h). **Photo:** Third prototype.

Rockwell International T-2 Buckeye USA

No prototype of the Buckeye was built and the first of the original series of 217 T-2A production models for the US Navy flew on 31 January 1958. This version, no longer in service, was a tandem two-seater with a 3,400lb (1,540kg) st Westinghouse J34-WE-48 turbojet, and was suitable for the complete syllabus of naval training. On 30 August 1962 North American flew the first of two YT-2B prototypes (converted from T-2As), built to evaluate the potential of the airframe when fitted with two 3,000lb (1,360kg) st Pratt & Whitney J60-P-6 turbojets. A total of 97 T-2Bs was built for the Navy in 1964-69; the first flew on 21 May 1965. During 1968, a prototype T-2C was produced by installing 2,950lb (1,339kg) st General Electric J85-GE-4 engines in a T-2B and the Navy took delivery of 231 in 1968-75; they were expected to remain in service until 1986/1988. 24 T-2Ds for Venezuela differ from the T-2C only in electronics and deletion of carrier landing capability; but the second batch of 12 was supplied with attack kits providing six underwing hardpoints for 3,500lb (1,588kg) of external stores. 40 T-2Es for Greece have similar attack capability. **Data** (T-2C): Span 38ft 1.5in (11.62m). Length 38ft 3.5in (11.67m). Gross weight 13,179lb (5,977kg). Max speed 522mph (840km/h). Range 1,047 miles (1,685km). **Photo:** T-2B

Rockwell International T-39 Sabreliner   USA

The Sabreliner prototype flew for the first time on 16 September 1958, with two General Electric J85 turbojets; but production models for military use have 3,000lb (1,360kg) st Pratt & Whitney J60 (JT12) engines. The T-39A (143 delivered) is a pilot proficiency trainer and administrative support aircraft in service with the USAF. The six T-39B aircrew trainers have Doppler radar and NASARR all-weather search and ranging radar. The US Navy's 42 T-39Ds have a Magnavox radar system for maritime radar training. Seven CT-39E rapid response airlift jets acquired by the USN are similar to the commercial Sabreliner 40, while 12 CT-39Gs have the longer fuselage of the Sabreliner 60. A further variant is the T-39F conversion of the T-39A, equipped to train 'Wild Weasel' ECM operators. **Data** (T-39A/D): Span 44ft 5in (13.54m). Length 43ft 9in (13.34m). Gross weight 17.760lb (8,055kg). Max cruising speed 502mph (808km/h). Range 1,950 miles (3,138km). **Photo:** Sabreliner 40A (TP86, Swedish Air Force).

Saab-91 Safir   Sweden

The Saab-91A two/three-seat basic trainer, first flown in prototype form on 20 November 1945, had a 145hp DH Gipsy Major 10. The Saab-91B changed to a 190hp Lycoming O-435-A engine and remains a standard basic trainer of the Swedish Air Force (75 delivered as SK50B) and Norwegian (25) and Ethiopian (16) air forces. The Saab-91C differs from the B only in having four seats and was sold to the Swedish Air Force (14 SK50Cs) and Ethiopia (14). Final version was the Saab-91D, which differs from the C in having a 180hp Lycoming O-360-A1A engine, propeller spinner, more powerful generator and rudder trim. Orders for the D were received from the air forces of Finland (35), Tunisia (15, no longer in use) and Austria (24). **Data** (Saab-91D): Span 34ft 9in (10.60m). Length 26ft 4in (8.03m). Gross weight 2,660lb (1,205kg). Max speed 165mph (265km/h). Range 660 miles (1,060km). **Photo:** Saab-91D, Finland.

Saab Supporter

Sweden

This aircraft had its origin in the MFI-9/Bölkow Junior series, designed by Bjorn Andreasson and used as lightweight attack aircraft by the Biafran forces in the Nigerian civil war. When Saab took over the MFI company, they supported development of the two/three-seat Saab-MFI 15 for military training and general-purpose duties. This aircraft was superseded in production by the Supporter (originally Saab-MFI 17), which differs primarily in having provision for six underwing attachments for up to 660lb (300kg) of rocket pods, wire-guided anti-tank missiles, droppable containers or other stores. Power plant is a 200hp Lycoming IO-360-A1B piston-engine. The Supporter entered production in the Autumn of 1972; orders have included 32 for the Royal Danish Air Force and Army, 20 for the Zambian Air Force and 16 for the Royal Norwegian Air Force. A total of 117 MFI-17s is being assembled or produced in Pakistan where the type is known as the Mushak (Expert). **Data:** Span 29ft 0.5in (8.85m). Length 22ft 11.5in (7.00m). Gross weight 2,645lb (1,200kg). Max speed 146mph (236km/h). Endurance 5hr 10min. **Photo:** Supporter, Pakistan.

Shenyang BT-6

China

One of the first aircraft of indigenous design to enter production in the Chinese People's Republic, the BT-6 is a primary trainer of conventional layout and at least in its configuration appears to owe something to the Yak-18A, which was built under licence in China as the BT-5. The BT-6 is powered by a 285hp Hou-sai-6 nine-cylinder radial engine, derived from original Soviet design, and production is reported to have run into hundreds, if not thousands, since 1961. Examples of the BT-6 have also been exported to such nations as Zambia, Bangladesh, North Korea and North Vietnam. **Data:** Span 35ft 1.25in (10.70m). Length 27ft 10.75in (8.50m). Gross weight 3,088lb (1,400kg). Max speed 178mph (286km/h). Endurance 3.5hr.

Shorts Skyvan Series 3M   UK

The prototype of this military version of the Shorts Skyvan Srs, 3 STOL utility transport flew for the first time in early 1970. It is powered by two 715shp Garrett-AiResearch TPE 331-201 turboprops and can carry 22 equipped troops, 16 paratroops and a despatcher, 12 stretcher cases and two medical attendants or 5,200lb (2,358kg) of freight. Entry to the cabin is via a rear loading ramp. Special equipment includes a Bendix weather radar on the nose, anchor cables for parachute static lines, inward-facing paratroop seats, stretcher mounts and roller conveyors in the cabin floor. Initial deliveries comprised two aircraft for the Austrian Air Force and the first of 16 for the Sultan of Oman's Air Force. Others are used by the Argentine Naval Prefectura (5), Royal Thai Police (3), the Nepalese Army (2), the Ghana Air Force (6), the Yemen Arab Republic Air Forces (2), and the Air Arms of Botswana, Lesotho, Panama, Yemen, Ecuador, Mauritania and Indonesia. The Singapore Air Defence Command acquired six in 1973. **Data:** Span 64ft 11in (19.79m). Length 41ft 4in (12.60m). Gross weight 14,500lb (6,577kg). Max cruising speed 203mph (327km/h). Max range 670 miles (1,075km). **Photo:** Skyvan, Austria.

Siai-Marchetti S208M   Italy

The prototype of the S208 five-seat light aircraft flew for the first time on 22 May 1967. It embodies many components of Siai-Marchetti's popular S205 series, but introduced one more seat and a more powerful (260hp) Lycoming O-540-E4A5 engine. In addition to civilian production, the company built 44 of a version designated S208M for the Italian Air Force. This differs from the standard model by having a jettisonable cabin door, and is intended for liaison and training duties. **Data:** Span 35ft 7.5in (10.86m). Length 26ft 3in (8.00m). Gross weight 3,307lb (1,500kg). Max speed 199mph (320km/h). Max range 1,250 miles (2,000km). **Photo:** S-208M.

Siai-Marchetti S211   Italy

Encouraged by the success enjoyed by the SF260 trainer and light attack aircraft, Siai-Marchetti (which is a wholly-owned subsidiary of the Agusta company) embarked upon the development of a lightweight low-cost basic jet trainer. Definition of the basic design of this S211 was completed by early 1979 but the decision to launch full-scale development was not taken until June 1979. Prototype construction then began, and the first flight was made during May 1981. The S211 is powered by a 2,200lb (1,000kg) st Pratt & Whitney JT15D-1 or 2,500lb (1,134kg) st JT15D-4 and is designed for the lowest possible first cost in its basic form, with a number of equipment options for customers who can afford them. Four wing hardpoints allow the carriage of up to 1,320lb (600kg) of weapons such as minigun pods, bombs, rockets or AAMs. **Data:** Span 26ft 3in (8.00m). Length 30ft 5.5in (9.28m). Gross weight 6,173lb (2,800kg). Max speed 414mph (667km/h). Range 1,245 miles (2,000km) with external fuel. **Photo:** Mock-up

Siai-Marchetti SF260 Warrior and Sea Warrior   Italy

The prototype of this two/three-seat aircraft, designed by Ing Stelio Frati, was built by Aviamilano as the F250 and flew on 15 July 1964. Production was undertaken by Siai-Marchetti, who exchanged the original 250hp engine for a 260hp Lycoming O-540-E4A5 and redesignated the aircraft SF260. In addition to manufacturing civil-registered SF260s, many for use as airline trainers, Siai-Marchetti received orders for military SF260Ms for the Air Forces of Italy (25), Morocco (2), Belgium (36), Zaïre (23), Singapore (22), Zambia (8), Thailand (12), Ecuador (12), Burma (10) and the Philippines (32). This version (first flown on 10 October, 1970) has a larger rudder and specialised equipment for military training. A strengthened and armed version, with wing pylons for up to 661lb (300kg) of bombs or rockets, is known as the SF260W Warrior and first flew in May 1972; 16 were ordered by the Philippine Air Force, 12 by Tunisia, 10 by the Irish Air Corps, 9 by Burma and a batch of about 8 was acquired by the Rhodesian Air Force through the Comores Islands. Production of 230 for Libya was underway in 1980. The SF260SW Sea Warrior has photo-recce and radar equipment in wingtip tanks, for surveillance, search/rescue and supply missions. **Data** (SF260W): Span 27ft 4.75in (8.35m). Length 23ft 3.5in (7.10m). Gross weight 2,866lb (1,300kg). Max speed 196mph (315km/h). Operational radius 57-345 miles (92-556km). **Photo:** SF260, Belgium.

Siai-Marchetti SM1019E

Italy

This two-seat light military STOL aircraft is a turboprop development of the Cessna L-19/O-1 Bird Dog which can be produced either as a new airframe or by extensive modification of existing aircraft. The entire airframe is updated to meet current operational requirements, and is fitted with new, angular vertical tail surfaces and a lengthened nose for the 400shp Allison 250-B17 turboprop. Up to 500lb of rockets, gun pods, missiles, bombs or camera packs can be carried on two underwing racks. The first of two prototype SM109s flew on 24 May 1969, and production of 80 aircraft for the Italian Army Aviation component was completed in 1978. **Data:** Span 36ft (10.97m). Length 27ft 11.5in (8.52m). Gross weight 3,196lb (1,450kg). Max cruising speed 184mph (296km/h). Range 840 miles (1,352km).

Sikorsky S-55 and H-19 (and Whirlwind)

USA

The H-19 is the military counterpart of the civil Sikorsky S-55, with accommodation for a crew of two and up to 10 troops or six stretchers. The parent company built 1,281, of which most went to the US armed forces. Others were manufactured in Japan by Mitsubishi. More than 20 air forces used versions of the S-55 and H-19 for utility transport, search and rescue, casualty evacuation and other duties. In the UK, Westland built more than 400 under licence, many with the 1,050shp R-R Gnome H.1000 turboshaft. A few of these remain in military service, but the last of the RAF's Whirlwind 10s was to retire in 1981. **Data** (S-55T): Rotor diameter 53ft (16.15m). Length 42ft 3in (12.88m). Gross weight 7,200lb (3,265kg). Max speed 114mph (183km/h). Range 370 miles (595km). **Photo:** Whirlwind HAR Mk 10.

Sikorsky S-58   USA
(H-34 Seabat, Choctaw, Seahorse)

On 30 June 1952, Sikorsky received a US Navy contract for a prototype anti-submarine helicopter to be designated XHSS-1. The aircraft flew on 8 March 1954, and was followed by 1,821 production helicopters of the S-58 series. Most were delivered to the US services, for a wide variety of duties under the names Seabat (Navy), Seahorse (Marines) and Choctaw (Army), but many were exported. For the French Army and Navy, Sud-Aviation built 166 S-58s, plus five for Belgium. Westland in the UK built

a turbine-powered version known as the Wessex (described separately). Few of the military S-58s remain in service and some that do have been converted to S-58T standard, with a 1,875shp Pratt & Whitney (Canada) PT6T-6 Twin-Pac twin-turbine power plant. **Data** (S-58T): Rotor diameter 56ft 0in (17.07m). Length 47ft 3in (14.40m). Gross weight 13,000lb (5,896kg). Max speed 138mph (222km/h). Range 278 miles (447km). **Photo:** S-58T, Thailand.

Sikorsky S-61B (H-3 Sea King)   USA

The Sikorsky S-61 was developed to provide the US Navy with an anti-submarine 'hunter-killer'. It was designed around two General Electric T58 turboshaft engines, with a watertight hull to permit operation on and off water. The prototype, designated XHSS-2, flew on 11 March, 1959. Deliveries of production HSS-2s to operational ASW units began in September 1961; altogether 255 were built, with 1,250shp T58-GE-8B engines. Their designation was changed to SH-3A Sea King in July 1962; conversions included 12 HH-3A armed search and rescue helicopters, 105 SH-3G utility helicopters, and SH-3H multi-purpose helicopters for ASW and defence against missiles. 41 CH-124s (similar to SH-3As) were delivered to the Canadian Armed Forces; 83 similar HSS-2s and 2As had been delivered to the JMSDF by Mitsubishi by 1979, when 16 more HSS-2As remained to be built. With uprated engines (1,400shp T58-GE-10s), the SH-3D appeared in 1965; 98 were built by Sikorsky,

including 22 for the Spanish Navy and four for the Brazilian Navy. Eleven specially-equipped VH-3Ds are operated by the Executive Flight Detachment based in Washington for VIP duties. SH-3Ds continue in production by Agusta as the AH-61B; in Britain, Westland produce a family of SH-3D variants as the Sea King and Commando (described separately). Other Sikorsky-built variants include four S-61D-4s (similar to SH-3D) for the Argentine Navy; nine S-61A transports (similar to SH-3A) for long-range air/sea rescue duties with the Royal Danish Air Force; and 38 S-61A-4 Nuri 31-seat transports for the Royal Malaysian Air Force. **Data** (SH-3D): Rotor diameter 62ft 0in (18.90m). Length 54ft 9in (16.69m). Gross weight 18,626lb (8,449kg). Max speed 166mph (267km/h). Range 625 miles (1,005km). Armament 840lb (381kg) of homing torpedoes, depth charges, etc. **Photo:** AH-61B, Peru.

Sikorsky S-61R (H-3 Jolly Green Giant/Pelican) USA

On 8 February 1963, the USAF ordered 22 CH-3C general-purpose helicopters, based on the S-61 but with new stabilising sponsons for amphibious operation, a hydraulically-operated rear loading ramp and built-in auxiliary power unit. An S-61R civil prototype flew on 17 June 1963, followed a few weeks later by the first CH-3C, with 1,300shp T58-GE-1 engines. By the time deliveries began in December 1963, another 19 had been ordered to fill a further USAF requirement for a long-range rotary-wing support system. In February 1966 production was switched to the CH-3E with 1,500shp T58-GE-5s; 42 were built to this standard, and the 41 CH-3Cs were modified to CH-3Es. Subsequently, 50 CH-3Es were converted into HH-3E Jolly Green Giants for the USAF Aerospace Rescue and Recovery Service, with defensive armament, armour plating, jettisonable fuel tanks and rescue hoist. 40 unarmed HH-3F Pelicans were built for extended search and rescue operations with the US Coast Guard. Basic accommodation of all models is for a crew of two or three, 30 troops, 15 stretcher patients or 5,000lb (2,270kg) of cargo. Agusta has built 12 HH-3Fs for SAR duties with the Italian Air Force, and the others for foreign operators. **Data** (CH-3E): Rotor diameter 62ft 0in (18.90m). Length 57ft 3in (17.45m). Gross weight 22,050lb (10,000kg). Max speed 162mph (261km/h). Range 465 miles (748km). **Photo:** HH-3E.

Sikorksy S-64 Skycrane (CH-54 Tarhe) USA

The highly-functional Skycrane consists of a 'backbone' structure carrying a cab for three crew at the front, two 4,500shp Pratt & Whitney T73-P-1 turboshaft engines and the main rotor above the centre of gravity, and a tail rotor. The underside of the backbone is flattened, enabling bulky cargoes to be clamped tightly beneath it, between the stalky main undercarriage legs. The payload can be carried in interchangeable Universal Military Pods, each accommodating 45 combat-equipped troops, 24 stretcher patients, a surgical unit or field command or communications post. The first of three S-64A prototypes flew on 9 May 1962. In June 1963, the US Army ordered six, as CH-54A Tarhes, to evaluate the heavy-lift concept as an aid to battlefield mobility. After trials in Vietnam, the Army ordered 73 CH-54As, followed by 10 CH-54Bs with 4,800shp T73-P-700 engines, high-lift rotor blades and gross weight of 47,000lb (21,319kg). Typical loads carried in Vietnam included 20,000lb (9,072kg) armoured vehicles and up to 87 troops; more than 380 damaged aircraft were retrieved. **Data** (CH-54A): Rotor diameter 72ft 0in (21.95m). Length 70ft 3in (21.41m). Gross weight 42,000lb (19,050kg). Max speed 126mph (203km/h). Range 230 miles (370km).

Sikorsky S-65A
(H-53 Sea Stallion and Super Jolly)

USA

On 14 October 1964, Sikorsky flew the prototype of the CH-53A Sea Stallion heavy assault transport for the US Marines, with accommodation for a crew of three, 37 combat-equipped troops, 24 stretcher patients or internal or external freight. Deliveries of production models, with two 2,850shp General Electric T64-GE-6 turboshaft engines, began in mid-1966. These aircraft were operational in Vietnam from January 1967, primarily to carry cargo, vehicles and equipment such as 105mm howitzers, loaded into the amphibious fuselage via rear doors. The first improved CH-53D, with 3,925shp T64-GE-413s, was delivered in March 1969, and the Marines received a total of 265 As and Ds. Simultaneously, the USAF Aerospace Rescue and Recovery Service acquired eight HH-53Bs, with 3,080shp T64-GE-3s, armament, flight refuelling probe and jettisonable external tanks;

followed by 64 HH-53Cs with 3,925shp T64-GE-7s. The German armed forces acquired 112 CH-53Gs, assembled under licence; Israel had about 30 CH-53Ds, the Iranian Navy six RH-53Ds and the Austrian Air Force has two S-65Oes for rescue work in the Alps. RH-53Ds supplied to the US Navy (30) have 4,380shp T64-GE-415 engines, special towing equipment to sweep mechanical, acoustic and magnetic mines, and max gross weight of 50,000lb (22,680kg). Nine HH-53Cs have been converted to HH-53Fs in the 'Pave Low III' programme to have enhanced night and bad-weather capability for service in Europe. **Data** (CH-53D): Rotor diameter 72ft 2.75in (22.02m). Length 67ft 2in (20.47m). Gross weight 42,000lb (19,050kg). Max speed 196mph (315km/h). Range 257 miles (413km). **Photo:** CH-53G, Germany.

Sikorsky CH-53E Super Stallion

USA

To meet a US Navy/Marine Corps requirement for a new heavy-duty multi-purpose helicopter, Sikorsky proposed this version of the H-53 with a third engine, larger-diameter rotor with seven titanium blades, and uprated transmission. The first of two YCH-53E development aircraft flew on 1 March 1974; the second has flown at a gross weight of 74,500lb (33,793kg), unmatched by any other helicopter outside the Soviet Union. Two pre-production CH-53Es have demonstrated their capability of performing the Navy's vertical on-board delivery mission for ships at sea, and 49 are to be acquired, with about two-thirds going to the Marine

Corps. In addition to removing battle-damaged aircraft from carrier decks, the CH-53Es will be capable of airlifting 93% of a Marine division's combat items, and of retrieving 98% of Marine tactical aircraft without disassembly. The first production CH-53E flew on 13 December 1980. **Data:** Power plant, three 4,380shp General Electric T64-GE-415 turboshaft engines. Rotor diameter 79ft 0in (24.08m). Length 79ft 9in (22.48m). Gross weight 73,500lb (33,339kg). Max speed 196mph (315km/h). Range 1,290 miles (2,075km).

Sikorsky S-70 (H-60 Black Hawk and Sea Hawk)   USA

Three YUH-60A prototypes were built initially, to compete with three Boeing Vertol YUH-61As, in the programme to provide the US Army with a new utility tactical transport aviation system (UTTAS). The first YUH-60A flew on 17 October 1974, and Sikorsky's design was declared the winner of a seven-month fly-off evaluation on 23 December 1976. Deliveries began on 31 October 1978 of an intended total of 1,107 production UH-60A Black Hawks, to replace UH-1s in selected assault helicopter, air cavalry and aeromedical evacuation units. Powered by two 1,543shp General Electric T700-GE-700 turboshaft engines, the UH-60A carries a crew of three and a fully-equipped infantry squad of 11 troops, four stretcher patients, internal cargo or 8,000lb (3,630kg) of slung cargo. Two side-firing machine guns can be fitted for protection during drops. The US Army has also contracted with Sikorsky for the development of the EH-60B version as a Stand-Off Target Acquisition System, with more than 100 required; the first of five YEH-60B prototypes flew for the first time on 6 February 1981. In addition, the US Navy ordered five prototype SH-60Bs in September 1977, to initiate development of the 204 aircraft that will eventually replace SH-2F Seasprites, as the Navy's LAMPS III shipboard ASW and ASV helicopters. The SH-60B Sea Hawk is similar to the UH-60A except for automatic blade-folding, added surface search radar, MAD, sonobuoys, two homing torpedoes and other specialised equipment. The first of the YSH-60Bs flew on 12 December 1979. **Data** (UH-60A): Rotor diameter 64ft 10in (19.76m). Length 50ft 0.75in (15.26m). Gross weight 20,250lb (9,185kg). Max speed 184mph (296km/h). Endurance 2.3hr. **Photo:** UH-60A.

Soko G2-A Galeb   Yugoslavia

First flown in prototype form in May 1961, the G2-A Galeb tandem two-seat basic trainer is conventional in design and, like many of its counterparts in other countries, is powered by a Rolls-Royce Viper turbojet. The second prototype embodied improvements and was representative of the production version, of which many are in service with the Yugoslav Air Force. The engine in the production G2-A is a Viper 11 Mk 22-6 of 2,500lb (1,134kg) st. For weapon training or light attack duties, it is fitted with two 0.50in machine guns and underwing racks for bombs and rockets. Two G2-A Galebs have been supplied to Zambia. Final export model was the G-2A-E, with updated equipment; a batch of 50 of these was built for Libya between 1976 and 1980. **Data** (G-2A): Span 38ft 1.5in (11.62m). Length 33ft 11in (10.34m). Gross weight 8,440-9,480lb (3,828-4,300kg). Max speed 505mph (812km/h). Range 770 miles (1,240km).

Swearingen Merlin IIIA   USA

This eight/eleven-seat pressurised transport has the same wings, undercarriage and basic engines as the longer-fuselage Metro II and Merlin IVA. The original Merlin III was certificated in July 1970; additional cabin windows, system and flight deck improvements and cabin refinements came with the current Merlin IIIA, which is powered by two 840shp Garrett-AiResearch TPE 331-3U-303G turboprops. Success as a commercial business transport led to a Belgian Air Force order for six, which were delivered in 1976. Four are operated by the Argentine Army. **Data:** Span 46ft 3in (14.10m). Length 42ft 2in (12.85m). Gross weight 12,500lb (5,670kg). Max cruising speed 325mph (523km/h). Range at max cruising speed 1,968 miles (3,167km). **Photo:** Merlin IIIA, Belgium.

Swearingen Metro/Merlin IVA   USA

The original Metro and current Metro III are equipped normally as 19/20-passenger pressurised commuter airliners, but have an easily convertible passenger/cargo interior. Kits are available for adaptation to business transport, air ambulance (ten stretcher patients) or air survey photographic configurations. The twin engines are 940shp Garrett-AiResearch TPE 331-3UW-303G turboprops. A more luxurious 12/15-passenger executive model is available as the Merlin IVA. Customers for this include the South African Air Force, which has six for VIP transportation and one equipped as an air ambulance. The Argentine Air Force has two fitted out for 'critical care' ambulance duties, with normal accommodation for two stretchers and five seated casualties or attendants, and with provision for four more stretchers in the rear of the cabin. Thailand has four, including two for the Royal Flight. **Data** (Merlin IVA): Span 46ft 3in (14.10m). Length 59ft 4.75in (18.10m). Gross weight 12,500lb (5,670kg). Max cruising speed 310mph (499km/h). Range at max cruising speed 1,575 miles (2,534km). **Photo:** Merlin IVA, SAAF.

Tupolev Tu-134A (NATO code-name 'Crusty') USSR

This 64/80-seat transport is basically a rear-engined development of the Tu-124, powered by two 14,990lb (6,800kg) st Soloviev D-30 turbofans. In the same class as the BAC One-Eleven and McDonnell Douglas DC-9, it is standard short/medium-range equipment of Aeroflot and other East European airlines. In addition, it is operated in small numbers by the air forces of the Soviet Union, Bulgaria, East Germany, Hungary and Poland. Examples can be seen with both western-style nose radome and a glazed nose with shallow undernose radome. **Data:** Span 95ft 2in (29.01m). Length 121ft 6.5in (37.05m). Gross weight 103,600lb (47,000kg). Max cruising speed 550mph (885km/h). Range with max payload 1,243 miles (2,000km). **Photo:** Tu-134A, Hungary.

UTVA-60 and UTVA-66 Yugoslavia

The Yugoslav Air Force has a number of these sturdy four-seat utility aircraft built by the Fabrika Aviona UTVA at Pancevo. The UTVA-60, powered by a 270hp Lycoming GO-480-B1A6 engine, was manufactured in utility and ambulance versions. In addition, there was a floatplane version, designated UTVA-60H, with 296hp Lycoming GO-480-G1H6 engine. The UTVA-60H is known to be in military service, as is the developed UTVA-66, which exists in the same versions and has a 270hp GSO-480-B1J6 engine, fixed leading-edge slots, larger tail surfaces, increased fuel capacity, provision for underwing armament such as gun packs, and other changes. **Data** (UTVA-66): Span 37ft 5in (11.40m). Length 27ft 6in (8.38m). Gross weight 4,000lb (1,814kg). Max speed 155mph (250km/h). Max range 466 miles (750km). **Photo:** UTVA-66.

Valmet L-70 Vinka

Finland

This side-by-side two-seat trainer was developed as the Leko-70, a name representing an abbreviation of 'Lentokone', the Finnish word for 'aeroplane'. The prototype flew for the first time on 1 July 1975. On 28 January 1977, the Finnish Air Force ordered 30 production models to replace its Saab-91D Safirs, and the first two of these were handed over in October 1980. Construction is all-metal; power plant is a 200hp Lycoming AEIO-360-A1B6, equipped for aerobatic flying. **Data:** Span 32ft 3.75in (9.85m). Length 24ft 7.25in (7.50m). Gross weight 2,756lb (1,250kg). Max speed 149mph (240km/h). Range 630 miles (1,015km).

VFW-Fokker VFW 614

Germany

The unique overwing engine pods of this twin-turbofan short-haul transport appeared to offer a number of attractions. The undercarriage legs could be kept shorter than with underwing pods, and there were none of the T-tail/deep-stall complications encountered with some rear-engine designs. However, the VFW 614 failed to find a commercial market in competition with airliners such as the Fokker F28, and the production line was closed in early 1978 after sales of only sixteen had been announced. Three of these are operated by the Luftwaffe as VIP transports. Powered by two 7,280lb (3,302kg) st Rolls-Royce M45H Mk 501 turbofans, the VFW 614 is equipped normally to carry either 40 or 44 passengers in four-abreast seating. **Data:** Span 70ft 6.5in (21.50m). Length 67ft 7in (20.60m). Gross weight 44,000lb (19,950kg). Max speed 443mph (713km/h). Range with 40 passengers 748 miles (1,204km).

Vickers Viscount UK

Of 444 Viscounts built and sold between 1948 and 1964, only a few were purchased for military use; secondhand deals, however, resulted in several others passing from commercial to military service. By 1980, few remained in the hands of military operators. One Series 781 was still in use as a VIP transport by the South African Air Force, based at Zwarkop with No 21 Squadron. Two ex-commercial Srs 800s serve in RAF markings with the RAE

Bedford and are dedicated to radio and radar development flying. The Viscount is powered by four 1,740shp Rolls-Royce Dart 506 turboprops. **Data:** Span 93ft 8in (28.54m). Length 81ft 10in (24.93m). Gross weight 64,500lb (29,256kg). Cruising speed 324mph (518km/h). Range 1,785 miles (2,872km). **Photo:** Srs 800, RAE.

Vickers-Slingsby T61E Venture UK

This side-by-side two-seat motor-glider had its origin in the German Scheibe SF-25B Falke (Falcon), of which Vickers-Slingsby manufactured 35 under licence in 1971-74. Impressed by the possibilities of the type for low-cost training and air experience flying, the UK Ministry of Defence evaluated a prototype (XW983) as Venture T Mk 1. It then ordered 15 of the improved T61E version, powered by a Rollason 1600cc Volkswagen car engine and with many components of glassfibre, including the plywood-encased wing main spar. Named Venture T Mk 2, these entered service at the Gliding Schools

used by the Air Training Corps. On 3 February 1979, a T Mk 2 flew with an electric self-starting system installed and an order was placed for 25 Venture T Mk 3s (T61F) with this feature. **Data:** Span 50ft 2.5in (15.30m). Length 24ft 9.25in (7.55m). Gross weight 1,350lb (612kg). Max speed 100mph (160km/h). **Photo:** T Mk 3.

Westland Commando (and Sea King 4)   UK

Based on the Sea King, the Commando is intended to operate primarily on tactical troop transport, logistic support, cargo transport and casualty evacuation duties. It can be used also for ground support and search and rescue. The Mk 1 version, which accommodates up to 21 troops and has a retractable undercarriage, is externally similar to the Sea King, except for the absence of the latter's search radar in a hump above the fuselage. Five were ordered by Saudi Arabia, on behalf of Egypt. The first of these flew on 12 September 1973. The more specialised Commando Mk 2 has two 1,660shp Rolls-Royce Gnome H.1400-1 turboshaft engines, a fixed undercarriage, provision for a wide range of guns, missiles and other weapons, and accommodation for a crew of two, up to 28 troops, internal or external freight or stretchers; it flew for

the first time on 16 January 1975. Saudi Arabia's contract included 19 of this version, two of them furnished as VIP Mk 2Bs. Three Mk 2As and a VIP Mk 2C were ordered by the Qatar Emiri Air Force. Fifteen Commandos ordered by the MoD in 1978 are designated Sea King HC Mk 4 and replace the Wessex HU Mk 5s in two RN squadrons in the commando support role. First flight was made on 26 September 1979. The export-model Commander 3 is a multi-role version with Sea King type undercarriage, and a variety of armament options; Qatar has ordered eight. **Data** (Mk 2): Rotor diameter 62ft 0in (18.90m). Length 55ft 10in (17.02m). Gross weight 21,000lb (9,525kg). Max speed 137mph (220km/h). Range 276 miles (445km) with max payload. **Photo:** Mk 2A, Qatar.

Westland Sea King   UK

This is the Sikorsky SH-3D Sea King (separately described), built under licence initially for the Royal Navy, whose HAS Mk 1 differed in having 1,500shp Rolls-Royce Gnome H1400 engines, an automatic flight control system, long-range sonar with Doppler processing, AW391 search radar in a dorsal hump fairing, Doppler navigation system and armament of four Mk 44 homing torpedoes or Mk 11 depth charges. After four imported S-61s, the first of 56 HAS Mk 1s for the Royal Navy flew on 7 May 1969; the first of 21 uprated HAS Mk 2s with 1,660shp Gnome H1400-1 engines, followed on 18 June 1976, and most Mk 1s have been modified to similar standard including a few with Jezebel passive sonar. These aircraft equip five operational squadrons, two flights and a training squadron and are being supplemented from 1980 by 17 HAS Mk 5s with

new Sea Search radar in an enlarged radome and other changes. Sixteen Sea King HAR Mk 3s began to re-equip RAF search and rescue (SAR) squadrons in 1978; first flight was made on 6 September 1977. Export orders have included 22 Sea King Mk 41s for SAR duties with the Federal German Navy, 17 ASW Mk 42s for the Indian Navy, 10 SAR Mk 43s for the Norwegian Air Force, 6 ASW Mk 45s for the Pakistan Navy (three with provision to carry Exocet ASMs), 6 ASW Mk 47s for the Egyptian Navy, 5 SAR Mk 48s for the Belgian Air Force, and 10 Mk 50s for the Royal Australian Navy, with Gnome H1400-1 engines and improved sonar. **Data** (Mk 2): Rotor diameter 62ft 0in (18.90m). Length 55ft 9.75in (17.01m). Gross weight 21,000lb (9,525kg). Max speed 137mph (220km/h). Range 764 miles (1,230km). **Photo:** Sea King HAS Mk 5.

Westland Wasp/Scout UK

The anti-submarine Wasp and Scout light liaison helicopter are variants of the same design, which had its origin in the private-venture Saunder-Roe P531. Evaluation of three early models led to a Royal Navy contract for development and production of the Wasp HAS Mk 1, with a 710shp (derated) Rolls-Royce Nimbus 503 turboshaft engine, folding tailboom, four individual undercarriage legs with castoring wheels, armament of two Mk 44 homing torpedoes or other external stores, and accommodation for a crew of two, with provision for three passengers or for a stretcher across the rear of the cabin. The first Wasp flew on 28 October 1962, and aircraft of this type were being progressively replaced by the Lynx from 1978 onwards. Export customers included South Africa (17), New Zealand (3), Netherlands (12) and Brazil (9). The first pre-production Scout for the British Army Air Corps flew on 4 August 1960; the production Scout AH Mk 1 has a 685shp Nimbus 101 or 102 engine, skid undercarriage, fixed tail and gross weight of 5,300lb (2,404kg). Export customers were the Royal Australian Navy (2) and Uganda Police Air Wing (1). **Data** (Wasp HAS Mk 1): Rotor diameter 32ft 3in (9.83m). Length 30ft 4in (9.24m). Gross weight 5,500lb (2,495kg). Max speed 120mph (193km/h). Range 270 miles (435km). **Photo:** Scout AH Mk 1.

Westland Wessex UK

The prototype for the Wessex was a Sikorksy HSS-1 (S-58) imported by Westland, re-engined with a Gazelle turboshaft and first flown in this form on 17 May 1957. The Royal Navy ordered a production version, designated Wessex HAS Mk 1, for anti-submarine duties in the hunter-killer role; the first operational squadron was commissioned in July 1961. The HAS Mk 1 had a 1,450shp Gazelle 161 engine, dipping sonar and strike weapons, and carried a crew of four. An assault transport version, carrying 16 troops, entered service in 1962. The HAS Mk 1 was superseded by the HAS Mk 3, with 1,600shp Gazelle 165 and large dorsal radome. In service for Commando assault, training and fleet requirements until the delivery of Sea King HC Mk 4s is completed were two squadrons of Wessex HU Mk 5s, with a 1,550shp Rolls-Royce Gnome 112/113 twin-turbine power plant. The RAF has three squadrons of similar, twin-engined Wessex HC Mk 2s; two airframes were converted to HCC Mk 4 standard for The Queen's Flight and others became HAR Mk 2s for the search and rescue role, replacing Whirlwinds. Export models were delivered to the Royal Australian Navy (27 HAS31B with 1,540shp Gazelle 162) and Iraq (9 Mk 52, similar to Mk 2). **Data** (HU Mk 5): Rotor diameter 56ft 0in (17.07m). Length 48ft 4.5in (14.74m). Gross weight 13,500lb (6,120kg). Max speed 132mph (212km/h). Range 478 miles (770km). **Photo:** Wessex HC Mk 2.

Westland WG30   UK

This enlarged development of the Lynx (with the same dynamic system) was undertaken as a private venture by Westland to provide a helicopter suitable for a variety of military and civil rôles. The first of two prototypes flew on 10 April 1979 and had flown more than 200 hours a year later; the second prototype was to fly in spring 1981 after lengthy structural integrity tests. During its first year, the prototype WG30 flew in both civil and military guise; in the former, it can accommodate up to 22 passengers in a high density layout, and a similar number of troops can be carried when the WG30 is used in the air mobility role. Engines in the first production batch, which were in hand in 1980 for delivery from 1982 onwards, are 1,120shp Rolls-Royce Gem 41-1 turboshafts; more powerful versions of the Gem will be available later. **Data:** Rotor diameter 43ft 8in (13.31m). Length 52ft 2in (15.90m). Gross weight 11,750lb (5,330kg). Max speed 155mph (250km/h). Range 300 miles (483km).

Westland/Aérospatiale Lynx   UK/France

The Westland WG13 was one of three helicopters included in the Anglo-French helicopter programme launched in February 1967 and it was subsequently developed in two distinct versions (Navy Lynx and Basic Lynx) primarily to meet the requirements of the French and British Navy and the British Army. These differ externally in the type of landing gear (wheels for deck operations, skids for land use) and in the equipment fit. The first of 13 development Lynx flew on 21 March 1971 and by end-1980 orders for production versions totalled 307, including 114 Lynx AH Mk 1 for the British Army, 80 HAS Mk 2 for the RN and 40 HAS Mk 2 for Aéronavale. Service use began in September 1976 with the formation of a joint RN/Royal Neth Navy Intensive Flying Trials Unit, followed by the first RN operational unit in December 1977. Export customers are the Royal Netherlands Navy (six Mk 25 UH-14A, 10 Mk 27 SH-14B and eight Mk 81/SH-14C); Brazilian Navy (nine Mk 21); Argentine Navy (eight Mk 23); Royal Danish Navy (eight Mk 80); R Norwegian AF (six Mk 86); German Navy (12 Mk 88) and Qatar (one Mk 28 and two Mk 84). **Data** (HAS Mk 2): Rotor diameter 42ft 0in (12.80m). Length 39ft 1.25in (11.92m). Gross weight 10,500lb (4,763kg). Max cruising speed 167mph (269km/h). Range 390 miles (628km). **Photo:** Lynx, Aéronavale.

Westland/Agusta EH-101 UK

To provide the Royal Navy with a replacement for its Sea King anti-submarine helicopters, the Westland WG34 design was chosen in the late summer of 1978 from a number of alternative projects and construction of three WG34A prototypes was put in hand, to be powered by General Electric T700 turboshafts. In addition, the MoD contracted for a single Sea King 4X to serve as a development airframe for the WG34 transmission and rotor system, using the basic Sea King HC Mk 4 fuselage. After the Italian Navy had confirmed its interest in a

broadly similar type of helicopter, Westland and Agusta set up a joint company, EH Industries Ltd, to manage the programme and the helicopter was redesignated the EH101. During 1980, final definition was proceeding to meet the combined requirement for 80-100 EH101s, which are expected in service in the late 1980s. Production aircraft may have the Rolls-Royce RTM321 engine; gross weight is about 28,660lb (13,000kg) but no other data has been given.

Yakovlev Yak-18 and Yak-18T (NATO code-name 'Max') USSR

In a variety of forms, the sturdy all-metal Yak-18 has been the standard primary trainer of the Soviet Air Force and civil flying schools since 1946, and is also in service in a dozen other countries. Numerous versions have appeared since the early tandem two-seat Yak-18 ('Max') with 160hp M-11FR engine and tail-wheel landing gear. These include the Yak-18U with nose wheel and longer fuselage; Yak-18A with 300hp AL-14RF engine; Yak-18P single-seat version of the -18A with forward retracting or inwards-retracting landing gear; Yak-18PM single-seat aerobatic version; Yak-18PS tailwheel version of the PM; and the four-seat

Yak-18T, with wider centre fuselage and enclosed cabin, which entered service in the early 1970s and was still in production in 1981. At least one prototype Yak-18 has been flown with a Glushenkov TVD-10 turboprop fitted. Both the basic Yak-18 and the Yak-18A were licence-built in China from 1954 onwards; known respectively as the BT-3 and BT-5; they remain in service there. **Data** (Yak-18T): Powered by 360hp Vedeneev M-14P engine. Span 36ft 7.25in (11.16m). Length 27ft 4.75in (8.35m). Gross weight 3,637lb (1,650kg). Max speed 183mph (295km/h). Range 560 miles (900km). **Photo:** Yak-18T.

Yakovlev Yak-52   USSR

The Yak-52 is the latest in a long line of primary and basic training aircraft developed by the Yakovlev design bureau. First flown in 1977, it was evolved in parallel with the single-seat Yak-50 aerobatic monoplane, from which it differs primarily in having tandem seating for pupil and instructor, and a semi-retractable undercarriage, the nose and main legs of which fold to leave the wheels exposed under the fuselage and wings where they can help to reduce damage in the event of a forced landing. Production of the Yak-52 has been entrusted to the IRAvB

factory at Bacau, Romania, under the terms of the COMECON (Council for Mutal Economic Assistance) programme and as a replacement for the Yak-18 at Soviet flying training schools the Yak-52 is expected to be built in very large numbers. Production deliveries began late in 1980. **Data:** Span 31ft 2in (9.50m). Length 25ft 2.25in (7.68m). Gross weight 2,844lb (1,290kg). Max speed 177mph (285km/h). Max range 241 miles (550km).

Index